Mortals, Money, and Masters of Thought

Collected Philosophical Essays

by

Giorgio Baruchello, PhD

NORTHWEST
PASSAGE
Books

Gatineau, Quebec, Canada

Mortals, Money, and Masters of Thought

Collected Philosophical Essays

by Giorgio Baruchello, PhD

ISBN: 978-0-9939527-4-6

Published by
Northwest Passage Books
Gatineau, Quebec, Canada

In loving memory of Eleonora Bennati and Corrado Panzanera,

who departed this life while the present book was being written.

Table of Contents

Preface

Candidly and with a modicum of trepidation, if not even with a slight sense of shame, I must confess that death has intrigued me since childhood. Not as a morbid obsession. Not as a source of fear and trembling. Not as a zoological or pathological curiosity. Not even as a personality-defining focus point for my psyche—*à la* Fromm, so to speak. Rather, it has fascinated me as a contradictory and constant presence in life. Death is everywhere; literally. Everything that lives passes away. As a child, I was perplexed by the way grown-ups seemed aware of the inevitability of death as well as of its widespread and commonplace presence in our lives—and how couldn't they be? Yet, in my experience, they tried to avoid it in conversations, showing often discomfort when asked about it, or even getting annoyed when it happened. And it did happen, myself being an inquisitive and persistent, if not obstinate child. They uttered the word itself more softly than the others, almost timidly; their talking turning into a whisper. No other topic seemed equally uncomfortable for them to tackle or to be questioned about. Perhaps only the issue of the devil or Satan, at least with my older Catholic relatives, drew comparably negative responses and as soft a tone of voice.

I know now that, for the most part, those grown-ups believed that they were protecting me from a dreadful aspect of existence; one that children should hardly contemplate at their young age. There would be plenty of time later on in life to consider, experience and face death. As an older man and a parent, I can comprehend the reasons for their actions. Still, back then, I was somewhat pleased and certainly relieved to discover that there were, in fact, several grown-ups who had spent time and thought about this topic and that had debated openly and extensively upon it. They were, for the most part, dead grown-ups, as far as I could determine. They were more or less famous poets, novelists, theologians, but above all philosophers, who had written extensively about death and mortality, which was the actual issue that, as I came to realise later, truly intrigued me.

Thus, to some extent, I can say that it was the issue of mortality that drew me towards philosophy and subsequently led me into philosophical studies, which turned out to be my eventual profession and, to a deeper level, my genuine vocation in life.

Over the many years that I have spent working as an academic, I happened to write a number of articles and book chapters devoted to the issue of mortality, if not death at large. I cannot claim that the philosophical study of mortality and death has made me an expert about them, or that it has granted me some profound insight in mortality and death that no man or woman has ever possessed before. Rather, my frequent philosophical musings have made mortality and death even more familiar to me, perhaps slightly more acceptable, and hopefully less terrifying than they might prove otherwise. Above all, such musings have functioned as a regular and reliable reminder of the fleeting and incredibly frail character of human life, the paramount value of which has then emerged before my mind in its utmost significance and greatest urgency. If this is wisdom, then it is the wisdom that philosophy, which etymologically means love of wisdom, has taught me in its simplest and most forceful expression.

Acknowledgements

I wish to thank, first of all, Dr. Brendan Myers, chief consultant at Northwest Passage Books, for encouraging me and helping me to combine my previous work on mortality and death into one book. A friend of mine and a proud fellow graduate from the University of Guelph, he made the present contribution possible. On the one hand, this book is meant to expand the diversity and increase the visibility of Northwest Passage Books. On the other hand, I myself have benefitted enormously from Dr. Myers' philosophical feedback, professional expertise and publishing services. Also, I must thank the editors of the academic books and scholarly journals in which my enquiries into mortality and death were previously published; namely Drs. Charles Tandy for Ria University Press, R.T. Allen and Simon Smith for *Appraisal*, Maurizio Tani for *Nordicum-*

Mediterraneum, and another Guelphite, Antonio Calcagno, for *Symposium*. All of them have agreed and allowed me to republish here those book chapters and articles, in slightly modified form. I must likewise express my sincere gratitude to the rector and senior management of the University of Akureyri for granting me a sabbatical leave in the academic year 2016–2017, during which I could devote myself to a number of research projects, including the present one. Dr. Enrico Albanesi and Prof. Carlo Penco of the Università degli Studi di Genova should also be thanked, since they allowed me to access key facilities of said Italian university and provided me with much-needed office space. A special note of thanks must be extended to my Italian parents, who helped me to take care of my two young sons while I worked hard on my research projects and their mother, another equally unremitting academic, worked hard on her own. Finally, I wish to acknowledge two long-time collaborators and friends, namely Profs. John McMurtry and Valerio Lintner, whose learning and understanding inform profoundly the present book, especially as concerns fundamental issues of value and economics. If any imprecision or error is still to be found in the pages to follow, however, the responsibility lies solely with me.

Introduction

Thanks to the interest of Northwest Passage Books, I combine together in this volume my past articles and book chapters on the subject of mortality and death, in order to bring the little wisdom that I may have gathered as a philosopher to the public outside academia; that is, in addition to the readers of the scholarly journals and academic books in which the articles and chapters were published in the first place. Although revised to ensure consistency, avoid redundancies, update some references, explain a handful of lesser-known Latin and foreign phrases, and eliminate the occasional linguistic oddity, misprint or plain error that survived prior editorial reviews, my older articles and book chapters form, together, the near totality of the conceptual, critical and bibliographic material presented in this volume. As a general rule, I have tried to keep the modifications to a minimum, despite the temptation of revising thoroughly my older texts which, sometimes many years after their original publication, no longer satisfy my own scholarly standards and preferred lines of argument. However, being too thorough in this sense would have meant writing entirely new essays, which is not the aim of the present book. Consequently, the essays collected here reflect the time and circumstances under which they were written.[1] Still, their theoretical core and main thrust are, in my view, as good (or as bad) now as they were then—indeed, as the economic considerations presented in the second part are concerned, they proved largely correct.

I reissue here ten book chapters written between 2003 and 2017 for as many volumes in the series entitled *Death and Anti-Death* (i.e. 1, 3–10 and the forthcoming 14), published by Ria University Press in the United States of America [hereafter USA] and edited by Charles Tandy. Also, I redraft here my 2005 "Notes on Pessimism", which appeared originally in issue 5(3) of the British Personalist Forum's journal *Appraisal*, plus a short 2013 paper entitled "Cruelty and Austerity. Philip Hallie's Categories of Ethical Thought and Today's Greek Tragedy", prepared for a 2012 symposium held by the research group number three of the Nordic Summer University and published in issue 8(3) of the Icelandic scholarly journal of Nordic and Mediterranean studies, *Nordicum-Mediterraneum*. Finally, I make use of the contents of a 2001 article entitled "Montaigne and Nietzsche: Ancient and Future Wisdom", published in issue 6(1) of the Canadian Society for Continental Philosophy's scholarly journal *Symposium*. All this material is organised in the present book's three parts, each of which comprises three (Part I) to four short chapters (Parts II and III).

The first part, which I have called "Mortals", offers a broad set of reflections on death and mortality as experiences functioning *qua* potential intellectual *cum* emotional means, by which we can better grasp the fundamental structures of value and meaning of human life. Specifically, I offer a synoptic account of positive appraisals of death and mortality in the history of Western philosophy, plus some references to Eastern thought too, as well as of representative cases of philosophical pessimism in general, and highlight how a more fundamental philosophy of life can emerge thereof (chapter 1). A related study of the original split in ancient philosophy between the world of everyday experience and a seemingly deeper, truer world revealed by reason alone is then offered, so as to cast further light on some of the most influential forms of just such positive appraisals, i.e. Socrates' and Plato's (chapter 2). Additionally, I tackle the philosophical assumptions of the modern scientific worldview, born with Descartes and Galileo in the 17th century, and flesh out their bearings upon the notions of death, mortality and, once more, life (chapter 3). Theoretically crucial in all three chapters is the work of Canadian philosopher John McMurtry, and in particular his deep and articulate theory of value, known by contemporary philosophers as *life-value onto-axiology*. McMurtry's theory of value is present in all of his major public addresses[2] and books, including both editions of his celebrated *Cancer Stage of Capitalism*.[3] However, his life-value onto-axiology is developed to its fullest extent in his entries for the encyclopaedia of philosophy entitled *Philosophy and World Problems*, volumes I-III.[4] These three large volumes are themselves part of the United Nations Educational, Scientific and Cultural

Organization's [hereafter UNESCO] monumental *Encyclopedia of Life Support Systems*, which is to date the largest repository of scientific and scholarly information on sustainable development, and for which McMurtry worked as honorary theme editor for several years.[5]

The second part, "Money", comprises reflections on the most powerful and widespread cause of *avoidable* death in the world today, namely the misconceived and misdirected structure of value operating at the very heart of the global economy. In this connection, much of the text expounded in the second part is based upon prolonged exchanges that I had with Valerio Lintner, professor of economics at London's Hult Business School, leading to co-authored contributions to the 2009 and 2010 volumes of the *Death and Anti-Death* book series of Ria University Press. Precisely, I begin by continuing the reflections on modern science's fundamentally *lifeless* worldview begun in chapter 3 and apply them to the modern social science of economics (chapter 4). An imaginary dialogue follows between Athena B., a philosopher, and Hermes L., an economist, in order to highlight, in a lighter tone, the core problems with contemporary economics and, above all, with the world's economies, so as to make the lifelessness discussed in the previous chapter more tangible in its everyday but nonetheless deadly character (chapter 5). Born as a simple dialogue between Prof. Lintner and me, it is the essay that required the most substantial reworking. Additional reflections on contemporary economic woes and their lethal aspects ensue, suggesting remedies and showing implicitly how philosophy can function as a lifeline of fundamental criteria (e.g. good and bad) for other disciplines' self-assessment and amelioration (chapter 6). In essence, philosophy is the unique and uniquely valuable discipline that can allow the specialists of all the other disciplines to pause and ponder upon why they are doing whatever they may be doing, and whether it may be wise to keep doing it or, instead, refrain from it and redirect their efforts. After all, while the focus of the other disciplines is firmly and valiantly set upon knowledge as such, philosophy's traditional and peculiar focus is wisdom. Being knowledgeable is not the same thing as being wise. This non-identity has been amply and frequently exemplified in human affairs. There have been talented physicists and hardworking engineers designing newer and deadlier weapons of mass destruction. Top-notch psychologists and gifted marketing experts concocting effective new ways to sell more fat- and sugar-laden addictive junk food to children and teenagers. Committed managers and capable software programmers who have been replacing human beings with machines that accrue to shareholder value and yet make high unemployment rates unswerving. Not to mention high finance's 'best and brightest' bringing about yet another economic collapse by means of mathematically complex tokens of highly paid technical wizardry and wildly celebrated financial genius, adding then, on top of it all, the wrong expert advice for recovery, as tragically and cruelly exemplified by the recent case of Greek austerity (chapter 7).

The third and last part, "Masters of Thought", contains explorations of past reflections on mortality and death by five great minds in the philosophical canon of the West: Michel de Montaigne (1533–1592), Giambattista Vico (1668–1744), Friedrich Nietzsche (1844–1900), Michael Polanyi (1891–1976) and Cornelius Castoriadis (1922–1997). All of them have been five masters of philosophical thought, from five different European countries of origin (i.e. France, Italy, Germany, Hungary and Greece), who wrote in remarkably different styles (e.g. first-person memoires and essays, lengthy treatises, collected aphorisms, scholarly articles, books and interviews) in different historical periods (i.e. the Renaissance, the early Enlightenment, the peak of European imperialism, the two World Wars and the Cold War) and personal contexts. For example, Vico led a private existence as a minor Neapolitan academic and a provincial tutor for patrician youngsters, fighting against severe bouts of depression throughout his life. Conversely, Castoriadis was an energetic and self-confident man, who fought as a Trotskyist partisan in the 1940s, worked until 1970 as an economist for the Organisation for Economic Cooperation and Development [hereafter OECD], and then started practicing as a psychoanalyst in 1973. Yet, jointly, these five thinkers show how philosophy can be the place where our questions about mortality and death are verily taken seriously and pursued most thoroughly, whatever the results may be, and whether we agree or disagree upon such results. In particular, Montaigne and Nietzsche are compared and contrasted in their deeply personal, self-centred, this-worldly philosophical understanding of human mortality (chapter 8). Then, in chronological order, further insights on the same subject are retrieved and discussed *vis-à-vis* the philosophies of Vico (chapter 9), Castoriadis (chapter 10) and Polanyi (chapter 11). All three of them cast light on the existentially pivotal given of mortality, yet *via* conspicuously different areas of emphasis and cultural entry points, which are, respectively, literature and anthropology for Vico, politics and psychoanalysis for Castoriadis, and epistemology and religion for Polanyi. Taken together with the other thinkers cited and discussed in the preceding chapters of this volume, albeit to inevitably uneven degrees of depth and breadth, the concluding four chapters allow this book to offer itself as a fairly comprehensive account of the many philosophies of death and mortality available in the history of, primarily, Western thought. As such, this book should be of interest to any reader who wishes to explore this history and/or the topics of death and mortality under the perspective of intellectual history. Above all, this book should extend an opportunity for meditating upon such topics, in the hope of helping the reader to cope with our quintessential finitude.

Original publication credits

The exact titles and publication details of the essays collected in this volume are as follows (they are not reiterated in the final bibliography):[6]

Chapter 1

Death and Anti-Anti-Death. A Cultural Exploration, in C. Tandy (ed.), *Death and Anti-Death Volume 1*, Palo Alto: Ria University Press, 2003, pp. 131–70.

Notes on Pessimism, *Appraisal*, 5(3) ("Other discussion papers"), 2005, pp. 148–50 and 159–60.

Chapter 2

Death and Life Support Systems: A Novel Cultural Exploration, in C. Tandy (ed.), *Death and Anti-Death Volume 3*, Palo Alto: Ria University Press, 2006, pp. 31–58.

Chapter 3

Mechanism, Galileo's *Animale* and Heidegger's *Gestell*: Reflections on the Lifelessness of Modern Science, in C. Tandy (ed.), *Death and Anti-Death Volume 4*, Palo Alto: Ria University Press, 2007, pp. 29–66.

Chapter 4

Deadly Economics: Reflections on the Neoclassical Paradigm, in C. Tandy (ed.), *Death and Anti-Death Volume 5*, Palo Alto: Ria University Press, 2008, pp. 65–132.

Chapter 5

Life and Death Economics: A Dialogue (with Dr. Valerio Lintner), in C. Tandy (ed.), *Death and Anti-Death Volume 6,* Palo Alto: Ria University Press, 2009, pp. 33–56.

Chapter 6
Life and Death Economics Revisited: One Year On (with Dr. Valerio Lintner), in C. Tandy (ed.), *Death and Anti-Death Volume 7*, Palo Alto: Ria University Press, 2010, pp. 35–54.

Chapter 7
Cruelty and Austerity. Philip Hallie's Categories of Ethical Thought and Today's Greek Tragedy, *Nordicum-Mediterraneum. Icelandic E-journal of Nordic and Mediterranean Studies*, 8(3), 2013, <http://skemman.is/en/item/view/1946/17322>.

Chapter 8
Montaigne and Nietzsche: Ancient and Future Wisdom, *Symposium*, 6(1), 2001, pp. 79–91.

Chapter 9
Homer, Heroes and Humanity: Vico's *New Science* on Death and Mortality, in C. Tandy (ed.), *Death and Anti-Death Volume 8*, Palo Alto: Ria University Press, 2011, pp. 33–52.

Chapter 10
Contingency, Autonomy and Inanity: Cornelius Castoriadis on Human Mortality, in C. Tandy (ed.), *Death and Anti-Death Volume 9*, Palo Alto: Ria University Press, 2012, pp. 27–54.

Contingency, Autonomy and Mysticism: Three Critical Remarks on Cornelius Castoriadis' Understanding of Human Mortality, in C. Tandy (ed.), *Death and Anti-Death Volume 10*, Palo Alto: Ria University Press, 2013, pp. 21–30.

Chapter 11
Religion's *Gestalt*. Reflections on Michael Polanyi, Tacit Knowing and Mortality, *Death and Anti-Death Volume 14*, Palo Alto: Ria University Press, forthcoming (2017)

.

PART I – Mortals

Chapter 1:
Death and Anti-Anti-Death. A Cultural Exploration

Throughout the history of Western thought and cultures, there have existed a number of religious and philosophical lines of thought, all of which share the notion that death is, can, or even ought to be a positive given of human existence. I do not mean an experiential given for the individual with regard to himself, of course, but an experiential given of the individual with regard to other selves.[7] In this sense, death can be a *desideratum* [something desired], or even a *desiderandum* [something to be desired], and not, as it is commonly heard, a hopeless doom, an unavoidable tragedy, or, more rarely, a fact of no actual importance. As a consequence, I exclude *ab initio* [from the beginning] all the positions that bring forth a variously formulated denial of death, either as a nightmare to be kept as far-off as possible, or as a condition of which nothing is known, and *ergo* [therefore] about which nothing has to be done. An instance of the former kind of denial is the cult of Isis, which was extremely common throughout the Roman Empire at the dawn of the Christian age, and which centred upon the regular performance of rituals aimed at insuring good health, sexual power, and, above all, longevity. An instance of the latter kind of denial is the Epicurean tetrapharmakos or "four-part cure", namely the doctrine teaching how not to worry about the gods, the ills of life, unfulfilled desire, and, above all, about death. As a late Epicurean put it concisely: "Don't fear god, don't worry about death; what's good is easy to get, and what's terrible is easy to endure."[8]

In what follows, I arrange my sources in two quadripartite sets or, as I refer to them henceforward, in two tetralogies of death.

The first tetralogy of death is meant to give structure to the material I cite. As such, this first tetralogy is undoubtedly arbitrary, uncompromisingly concise, and historically incomplete—a systematic thinker like Kant would probably call it "rhapsodic". Still, just as rhapsodists did utilise meters and other lyrical arrangements in order to compose understandable expressions of poetical insight, so do I benefit from the employment of an expository classification in order to present the bearings of the broad cultural exploration opening this book. The final goal of my exploration is to individuate the ground of value that makes this particular approach possible. It is my hope to be able to identify a shared pattern of understanding lurking behind the cultural phenomena gathered under the four 'pigeonholes' of my first tetralogy.

The second tetralogy of death comprises a fourfold comparative scrutiny of the material presented in the first tetralogy. The first form of scrutiny is analytical, i.e. aimed at furnishing a few relevant conceptual distinctions. The second form is axiological, i.e. aimed at probing the most significant dominions of value related to death. The third form is ontological, i.e. aimed at configuring the modes of connectedness with death. The fourth form is existential, i.e. aimed at evaluating the relevance of death for the individual's life. Though logically distinct from one another, all four forms of scrutiny are mutually intertwined.

The First Tetralogy of Death

[I] *Contemptus mundi..*[9] If "death is annihilation, and the dead has no consciousness of anything… I call it gain", says Socrates:

If there is no consciousness but only a dreamless sleep, death must be a marvellous gain. I suppose that if anyone were told to pick out a night on which he slept so soundly as not even to dream, and then to compare it with all the other nights and days of his life, and then were told to say, after due consideration, how many better and happier days and nights than this he had spent in the course of his life – well, I think that the Great King himself, to say nothing of any private person, would find these days and nights easy to count in comparison with the rest.[10]

This passage highlights the first of two possible conceptions of death that Socrates discussed before the Athenian jury in his *Apology*: life is a valley of tears. Pain, misfortunes and sorrows are the daily bread of the human being. Or, at least, such seems to be the destiny of most human beings, to whom death represents actual liberation from their painful existence. Consistently with this realisation, the universe in which we are condemned to live deserves mere contempt. Representatively, Michel de Montaigne quotes from the Greek gnomic poets, first among many a voice in the millenary history of anthropological pessimism: "*Either a painless life, or else a happy death. / To die is good for those whom life brings misery. / 'Tis better not to live than live in wretchedness.*"[11] Since most human beings dwell in a condition of "wretchedness", then death is highly desirable. Only death can rescue them from their miserable existence and bring about eternal peace and the relief that "it is all over".[12]

[II] *Immortalis eris.*[13] If death is "a change, a migration of the soul from this place to another", says Socrates:

> *If... death is the removal from here to some other place, and if what we are told is true, that all the dead are there, what greater blessing could there be than this...? [H]ow much would one of you give to meet Orpheus and Musaeus, Hesiod and Homer? I am willing to die ten times over if this account is true... [I]t would be a wonderful personal experience to join them there, to meet Palamedes and Ajax the son of Telamon and any other heroes of the old days.*[14]

This passage highlights the second of Socrates' possible conceptions of death. Death could be just a moment of transition. Death could be a dramatic and startling gate to be crossed in order to attain further life, as in the doctrines entailing the notion of metempsychosis (e.g. Pythagoras and Hinduism); or a completely different life, possibly a blessed life of eternal joy, as in the doctrines contemplating the existence of heaven (e.g. the Christian and Muslim creeds). Maybe this process involves a cycle of reincarnations, and therefore a sequence of several births and deaths (e.g. the Buddhist doctrine of *samsara*). Maybe it involves a period of unconscious rest (e.g. the condition of the dead awaiting the *dies irae* [the Day of Wrath] in Saint Paul's *First Letter to the Thessalonians*). Or maybe it involves a period of harsh penitence (e.g. Dante's *anime purganti* [expiating souls] in his *Comedy*). Still, *intermezzi* [interludes] apart, the eventual outcome is going to be a better life. Death, consequently, becomes desirable, since it can lead to a superior form of fulfilment. Life, in spite of death, or better, through death, continues and, if possible, improves.[15]

[III] *Bona mors.*[16] Death may be an accomplishment in at least three major senses (respectively [IIIa], [IIIb] and [IIIc]).

[IIIa] There are many ways in which to die. Not all of them are alike and, more importantly, not all of them are equally commendable. Some ways can be pathetic—the final painful agony of death after the long, callous torture of old age, about which Egill Skallagrímsson, the dubious hero of the homonymous saga by Snorri Sturluson, sighs miserably: *"My bald pats bobs and blunders / I hang it when I fall; / My cock's gone soft and clammy / And I can't hear when they call.*[17] Some others can be glorious—a warrior's end to be celebrated as the most honourable victory, like the death of the valiant Gunnar of Hildarendi in the saga of Njál the Burnt, of whom Thorkel sang proudly:

We have heard from the south
How Gunnar, warrior of many seas,
Passionate in battle,
Wielded his mighty alberd.
Waves of foemen broke
On the cliffs of his defence;
He wounded sixteen men
And killed two others.[18]

Some other ways can be horrendous—dying alone and in exile, like the death that Ugo Foscolo feared and that he did die as an Italian expatriate in the cold, foggy streets of London, far away from his Hellenic *"amate sponde"* [beloved shores].[19] Some others can be more simply appropriate—a serene passing away, as natural as falling asleep, like those deaths praised by Turgenev, Tolstoy and Solzhenitsyn with reference to the stoical, resilient *muzhiki* [peasants] of Russia: "[M]y death has come, that's that."[20] Death can be desirable, then: it can be an accomplishment, it can crown one's life; and it can be a 'good death' for the individual who dies. In a variety of appraisals and circumstances, honour, dignity, remembrance, fame, love, harmony, or reconciliation can still come to pass at the moment of death, if not especially at the moment of death. The social web within which all human beings are generated, nourished, raised and evaluated determines the method to encounter a proper death and, conversely, to avoid an improper one. A "good death", as Robert C. Solomon writes, may be dictated by "petty selfishness wrapped up in enigma", as in "one of favourite forms of male suicide[:] a pistol or shotgun barrel in the mouth, blowing out the brains but leaving the face untouched." In other words: "The pain is negligible, but the threat to one's vanity is overwhelming." What counts, then, is dying in a proper manner, as determined by "the social dimension of death… When I worry about how I will die, bravely or badly, it is for others that I am concerned." [21]

[IIIb] Conversely, not only the dying individual may benefit from a "good death", but so may do a household, a community, or a whole country. They all may be materially aided, or taught an important lesson, or paid more respect by their neighbours, by means of a member's "good death". Martyrs, patriots, brave firemen, policemen and doctors have exhibited most clearly this possibility. Moreover, also 'bad deaths' can be beneficial, as they can become an instrument to promote more life within the very same social web in which they take place. A 'fool's death', however that may be accomplished, can be a true blessing to a community or a country that is sick of her foolishness (e.g. King Carlo Felice's death in 1831, which meant the end of reactionary conservatism in the Kingdom of

Sardinia).[22] In brief, from a social point of view, individual deaths can be desirable: they represent a way in which a life's end is turned into a step towards the improvement of other lives. A "good" or "happy death" is possible there too.[23]

[IIIc] Recognising one's own mortality can be a crucial moment in a person's process of self-understanding. In Heidegger's philosophy, for instance, the realisation of one's "being-towards-death" is a fundamental moment in the *Dasein*'s itinerary towards authenticity.[24] Four centuries before him, Montaigne had written: "[P]remeditation of death is premeditation of freedom... He who has learned how to die has unlearned how to be a slave. Knowing how to die frees us from all subjection and constraint."[25] Death can be desirable, then: the awareness of its presence can enhance a wiser attitude towards life. Maybe death cannot be good *in se* [in itself], but it can be good *per se* [for itself], as it opens the gates to a better life, which is enriched by a deeper comprehension of oneself and possibly lived more richly by the more self-aware individual. Heidegger and Montaigne are not the only philosophers who regarded death as a source of enlightenment and wisdom. In the West, Epicurus, Lucretius, Seneca, and Pascal, just to mention a few, shared analogous views, and so did in the East Dogen, Shosan, Tagore, and Nishitani. It is interesting to notice that for all these authors, and for several others that could be added, the illumination provided by reflecting upon our mortality implied an austere acceptance of life and a flight from its vain pleasures. Nonetheless, this is not the only response that can be logically inferred from the increased awareness of one's finitude. Lorenzo de Medici, for instance, sang a very different song, namely the song of hedonism:

Questa soma, che vien drieto
sopra l'asino, è Sileno:
così vecchio è ebbro e lieto,
già di carne e d'anni pieno;
se non può star ritto, almeno
ride e gode tuttavia
Chi vuol esser lieto, sia:

di doman non c'è certezza.[26]

[IV] *Intra vitam*

Death may not be what it seems. Many religions and philosophies tend to place life and death in sharp contrast with each other. However, not everybody agrees on the actuality of this division. Several authors describe life and death under a different light: as deeply intertwined; as correlated to each other; even as undistinguishable from each other. Such are the cases of Chuang-Tsu's and Lao-Tsu's Taoist doctrines, for instance, which agreed upon the following point: "life and death are human distinctions made by those who do not understand the unity of all things in the Tao."[27] What we regard as death and life are actually accidental changes within the same substance, distinguishable but not separate modes of being of the same nature, "condensing and expanding" moments of the "field of psycho-physical energy" constituting the whole cosmos (or *qi*).[28] That which we call "death" has to be welcomed, according to these authors, since it perpetuates the ecstatic flux of continuous "transformation of things" (or *wuhua*) that permeates all realities.[29]

On the other hand, in the case one did not share such a positive interpretation of temporality, which is exemplified by Taoism in Asia and, in Europe, by philosophers like Friedrich Nietzsche and Gilles Deleuze, a slightly different perspective is offered by a number of philosophies and mystical doctrines.[30] Among these, several Buddhist schools provide a significant instance by considering the death of the individual as an encouraging event. This occurs because, first of all, such a 'breaking down' of the individual is likely to activate a new individual somewhere else, consistently with the belief in the reincarnation of the soul. Life, in other words, is being transmitted and not dispersed. Secondly, were this activation not the case, then that would mean that an even better result was attained, namely that the individual soul succeeded in escaping from the cycle of *samsara*. The state of 'unestablished consciousness' (or *nirvana*) would have been reached. Life would have realised its potential for utmost perfection.[31] Death, once more, becomes desirable, as it is revealed as a ripple on the surface of the vast ocean of being, or as a splendid moment of transformation or, in a less Heraclitean way, as a gate to enter, or to re-join, the permanent state of perfection, with which the living had lost touch. Indeed, under the latter respect, i.e. that of permanent perfection, Buddhism (and Hinduism) echoes the blissful Christian and Muslim heaven discussed in [II].

The Second Tetralogy of Death

(1) The analytical dimension of death: To die, to be dying, and to be dead.

The first moment of this second tetralogy intends to outline a brief conceptual analysis aimed at showing a few relevant distinctions, which are often neglected in the scholarly and non-scholarly treatment of the issue of death. I proceed by comparing [I]-[IV] with one another, in order to work out these distinctions. However, before I move on and comply with this task, I wish to resume the four major positions outlined in the first tetralogy of mine:[32]

[I]	*Contemptus mundi* (contempt for the universe)
[II]	*Immortalis eris* (continuation or perfection of life)
[IIIa]	*Bona mors* 1 (individual accomplishment)
[IIIb]	*Bona mors* 2 (collective accomplishment)
[IIIc]	*Bona mors* 3 (wisdom or better sense of life's worth)
[IV]	*Intra vitam* (transformation within the whole)

The first distinction is between to die (or the event of death) and dying.

[I], [II], [IIIa–b], and [IV] seem to deal mostly with the event of death; while [IIIc] deals mostly with the consciousness of mortality or, more broadly, with the process of dying. I do not mean to say that the process of dying is excluded by [I]–[IIIb] and by [IV]. Rather, I intend to highlight the fact that their emphasis is placed on the event of death, rather than on the ongoing dying of the subject that accompanies her living throughout: "Death is the condition of your creation, it is part of you… The constant work of your life is to build death. You are in death while you are in life… During life you are dying."[33]

[I] emphasises the event of death by stressing the liberating function of the self's annihilation, which, incidentally, does not necessarily coincide with death. In truth, if we identify the self as the capacity of reacting to stimuli or with retaining certain mental faculties, then patients in permanent vegetative state or unrecoverable alcoholics may be hardly attributed any tenable principle of selfhood: they may be (and, indeed, sometimes are) regarded as tantamount to dead persons.[34]

[II] operates analogously to [I], but *via* several forms of *memento mori* [reminders of mortality], all of which underline the importance of reaching the fatal moment with an active balance on one's *liber vitae* [book of life]. It is only with a clean, good record—whatever "good" may mean in a doctrine's lexicon—that one can happily commute from this world to the next (and join the cherubs or the Valkyries).

[III] teaches a similar approach in [a], by insisting on the nobility, beauty, and on the goodness of determinate types of death. In [b], instead, it concentrates its scope on the usefulness of death. Still, in both [IIIa] and [b], the stress is placed upon the moment of death as an individual act or opportunity. This is done in connection with possible positive outcomes, such as enduring social memory, sincere mourning, or collective gain. [III] differs in [c], which does not orbit around death as such, but around the notions of mortality, finitude, or "being-towards-death". This type of *memento mori* is not concerned with the final event and with the mystical or social transmutation of the individual. On the contrary, the accent is posited on the *hic et nunc* [here and now], i.e. on the present mundane life of the individual, and on how the awareness of one's temporality should pave the road towards true wisdom for this life.[35]

[IV], finally, seems to prioritise death on dying, insofar as it stresses the ways in which the self may dissolve and join the underlying texture of the universe. In several cases (e.g. Japanese

Zen, Madhyamika Buddhism) the process of dying is translated into the very fatal moment of death, which just presents itself at every moment of that which we call "life". Every exhaling, every diastole, every subsiding thought, every night of sleep, every day passing by are seen, in fact, as a little death: "[T]he alternating current of life appears to flow on, oscillating over the abyss, and flowing off continually".[36]

The second distinction is between death as the last event in life and death as a permanent condition, i.e. the status of being dead.

[I] and, more modestly, [IV] focus on the permanent state of selflessness following the event of death. [II] and [III] deal mainly with the very last moment of one's life. [I] promises peace and release at the highest degree. Its point of strength is the total dissolution of the conscious self, the bearer of all the pain, to which, apparently, the existence of the human being pertains:

> *Or poserai per sempre,*
> *Stanco mio cor. Perì l'inganno estremo,*
> *Ch'eterno io mi credei. Perì. Ben sento,*
> *In noi di cari inganni,*
> *Non che la speme, il desiderio è spento.*
> *Posa per sempre. Assai*
> *Palpitasti. Non val cosa nessuna*
> *I moti tuoi, nè di sospiri è degna*
> *La terra. Amaro e noia*
> *La vita, altro mai nulla; e fango è il mondo.*
> *T'acqueta omai. Dispera*
> *L'ultima volta. Al gener nostro il fato*
> *Non donò che il morire. Omai disprezza*
> *Te, la natura, il brutto*
> *Poter che, ascoso, a comun danno impera,*
> *E l'infinita vanità del tutto.*[37]

[II] and [IIIa–b] privilege the perspective of death as an event, i.e. as the last moment of a life and, consequently, as the most significant moment of an individual's entire existence, if not even the true climax. They teach to the individual or to the community about how to make the most of this event, either by gaining an afterlife, or dignity, or whatever positive gain may come out of death. [IIIc] does nearly the same as [II] and [IIIa-b], but in a more intellectual fashion. In this case, in fact, the stress is placed upon the awareness that one day, inevitably, death shall come. Thus, by keeping this very notion firm in one's own mind, the person may return to her life serenely and ready to enjoy it more maturely and more inclusively. As Montaigne wrote: "[A]ll the wisdom and reasoning in the world boils down finally to this point: to teach us not to be afraid to die."[38]

[IV] constitutes a rather ambiguous case. Death as an event is in fact dissolved or treated as poorly relevant. Death as a permanent state seems to disappear as well, at least insofar as the gaze is directed on the eternal flux of being which underlies all phenomena, and which is generally described in terms of boundless consciousness or energy. The self is gone, but something quasi-living or quasi-thinking persists. In this sense, exceptional are those Indian schools embracing a radical materialist ontology (e.g. the Carvakas of the 7th century B.C.), which anticipate the de-humanization of the human being that we encounter in much of modern and post-modern Western philosophy (e.g. Friedrich Nietzsche or Gilles Deleuze). In these cases, the whole to which the dead returns is that of nature in its inorganic and organic components, rather than a quasi-mystical realm of non-spatial consciousness or energy.[39]

(2) The axiological dimension of death: The value of death

The second moment of this second tetralogy of death is intended to individuate briefly the major elements of value connected with the accounts of death considered in the first tetralogy. As a general consideration, the phenomenon of death appears to be culturally laden with negative and/or positive implications of value, both as a reason for taking it into consideration, and as an outcome of having taken it into consideration. However, I do not spend many words on this second moment, since this chapter is axiologically biased *ab origine* [from the start]. As mentioned in the introductory remarks, I have chosen only positions that deem death to be desirable, even if for different reasons and under different circumstances.

[I] is probably the most radical case in terms of its approval of death. Death is a blessing, a fortune, or a goal to be eager of. Some thinkers (e.g. Arthur Schopenhauer) did even preach for absolute chastity in view of the extinction of the human race. After all, if one looks at life as a disvalue, what else could be more valuable than its total annihilation?

[II] and [III], whether dealing with death as the final step, or with death as dying, still regard both cases as valuable.[40] The difference between the two approaches concerns the modality in which they do it. [II] considers death as a crucial moment in human life, so that much of its teaching is directed to providing the human being with an adequate structure of understanding, in order for her to be able to cope with it. [IIIc] is often equally emphatic about death, as with Heidegger's insistence on the epiphany of Being *via* death-induced "*Angst*" [(existential) anxiety], or with the Zen's *Leitmotiv* [recurring theme] of living having let go of life.[41]

[IIIa–b], instead, are far more context-dependent. In fact, not always one can choose how to die, and therefore make the most of death; nor can or may a community benefit always from a member's death. Plausibly, the only thing that may be done nearly always is the creation of those conditions that allow for the maximisation of the number of good or useful deaths. Education, myth-making, and social pressure on the one hand, testaments, ritual cannibalism, and funeral business on the other, are all forms in which this kind of preparatory, good-death-enhancing settings can be instituted and maintained.

[IV], once again, is the most ambiguous case. Its denial of the actuality of death would seem to lead towards indifference to both life and death. Yet, as Mahayana Buddhism exemplifies, the concern about life and death is present, for the fact itself of teaching about life and death implies an axiological investiture of the two.[42] Similarly, Taoism, Jainism, and Hinduism, in all of their forms, do want to teach us how to avoid suffering and, *a fortiori*, how to live and how to die. The same can be said about the Western voices mentioned in my work: death may be proclaimed not to exist, not to be real, not to be much at all; still, it remains something to be explained, understood, accepted and, in certain cases, enjoyed (e.g. Nietzsche's principle of *amor fati* [love of destiny] or Montaigne's belief that "to philosophise is to learn to die").[43]

(3) The ontological dimension of death: Who dies?

A complex structure of ontological presuppositions lurks behind the various positions on death as a *desideratum* (or *desiderandum*) we have encountered. In order for a *desideratum* to be, in fact, there must be an individual or collective *desiderans* [somebody who desires], one or more actual or virtual *desiderabilia* [possible objects of desire], and an origin or a cause of such *desiderabilia*'s becoming *desiderata/desideranda* [objects of desire/objects to be desired], which I call *ratio desiderii* [the ground for desiring].

[I] comprises a clear *desiderans*: the self. It is the individual, in fact, who sets death as a positive end, i.e. as a *desideratum*. She sets it so axiologically, for she evaluates it positively. It may even set it so ontologically, for she may commit suicide: this, because there are no other or no better *desiderabilia*. Virtually, or hypothetically, there would be only the very opposite of death i.e. life—a life without pain, without suffering, without all those defects that make it unbearable. Yet, a painless life is a mere dream—a tragic, frustrating, unattainable *desideratum*. The *ratio desiderii* is the sorrowful realisation of this disturbing truth: this valley of tears shall never be dry—may the self dwell in it no more.

[II] comprises more or less the same *desiderans* as [I]. The self is the one who has to gain access to the further- or after-life. Depending on the doctrine, a certain part of the self, variously called "soul", "spirit", "pneuma", etc., is often the protagonist of this longing for death. The individual body may break down, but the real self (i.e. its *principium individuationis* [principle of individuation]) does not. Instead, it persists and moves on to a new form of being. The *desiderabilia* of this afterlife are variously depicted among the diverse human creeds, mythologies, and doctrines that [II]

15

comprehends. Socrates, for instance, proposed an eternity of intellectual contemplation; Teresa of Avila a perpetual state of ecstatic bliss; Mohammed and the Vikings agreed upon a hyperbolic multiplication of mundane pleasures (whereas the former spoke mainly of food and virgin sexual partners, the latter focused on good ales and fighting). The *desideranda* can vary in a surprising manner. Still, a common *ratio desiderii* may be individuated in the appreciation of the goods that this life may give only in a limited way. That which shall come after this life, if properly earned, is an unlimited and ameliorated version of them. It could be objected that, in a number of doctrines, the body, as opposed to the soul, aims at different forms of fulfilment, which may be denied in the afterlife. This may appear to be true if one takes an external point of observation with respect to the doctrines. From an internal point of observation, in fact, this dismissal is absolutely consistent, since the body is not the true self, and its cravings are erroneous and ill-directed.

[III] extends the understanding of death to the social dimensions attached to it. In [a], and even more evidently in [c], it is still the self that plays the major role as *desiderans*. However, his looking at death as a *desideratum* is heavily dependent upon what the community in which she lives, or the exclusive judgment in which she trusts, regards as *desiderabilia*. It is up to the context in which she dies to transform such possible achievements into *desideranda*. In [b] it is the social body that takes over the part as *desiderans*, making it explicit how the self is more than a physical entity and more than a natural creature: it is a social being. Yet, all three sub-cases of [III] seem to offer the same *ratio desiderii*: life may grant us a few positive things, even with respect to the element of death that it necessarily entails. [c] elects wisdom and its correlated fullness of life as the most precious gain possible. [a] and [b] vary quite a lot, instead, but they do agree on the fact that death does bring forth some good whenever it enhances life, whether this is understood in terms of immortality, survival, fruitful legacy, exemplarity, enduring heritage, etc.

[IV] shifts too the attention from the self to the whole. The self is here discarded as a fictitious cluster of matter and laws thereof, or of instances of consciousness and laws thereof, according to the basic ontology endorsed by the various different doctrines. Death is a *desideratum* just because it destroys this temporary cluster and allows the whole to proceed further. Somehow, the *desiderans* is the self, who is taught to appreciate the idea that she shall die and re-join the totality in which she is already immersed and without which she would have never been. *Desiderabilia* are the ontological stages of collapse of the self's isolation, which enlarge her horizon and manifest the interdependence of all the manifestations of being. The *ratio desiderii* seems to be rather unselfish, hence difficult to connote as a gain for the self. The states of boundless consciousness or of vital energy-flow, of chaotic flux of matter inside which she is bound to vanish, are most selfless. Life, nevertheless, seems to persist in spite of all, or better, as all that which is there, i.e. as the whole of being embracing the particular beings as the ocean embraces its drops (interestingly, *nirvana* is often described as an *oceanic* field of boundless consciousness).

(4) The existential dimension of death: Who does really care?

Various existential attitudes can be derived from the previous three elements of the tetralogy. Once again, my analysis is brief, since I have delimited my field of analysis to a precise set of possible reactions to the *datum* [given] of death, namely those involving a positive response.[44]

[I] suggests that death should be sought after by all means. Existence is horrible; hence we should try to get rid of it. Whether by very direct means, such as suicide, or indirect ones, such as asceticism, we must flee from the world's cage.

[II] is somehow similar to [I], in the sense that the sooner one crosses the final threshold (in the appropriate manner), the sooner one crosses from the domain of imperfection into that of perfection. Once again, the modalities in which this can be done are diverse, but the underlying logic is one and the same. [I] and [II] entail several ways in which somebody can rush towards death: committing suicide, engaging in mortal fights, leading a Byronesque lifestyle (an *ante-litteram* [before the word was coined] Romantic version of the motto "sex, drugs, and rock'n roll"), or leading a Pachomian monastic life-style (inclusive of self-deprivation).

[IIIa–b] espouse a more moderate approach. Death has not to be longed for under all circumstances. It is only when death is appropriate that it is to be sought after. Death must be faced in the right way—with the sword or the pen in one's hand. If it is not right, it is wrong—indeed a reason for scorn, shame, or oblivion. [IIIc] invites the sage to "familiarize with death", so that the day death comes she will not be unprepared.[45] In this perspective, [IIIc] is a variation along the lines of [IIIa–b]. The right death is one to which the sage arrives *qua* sage, and not as a timorous, doubtful, unprepared commoner, who has wasted or not enjoyed the opportunity of leading an enlightened, authentic existence.

[IV] calls for a similarly enlightened, serene acceptance of death. Death is hardly anything, in fact, for our own life is hardly anything as well. All that dwells in the contingent is nothing but a fleeting construction, an illusion, an epiphenomenon, a temporary concretion of a more fundamental energy, which survives unscathed. Such an approach cannot but reduce the weight and the meaningfulness of the individual *qua* individual and, *a fortiori*, the traumatic impact of her death. Under this perspective, Nietzsche represents an *unicum* [unique case] in the history of Western thought, as far as [IV] is concerned. In spite of his recognition of the inhuman nature of the human being (e.g. our constitutive, utter and inescapable cruelty), in spite of his Schopenhauerian background regarding the overwhelming power of blind instincts and natural drives, in spite of his pulverization of any superior meaning of life following the recognition of the universal power of chance in the endless recurrence of the same, Nietzsche still wants us to accept reality as it is and to rejoice in it. The individual is almost nothing, but she is also all that she can be. Turning the French mystic Blaise Pascal upside-down, Nietzsche dives into infinite contingency, ready to play with all that is to come along, sorrow included. Under this respect, his key notions of the *Übermensch* (or "superman") and of the "revaluation of all values" become extremely significant: only an utterly new human being can say "Yes" to life (and to death) under such conditions, thus becoming the creator of her unique (yet recursive) life-path [46]

The Complexity of the Ontology of Death

It is important to reflect further on the implications of the ontological dimension of death explored in (3) and, by means of it, on the mutual interconnectedness of (1)–(4). It is important to realise the number of ontological levels at which the human beings spend their existence, often in a state of complete unawareness. Language, chemistry, cellular activity, electric exchanges with the environment are, ontologically speaking, as truly part of 'us' as will, desire, and parental functions. Life and death can be consequently read at several different levels, and they do not necessarily coincide with the body's disintegration. In truth, humans are given many a form of immortality, and as many of mortality. If we consider just the level of the body, for example, then we must notice that the individual's death liberates energies from the temporary form or concretion inside which they had been trapped, i.e. inside the individual herself. The same consideration applies to inorganic matter, which, from a physical point of view, is equivalent to energy. Thus, if the universe is going to exist after our death—if energy will keep flowing—part of the merit goes to the dying ones.

At a different level, such as the biological one, the death of an individual does not imply the destruction of her unique genetic information. The individual may have had children, in fact, who are likely to carry a relevant amount of that information for at least another generation. And still at the biological level, the individual's death may often involve the growth and flourishing of other forms of life, such as earthworms and fungi that are going to take care of the individual's process of decomposition: the individual does not abandon the food chain till her corpse is completely vanished, as this is slowly metabolised in the *apparatus* of snails, microbes, and of other life-forms.

What really matters, then, in order to have any kind of bodily survival at all, is that something related to the body survives the threshold-event that we call "death". All this may seem obvious, if not even trivial; still, it is most relevant. It is relevant in order to get a picture of how complex the human being's ontology is. In other terms, we are much more than the 'we' we think of being in our ordinary experience. Perhaps, it is hardly relevant for the dead, at least after the event of death. It could be of some relevance, or consolation, to the not-yet-dead (the living, or to-be-dead aka *moriturus*), since she would know that, after death, she can return to nature a good deal of that which nature had given to her (quarks, oxygen, water, or whatever we may pick as an instance). However, after death, does this really mean anything to the dead?

This is the kind of problem that is bound to accompany any philosophy of death: understanding death is an issue for the dying individual, i.e. everybody who is alive; while for the dead, as far as we can know, nothing is seemingly an issue any longer. Yet, this line of argument is based on a series of evaluative assumptions (e.g. understanding may help to deal with issues, issues may be relevant, new meanings may change attitudes, annihilation may be a source of anxiety or of relief, etc.), as well as a number of ontological assumptions (e.g. the non-existence of a soul, the persistence of a person's consciousness in another material structure, etc.). These assumptions do not solely show the interconnectedness of (1)–(4), but also how much the third perspective of my first tetralogy (*bona mors*) may be presupposed fairly easily in the secular scholarly context of the 21st century. Until a few generations ago, many a supporter of [II] or [IV] would have regarded these views as short-sighted reductions of the complex reality in which we live to the level of physical reality alone. Perhaps, such views would have been discarded as naïve and poorly supported by either evidence or authority or both. Such views might even be right: this issue is not something that I can resolve hereby. What matters here, instead, is to highlight how varied, comprehensive, and inexhaustible is the ontology related to the body's death.

Analogous considerations can be developed with regard to the level of consciousness as well, i.e. the level at which evaluations and ontological assumptions take place *qua* evaluations and assumptions (and at which issues of identity and existence are most commonly addressed). With regard to consciousness, in fact, the individual's thoughts, words, and experiences are not necessarily bound to disappear when the body ends. Her recorded memories, even as a mere name on a gravestone, are left to those who will have access to them. In addition, one's legacy (moral, artistic, educational, criminal, etc.) does not vanish with the end of the possibility for the individual's consciousness to have access to her own products. In truth, the importance of these legacies is made evident by the individual's interest in them during her own lifetime, i.e. prior to her own death. People want to be remembered as models of virtue, skilfulness, integrity, capacity, etc. They want their work—their poems, paintings, companies, collections, etc.—to survive after their death. The poet Ugo Foscolo saw his sonnets as the road toward immortality. The millionaire chemist Alfred Bader saw philanthropy as an alternative way to obtain the same result, as seven centuries before him did the Scrovegni family, who commissioned to Giotto the decoration of the famous Scrovegni chapel in Padua. Even murder, if well-designed and visibly accomplished, may guarantee similar results, whilst others become blunders—Jack the Ripper *docet* [teaches]. What really matters, in terms of survival of the fruits of one's consciousness, is that at least others may survive and preserve these fruits from extinction (naturally, it can be hard to imagine that one may be concerned with this kind of problem after her death).

Once we see how many forms of immortality we are granted, one may then conclude: "well, then my death is not such a big deal, for I shall live on in so many other ways!". On the other side, one could reply as well: "yes, but where do I, Jacques Bonhomme, have a place in these forms of immortality?" [I], [II], and [IIIc] would represent most plausible places for this latter type of question to arise. [IIIb] and [IV], instead, would seem to favour the former type of consideration. The crucial point does not seem to be merely a choice between life and death, but rather between an understanding of both life and death as affecting an eminently individualised or interrelated reality. We partake of both spheres, why should we reject one or the other? It is true that most of the bodily, conscious, and variously extra-individual, process-related determinations that have discussed under [IIIb] and [IV] are generally indifferent to life and death. In effect, they are present during both the life and the death of the individual. Instead, interrelatedness persists and insists *post mortem* [after death]. It is the individual *quid* [quintessence], though, that which seems to make the difference. Even if some part of a particular individual may persist, in fact, another part of her is annihilated—her original identity is annihilated. The value that we place on it is that which seems to make certain perspectives on death more or less appealing. However, this appeal may be explained in terms of cultural habits, which turn certain deaths into 'good deaths', and others into 'bad deaths'. The doctrines mentioned in [IV] (with the notable exception of Friedrich Nietzsche's) seem to suggest that our cultural obsession with individuality is at the origin of many an existential problem, some of which may even lead to the tragic conclusions mentioned in [I]. Who is right? Can anybody be right? Or is there any way in which these two questions can be harmonised together?

I have not provided here a criterion to select one stance rather than another: this is not the goal of my work. I leave it to the reader to decide where to leap with her faith—or where to follow her reason, if reason can guide one that far. Certainly, I hope to contribute to the reasons one may have for reflecting about these issues. In fact, I believe that it is possible to encompass both sides of the problem, i.e. individual and interrelated, without denying the correctness of the insights that come from both of them. Specifically, we can accept our living and dying in many ways and times throughout our individual existence. Nonetheless, why should we underestimate the impact that death has at these various levels, hence also (if not mainly) at the personal level? I do not intend to deny that the end of that process that we call one's life has a dramatic side. I do not reject individual will, desires, hopes, achievements, as mere illusions, which is what part of the doctrines mentioned in [IV] does. This refusal to reduce the individual experience to an underlying 'real' form of reality, to which we are re-joined by death, is that which allows us to place value on what we call one's "own" life. Still, the acceptance of the perspicuous identity of different, although interrelated, ontological levels is that which can make sense of any determination of value pertaining to anything that be other than the individuating substratum's; hence also of the recognition of the importance in one's "own" life of the opinion of our peers, of the proper upbringing of one's children, and of the well-being of the future generations (human and non-human), etc. In truth, one is likely to be able to be preoccupied with her *post-mortem* approval, fame, success, etc. only whilst she is still alive, as it seems plausible that one can do something about it only whilst she is still alive. Yet, once again, this is a plausible option if we take for granted that [III] depicts the reality of things, which, as I stated before, is something that has not been assessed for certain. As I said, I do not intend to solve this issue hereby. Rather, what matters to my end, is to reflect upon the interconnectedness of the various levels I have just presented separately in my two tetralogies.

The possibility itself of building one's legacy or one's fruits whatsoever *intra vitam* is dependent upon a number of other concomitant conditions: the presence of other human beings, for instance. Nobody was ever born by herself, as well as nobody was ever granted any form of approval, success, etc. without some kind of interaction with other humans. More generally, no value, or even no language, meaning, or self-understanding seems possible without the concomitant presence of other human beings (or medium-sized social mammals, at the very least). And the interactions with such other creatures must be organised in some way: there must be cultural patterns, regularities, and standards. In other terms, nobody lives outside a *polis* of some kind, at least until she decides to abandon it. Quite often, one does not leave it at all, no matter for how long she may have abandoned it: in Scotland, they still take flowers to William Wallace's grave. In brief, several interconnected dimensions of being can be inferred from the scrutiny of the death of consciousness. The social sphere is one (especially with [IIIa–b]). The political is another, as it can be inferred from the given of the mortality of one's consciousness, since no society can survive without some form of distribution of competence and power amongst the consciousness of the citizens (see again [IIIa–b]). Analogously, the linguistic sphere can be deduced, since there must be some form of communication in such a society—and so on with whatever super-subjective sphere one may desire to think of. As it was the case with the death of the body, so it is with the death of the consciousness: it relates to a varied, comprehensive, inexhaustible catalogue of determinations of being. So vast and diverse is the catalogue of these determinations, that one may even conclude by stating that death is a monad, as it contains the universe within itself (but what amidst the existing beings is not, after all, a monad related to all there is?).[47]

Speaking *à la* Leibniz, then, death is a perspective on the whole. All possible dimensions of being seem to be related to it, whether directly or indirectly. All possible dimensions of value do seem to impinge upon it, as do the existential ones. Whether it is riches, wisdom, love, or respect that we want, either individually or collectively, we want them before and/or after our death (depending on our ontological presuppositions), and we are ready to spend our whole life trying to get that which we want. Whatever that which we want is, our wanting is possible because, ontologically, there are the 'we', the desires, the capacity of having them, the reality within which we try to fulfil them, etc. Whether some of these dimensions are more basic than others, it is a problem that I do not intend to discuss here: my work intends to be a cultural exploration and not an assessment on the many positions available in the field of philosophical ontology. Still, I hope to have expressed and exemplified sufficiently the complexity of the themes that an investigation in the phenomenon of the desirable death may evince. In effect, it would seem that the whole universe can be shown through this particular monad.

The Dialectic of Life and Death

As for the focus of our monad, however, something more specific seems to come out of the exploration that I have led. The perspective on the whole that death represents, in fact, seems to be pointing toward a particular ground of value. Throughout this brief scrutiny of the main trends in the positive approaches to the phenomenon of death, death seems to be of some relevance for life itself. Montaigne and Nietzsche had already suggested that to be able to face the issue of death is a way to cast some light on life itself (cf. [IIIc]). Along those lines, what I am suggesting hereby is that every philosophy of death that regards death as a positive reality is, ultimately, a philosophy of life, the most articulate contemporary token of which is offered by the Canadian philosopher John McMurtry who, in his life-value onto-axiology, claims that life constitutes the most fundamental value (or source of value) across individuals, cultures, and epochs. By arguing in this direction, McMurtry moves daringly against the dominating post-modern trend spreading value-relativism in all disciplinary fields, and especially in the humanities. He endorses the idea according to which, by carefully analysing Western as well as Eastern religions, the declared goals of left- as well as of right-wing political ideologies, the justifications of conservative as well as of progressive social programmes, the appreciation as well as the condemnation of novel artistic creations, we can individuate a common ground of value. This ground of value can be cast as a "Primary Axiom of Value" or "value of all values" that is expressed as follows:

> *X is value if and only if, and to the extent that, x consists in or enables a more coherently inclusive range of thought/feeling/ action than without it.*

> *Where these three ultimate fields of value are defined as:*

thought = internal image and concept (T)
feeling = the felt side of being (F) / senses, desires, emotions, moods
action = animate movement (A) *across species and organizations*

Conversely:

x is disvalue if and only if, and to the extent that, x reduces/ disables any range of thought/experience/action.

Symbolically expressed:

$+V => LR + and -V = < LR$
where L= Range of T-F-A
and / = and/or[48]

The triplet comprising thought, feeling (aka experience) and action indicates what McMurtry understands life to be like. According to his theory, in fact, life encompasses three planes of being: [1] The plane of the organism's biological capacity for movement (e.g. being capable of moving freely one's limbs, or of breathing while asleep); [2] the plane of felt being, feeling, or awareness (e.g. being capable of feeling enlightened by this chapter, seeing it, or of being more vividly receptive); and [3] the plane of cognitive abstraction, or self-awareness (e.g. being capable of any mental representation whatsoever: from the simplest image-thoughts to the most abstract forms of mathematical demonstration). Thus, according to McMurtry, anything has value in proportion to the ranges of further biological movement, awareness, and self-awareness that it enhances. Food, emotions, education, taxation, or its reduction, are valuable–good–if and only if, and insofar as, they guarantee the attainment of a deeper and/or broader scope for action, felt being, and thought. Not only does McMurtry's theory of value suggest that actions, events, intentions, or phenomena have value insofar as they promote wider ranges of life, but also that valueless ones, i.e. life-destructive actions, events, intentions, or phenomena, can be mistaken for, or misrepresented as, life-promoting ones: one thing is to claim that x is value, another is that x is, in fact, value.[49]

All of the cases mentioned under [I]–[IV] address life in at least one of its constitutive dimensions. By referring to at least one of such planes, not only do they describe, or even prescribe, what life is or should be with respect to death; more deeply, they describe, or even prescribe, death as function of life: life is that which makes death desirable.

In [I], for instance, death is desirable because it may rescue a person from a life that she despises—since she would like to have another life so powerfully, that its denial makes her opt for no life at all. Life, as the thought of a fulfilling existence and as the realisation of its impossibility, is the actual engine of the person's preference for death. It may not surprise that Montaigne, faithful to the tradition of Stoicism, regarded suicide as a sensible way to escape from life, which is to be employed whenever life should become too hard to bear. Arthur Schopenhauer will provide an analogous account of suicide three centuries later, yet not to justify suicide, but to condemn it. Killing oneself because of life's harshness, in fact, was seen by Schopenhauer as an extreme act of affirmation of life itself, namely as a further and most dramatic expression of the universal, eternal, uncreated, undirected *Wille zum Leben* [will to live], which blindly guides most, if not all, individual existences, in the guise of the unconscious spring of desire.[50] With suicide, for Schopenhauer, the life-directed *voluntas* [will] of the individual does not negate life: the subject commits suicide since she cannot get the kind of fulfilment she would like to be enjoying. Life should be denied, instead, *qua* life, i.e. because of its being the source of all human sorrows, for life affirms itself each and every time the individual desires something. Suicide is not the negation of life, then, because it is performed *in nomine vitae* [in the name of life] and not *in nomine mortis* [in the name of death]: it is performed in order to fulfil a desire. Aesthetic contemplation, *pietas* [piety, compassion, humanity] and asceticism, on the contrary, are the right ways to demonstrate proper *noluntas* [un-will], i.e. to deny life's domain over oneself, for they abstract the individual from the realm of desire (more is to be said on Schopenhauer and philosophical pessimism in the pages to follow).

In [II], [IIIa] and [IIIc], instead, death is desirable because it may bring forth more life to the one who dies—since it grants access to a never-ending life (e.g. the Valhalla), or to a somewhat more modest form of immortality (e.g. fame), or to a superior form of life (e.g. the examined life of the sage). In [IIIb], death is desirable because it may bring forth more life as such—the extinction of the individual may be a necessary sacrifice in order to increase the quality and/or the quantity of life around her (e.g. the patriot's self-sacrifice for the good of the community). In [IV], death is desirable because it may be just a misunderstood face of life—nature, the universe, the oceanic field of consciousness that flows eternally; what we regard as individual lives and deaths are just ripples on the perpetual flux of a deeper form of life through the eons of time.

It could be easily replied that death, as, perhaps, any other concept, entails its own opposite, i.e., in this case, life. The dialectic between death and life hereby individuated would be, in other words, mere conceptual blatancy. The problem with this reply, however, is that it focuses only on the logical (or semantic) aspect of their interrelation, which is only one of the many possible approaches one can take (as exemplified by my four approaches [I]–[IV]). In truth, this assertion condemns this dialectical insight to a lower status of philosophical complexity just because it does not dare to look at other possible dimensions of inquiry, such as the axiological, the ontological, and the existential. Besides, it should be stressed that death, as very few other issues, appears to be an eminently axiological and existential issue, even before it may be reduced to a specimen for intellectual scrutiny. All societies, since the very dawn of humankind, have always shown a particular reverence towards this phenomenon, long before they ever started formulating philosophical or religious hypotheses in any codified fashion. Most humans, in addition, seem equally concerned with such a given of their existence, insofar as they tend to deal with it in a non-trivial manner, both in the case in which they try to avoid it as a threat, and in the case in which they call it upon themselves as a blessing or as a last resource (as seen with [I]). The reason for which death is regarded in such a non-trivial manner is because of its capacity of making the difference in one's life (or in the life of a family, of a tribe, of a community, as seen with [IIIb]). Whether death interrupts 'prematurely' a life, or does come 'at the right time', or is not actually the end, the evaluation of its in-/opportunity is always made in view of life itself (if, at least, my rendering of life *via* life-value onto-axiology is granted some plausibility).

Specifically, for the cases that I have been discussing (for all of which death is desirable), it seems appropriate to state that the key-element determining the desirability of death is exactly its capacity of affecting life in life's own terms. As my cultural exploration can help us realise, the more one investigates into the mystery of death, the more one finds out remarks, reflections, insights, perspectives on life. Death is a mirror: the more one looks at it, the more one sees herself; the more one looks at its features, the more one sees her own looking eyes. If one desires death, in one or more of the forms discussed in this succinct account of mine, then she actually desires a different life—a painless life, a happier life, a brighter life, a truer life, etc. Life shines most brightly in death's mirror—Medieval Christianity spoke, for one, of the *speculum mortis*: "the mirror of death".

Notes on Pessimism

This game of mirrors applies most emblematically to philosophical pessimism, namely the stance that would seem to pose the strongest challenge to life-value onto-axiology.

I do not intend to explain in further detail or criticise the triplet of dimensions that, for McMurtry, define life. I find it sufficiently clear and compatible with our notions of common sense about life; hence, I take it as valid. Rather, I intend to tackle the more basic issue of life being actually such a fundamental value (or source of value). Too many, in fact, are the voices that, from time immemorial, have utterly deprecated life. As early as in the sixth century B.C., the Greek poet Theognis of Megara wrote: "The best lot of all for man is never to have been born nor sees the beams of the burning Sun; this failing, to pass the gates of Hades as soon as one may, and lie under a goodly heap of earth."[51] And in his Oedipus Tyrannus, Sophocles echoed: "we must call no mortal happy until he has crossed life's border free from pain."[52]

With respect to the history of thought, this negative attitude towards life took probably its most dramatic form in the 19th-century constitution of philosophical pessimism as a legitimate speculative current, the distinctive feature of which was the open negation of life as a value. Here, I make use of two famous, representative 19th-century pessimist thinkers in order to test the validity of John McMurtry's thesis, and to assess whether life can be consistently denied as a value (or as a source of value); or whether, as McMurtry's thesis implies, life cannot but be the axiological basis for all discriminations of value–even for those of the pessimist itself. Before proceeding, it is important to note that the philosophical and religious positions that I am bringing about are *explicitly* criticising a positive consideration of life. They are not denying life as a value because they are forgetting about it. A forgetfulness or oblivion of life is revisable, for example, in the case of the scientific-technological *Weltanschauung* [worldview] that, according to Martin Heidegger, has been dominating the 20th century, or in the case of the liberal market-economy paradigm, which, according to John McMurtry, can only deal with reality by reducing it to a collection of predictable, invariant series of phenomena that are assumed to behave like the inanimate objects of physics. Both cases represent two life-blind value-programmes, whose conceptual-methodological endorsement of a late Newtonian mechanistic epistemology rules out *a priori* life as a possible variable in their calculations, as I explain in chapters 3 and 4.

The first representative author that I wish to consider is the Italian poet and philosopher Giacomo Leopardi, whom I have already quoted in this chapter. Encyclopaedically familiar with classical literature at a very early age, he knew extremely well the tragic streak that, from Sophocles to Lucretius, had depicted life as a miserable, dreadful journey through valleys of tears, hells of pain, seas of sorrows, labyrinths of incomprehensible riddles. "Pleasure is the son of suffering",[53] for pleasure can occur if and only if we find momentary respite from unhappiness; for instance when "you sleep without dreaming, or have fainted, or somehow have the use of your senses interrupted",[54] namely when you are enjoying "anticipation of death".[55] In one of his most famous *Operette morali*, Leopardi describes "our common mother" Nature as "an immense female shape, sitting on the ground with her torso erect, leaning on the side of a mountain... with a face partly beautiful and partly frightening, and with the darkest eyes and hair".[56] An unfortunate Icelander, who was vainly trying to escape from her dominion, meets this sublime giantess accidentally in the African savannah, and is addressed by her with these words:

Did you believe that the world had been created for you? You must know that in my makings, orders, and operations, and with very few exceptions, I have always had and still have intents that do not contemplate men's happiness or unhappiness. Whenever I offend you in any way or fashion, I don't realise it, if not in very rare cases; and usually, if I please or help you, I don't know it; I didn't do, as you believe, such things or actions to please you or to offer you aid. Indeed, if it happened that I make your entire species extinct, I would not be aware of it.[57]

According to Leopardi, nature does not care about human fortunes. Our suffering is of no point or interest to her. If there is any logic behind Mother Nature's work, we will never know it. Most tellingly, just an instant before Nature reveals her plans to the Icelander, the poor man is assaulted by two lions or, according to another account, a sandstorm befalls upon him and mummifies his body. The ending of this parable shows how Leopardi was incapable of finding any meaning in human existence. Suicide might be a plausible solution, but one that, according to him, is almost impossible to select. Nature is a sadistic tyrant, in fact, and deprives most human beings of the strength of will that such an extreme action requires. For those who have some more strength than the average, though, the long wait for death called "life" is not the only alternative left on the scene. Our condition can be partially redeemed by one particular attitude: the stoical endurance of our cruel destiny. In the "Dialogue between Tristan and a Friend", we read:

If these convictions of mine originate from sickness, I don't know; I know that, whether I be sick or in health, I detest men's cowardice, I refuse any consolation or childish illusion, and I am brave enough to endure the absence of any hope, and to stare calmly at the desert of life, and not to lie to myself about men's infelicity, and to accept all the consequences of a painful, but true, philosophy, which may be useful to nothing else but allowing the strong man to see, with stoical gratification, all of destiny's cruel and hidden cloaks being stripped off.[58]

Still, it is at this point that doubts about the life-denying character of Leopardi's pessimism arise. The stoical gratification just praised by Leopardi is, in fact, a clear case, however minimal, of increase of life-ranges, specifically in terms of felt being and thought.[59] Certainly self-indulgence is contained within it, as the hero Tristan derives satisfaction from the almost warrior-like strength of his own soul, which can stand up against the terrifying sight of the truth about human existence. Similarly, Leopardi admires Tristan's intellectual attitude insofar as it is capable of embracing just this tragic truth, rather than fleeing cowardly from it, seeking refuge in the "childish illusions" of religion, which tell the human being that the delights that are denied in this life will be enjoyed in another life to come.[60] To a deeper scrutiny, Leopardi's apology of death itself appears to contain a life-based ground of value. Paradoxically, death is praised, or even called upon oneself, in the name of life. Even if somebody succeeds in killing oneself, she does so on behalf of the kind of life that she would like to possess, but which is being denied to her. What makes this dreamt-of life desirable is its fullness in action, felt being, and thought. That which makes the actually-lived life unbearable is that it does not resemble the former in any respect. Life is, then, the ultimate ground for value-discrimination.

The other pessimist philosopher that I intend to examine, Arthur Schopenhauer, as seen in the preceding section of this chapter, had already moved a critical remark on suicide analogous to mine. He did not accept suicide as a justifiable escape from life, because he believed that the reasons that people have to kill themselves are always connected with their frustrated desires for a better life, rather than with the sincere recognition of the impossibility of any better life, for life, as he argued, cannot be good in itself. Schopenhauer described all biological life as the superficial–epiphenomenal– expression of a deeper, eternal, infinite, uncreated, irrational, metaphysical energy: the so-called "will to live". This root of all being perpetuates itself through the eons of time by making all individual life-forms strive for survival. More complex creatures crave for pleasure and most significantly for the illusory sexual pleasure, which is as fleeting as it is attractive. In effect, there is actually no pleasure to be had. In this cunning way, every biological species continues to exist, making the individual believe that she is going to serve her own particular interests, when she is actually serving the interests of the species alone:

> *The ultimate aim of all love affairs, whether they are played in sock or cothurnus, is really more important than all other ends of human life, and is therefore quite worthy of the profound seriousness with which everyone pursues it. That which is decided by it is nothing less than the composition of the next generation. The dramatis personae who shall appear when we are withdrawn are here determined, both as regards their existence and their nature, by these frivolous love affairs. As the being, the existentia, of these future persons is absolutely conditioned by our sexual impulse generally, so their nature, essentia, is determined by the individual selection in its satisfaction, i.e., by sexual love, and is in every respect irrevocably fixed by this.*[61]

In reality, the individual's life oscillates always and only between *pain* and *boredom*. On the one hand, we desire, we need, we hope, we tend towards something else, something new, something that we miss, and the lack of which makes us dissatisfied. On the other hand, that very something else, for which we craved so much, once it has been reached, proves to be of no value whatsoever, for our contentment does not last, and, as long as we do not go back to desiring, needing, hoping, we are left with a sense of emptiness:

Human life must be some kind of mistake. The truth of this will be sufficiently obvious if we only remember that man is a compound of needs and necessities hard to satisfy; and that even when they are satisfied, all he obtains is a state of painlessness, where nothing remains to him but abandonment to boredom. This is direct proof that existence has no real value in itself; for what is boredom but the feeling of the emptiness of life? If life–the craving for which is the very essence of our being–were possessed of any positive intrinsic value, there would be no such thing as boredom at all: mere existence would satisfy us in itself, and we should want for nothing.[62]

All that we can hope for, according to Schopenhauer, is the interruption of this oscillation, which is not brought about by the satisfaction of any desire, but by the suppression of desire. Following the teachings of mainstream Buddhism, Schopenhauer strived for the creation of an articulated training directed towards the achievement of *nirvana*, namely the total annihilation of the will to live–the annihilation of desire. What matters most for my present study is that, by outlining exactly this will-suppressing training, Schopenhauer identified three specific ways out of the tragic fluctuation between boredom and dissatisfaction: art, humanity (aka piety, compassion) and asceticism—as outlined most notably in his famous book, *The World as Will and Representation*. At least two of these three specific ways out are, in fact, openly life-affirming:

[a] *Art*, which Schopenhauer intended as the aesthetic contemplation of the abstract forms of being, consists in nothing but

the enhancement of wider ranges of thought and, in particular, of felt being. Music, poetry, beautiful architectures are capable of lifting our spirits up to a higher dimension of experience, where we forget about our miserable existence. We become capable of embracing the universal, as if transcending the particular, which is our ordinary mode of existence.

[b] *Humanity* (aka piety or compassion) too is an enhancement of wider ranges of thought, felt being, and action. Schopenhauer depicted this form of negation of the will to live as human agency aimed at relieving other people and/or living creatures from their suffering, rather than fighting against them in view of ultimately unattainable pleasures. Whether the agent's life-range benefits directly from it or not, i.e. whether she feels morally good in being humane or not, the recipient of humanity is necessarily going to experience an increase of her own life-ranges.

[c] Only asceticism, which Schopenhauer represented as solitary self-maceration and chastity, appears to be a real denial of life, although I suspect that an element of life-affirmation is contained within it as well. In the course of the practices of self-maceration, in fact, it is not unlikely that mystical experiences may take place. Even if not necessarily, asceticism seems to leave room to peculiarly powerful openings of the plane of felt being, as the individual may lose her sense of selfhood and rejoice in that boundless field of consciousness which the nirvana, according to mainstream Buddhism, is supposed to be. Possibly, the entire project of Schopenhauer's negation of the will to live is merely an itinerary towards a higher, richer way of living.

Incidentally, there is another life-affirming point that can be seen as pertaining to Schopenhauer's case. His longevity and his love affairs—Schopenhauer was a notorious womanizer who never married and even cockled Lord Byron during a trip to Italy—suggest that he may have incurred into a performative contradiction, i.e. that he preached in favour of life-denial, when his own life was an extraordinary example of life-affirmation. In conclusion, my reflections lead towards the acceptance of McMurtry's life-value onto-axiology. Even the seemingly opposite theoretical position of philosophical pessimism appears to make use of this very same axiological basis. The two eminent pessimist philosophers hereby scrutinised did actually confirm McMurtry's main point.

Chapter 2
Death and Life Support Systems

In the previous chapter I investigated a number of religious and philosophical lines of thought claiming that death is a positive given of our existence. There, I concluded by observing how "life shines most brightly in death's mirror". This, it was argued, follows from the fact that even "the desirability of death" defended by many a philosopher is due to "its capacity of affecting life in life's own terms". In particular, the first chapter tackled the issue of the desirability of death from an axiological perspective. Its eventual goal was "to individuate the ground of value that makes this particular approach possible", along the lines of life-value onto-axiology. It did not face the challenge of explaining how, historically, so many religious and philosophical lines of thought had come to share in that ground of value, yet defending such a counterintuitive stance as the desirability of death. I describe this stance as counterintuitive because we can witness daily, if not hourly, how dearly and how daringly people as well as other living creatures struggle to survive, nearly with no exception and at almost any cost. Consistently with this observation, my former cultural exploration argued that life's own force and urgency were so powerful and pervasive, that they could be retrieved also behind such counterintuitive death wishes.

Still, one thing is to bow to life's own force and urgency by accepting life openly, another is to bow to life's own force and urgency by pursuing death. Life grasped *via* a life wish is not the same as life grasped *via* a death wish. It is the goal of this chapter to cast some light on the historical origin of this approach. Specifically, I investigate few but highly significant moments in ancient Western philosophy, which created a fracture between the world of nature and the human being, thus producing the conditions for the desirability of death. By no means am I the first to observe this fracture. Most famously, Friedrich Nietzsche attacked repeatedly Socrates and Plato for initiating it. His attack on Socrates reached its most defiant form in the section entitled "The Problem of Socrates" in his 1889 book *Twilight of the Idols: or How to Philosophize with a Hammer*, where Socrates is accused of being so pathologically in love with the perfect world of abstract reason, and so pathologically adverse to the imperfect world of corporeal reality, that he made it impossible for the city of Athens not to condemn him to death.[63] Nietzsche regarded Socrates' philosophical career as the moment of inception of 'negative nihilism', which he loathed. On the one hand, negative nihilism rejects contingent, material reality (e.g. the body, the instincts) for necessary, immaterial unreality (e.g. the soul, pure reason). On the other hand, 'positive nihilism' rejects the latter and recovers the former with a positive attitude, despite the awareness of the utter frailty of all. Nietzsche's preference went to the latter, of course.

My addition here wishes merely to suggest that this fracture started in philosophy before Socrates and Plato, and to highlight its implications *vis-à-vis* biological life and death's desirability.[64] It is my belief that Socrates and Plato perfected the conceptualisation of this fracture, leaving it as a far-reaching legacy to the men and women of the West, whose lives will be spent under its influence for at least twenty centuries after Plato's death. Nevertheless, the basic notions upon which Socrates and Plato operated had already been forged by other thinkers. The following pages endeavour to substantiate my belief.[65]

The Understanding of Life

As regards the understanding of life to be discussed here, I keep referring to John McMurtry's tripartite notion of life, as it was done in the first chapter. However, I integrate it here as well with UNESCO's idea of life support system:

A life support system is any natural or human-engineered system that furthers the life of the biosphere in a sustainable fashion. The fundamental attribute of life support systems is that together they provide all of the sustainable needs required for continuance of life. These needs go far beyond biological requirements. Thus life support systems encompass natural environmental systems as well as ancillary social systems required to foster societal harmony, safety, nutrition, medical care, economic standards, and the development of new technology. The one common thread in all of these systems is that they operate in partnership with the conservation of global natural resources.[66]

McMurtry's understanding of life underlies and underpins UNESCO's own approach to life. Yet, McMurtry's conception emerges from a strictly philosophical context. Instead, UNESCO's life support systems [hereafter LSS] synthesise the assumptions and expectations about life that, historically, the Western civilisation has come to prefer and crystallised into the wisdom of today's scientific community. In other words, whereas McMurtry's understanding of life is an effective theoretical tool to grasp that ground of value, after which I sought in the first chapter, UNESCO's understanding of life should be a tool capable of embracing the most widespread understanding of life in terms of contemporary scientific objectivity (at least in the sense of agreement amongst experts), if not even in terms of today's common sense itself. I suggest that UNESCO's notion may be able to capture today's common sense itself because it rests upon the assumption that "the life of the biosphere" means life in nature as we know and talk of it today in, say, newspaper articles about the 1997 Kyoto agreement and zoology journals. No clear-cut definition is given, but a widespread working consensus, which focuses on the planet-wide biological level as the fundamental level or life ground, the preservation of which is UNESCO's, if not the UN's, paramount mission. Under this perspective, UNESCO can be said to favour McMurtry's first plane of being (action) over feeling and thought, though not excluding them *a priori* either or ignoring them completely (e.g. UNESCO's defining concern *vis-à-vis* educational, scientific and cultural institutions).

UNESCO's use of the term "life" is broad and ecumenical. In a truly encyclopaedic fashion, the *Encyclopedia of Life Support*

Systems embraces many disciplines, each of which understands this term in a slightly different way. We know that physicists may define life as a system of locally reduced entropy; molecular biologists as replicating filaments of DNA competing, evolving, and adapting in a changing environment; physiologists as a biochemical system using energy from external sources to grow and reproduce; geophysiologists as a systemic flux of matter and energy maintaining an internal steady-state. Still, despite their differing definitions, scholars from all fields of inquiry have contributed generously to the *Encyclopedia of Life Support Systems*, for there is a general agreement upon the term at issue, which may be thorny to pinpoint semantically (especially when using predicates that are peculiar to each particular science) but which we recognise when we 'see' it. They all share a common ground of investigation, which they may define and describe in differing terms, but the importance of which they are not willing to dismiss with any seraphic shrug. Sustainability is enough of a serious problem to reduce the room for idle semantic disagreement. "Pragmatics", wrote once Gilles Deleuze, "becomes the presupposition behind all other [linguistic] dimensions and insinuates itself into everything". The *Encyclopedia of Life Support Systems*' meaning of "life" is resolved in the shared commitment to an end, i.e. the preservation of the life ground itself, upon which scientists and sciences stand.[67]

The Philosophical Neglect of Life Support Systems

Western philosophy and philosophers stand on the life ground. As long as they breathe, reproduce, eat and defecate, their involvement with the life ground is unavoidable. Nevertheless, until the emergence of life-value onto-axiology, no articulate and consistent frame of understanding has ever been developed in Western philosophy, which had LSS or LSS-analogues as its interpretative premise. Instead, there abound disconnected remarks about life, which tend to be secondary and partial. The study of LSS in the field of medical ethics represents itself only a recent development within the broad sphere of inquiry proper to Western philosophy, as philosophy constantly adapts its own old methods of theoretical analysis to the new advances of science and technology. The study of LSS conceived of as lying outside, and as prior to, the medical context, is even more recent and still alien to mainstream Western philosophy. To regard LSS as something more than particular medical devices, thus encompassing basic environmental and social systems promoting broader and deeper ranges of life in a sustainable fashion, means to step outside standard cultural and scientific categories of interpretation. Most commonly, philosophers: address one or few aspects of one or few human-engineered and/or environmental systems; contrast material life in the biosphere with higher, immaterial forms of life; neglect the issue of sustainability altogether; or limit the understanding of life in the biosphere to human life or to privileged portions of it. In fact, most philosophers have neglected or ignored all forms of life that were not the male, well-off, Western human individual that they themselves have tended to be throughout the history of the discipline. And even when focussing upon themselves alone, most Western philosophers have spoken of, or focussed on, the life of the intellect, soul, or spirit. Material life has not been crucial to their investigations. Under this perspective, the life ground has been largely rejected, neglected, or presupposed.

Were we even to consider the whole of ethics as an example of life-attentive philosophy, then we should recall that ethics has hardly ever been the principal area of philosophical investigation. With the notable exceptions of Hellenism and of the Enlightenment, metaphysics and epistemology have been, by large, the 'queens' of philosophical investigation. Even today, in the face of the world's environmental collapse, ontology and epistemology are generally assumed to be the most distinctive expression of philosophy, especially in the Anglophone world. For the sake of example, it is interesting to mention the case of a recent volume, *Great Thinkers A–Z*, edited by Julian Baggini and Jeremy Stangroom, and published by London's Continuum in the year 2004. It is a collection of brief entries on the hundred most representative members of the Western philosophical canon. In the Thematic Guide provided at the end of the book, we find the names of twenty-six philosophers that can be said to belong to the last three decades of the 20th century. Of these twenty-six philosophers, nineteen are categorised under labels referring to language- and mind-centred areas of research (e.g. philosophy of mind, philosophy of language) and only seven under labels referring to more 'concrete' areas of research (e.g. moral philosophy, political philosophy). This does not mean that the former group have nothing to say to the latter; or that the latter may not engage in discussions of abstract technicalities that keep the life ground as far from view as those of the former. Yet, it is significant that Western philosophers may perceive themselves as involved in inquiries that, nominally, relate to the life ground only limitedly or indirectly.

Thales of Miletus and His Immediate Followers

It is not my intention to affirm that LSS were never central to any investigation by a Western philosopher. On the contrary, one of the earliest recorded thinkers from the Mediterranean area, Thales of Miletus, stressed the utmost importance of water as the fundamental life support system. Water, for Thales, was the ultimate 'brick' with which the universe's edifice is built, the indispensable 'paste' that holds the edifice together, and the skilful 'hand' that varies the shape of the edifice in time. Thales said water to be the primary principle [*arché*] i.e. the fundamental constituent of reality, from which all things originate, to which all things return, and through which all change occurs. Thales' search for the primary principle represents possibly the first recorded attempt to individuate a unifying notion behind the apparent plurality of natural phenomena.

We can derive from Aristotle's account of Thales' philosophy that repeated empirical observations led him to reach this conclusion. For instance, Thales observed how "the nurture of all creatures is moist, and that warmth itself is generated from moisture and lives by it; and that from which all things come to be is their first principle".[68] "Besides this, another reason for the supposition would be that the semina of all things have a moist nature".[69] Thales noticed that all living being are generated in environments characterised by humidity (e.g. gills, eggs and uteri). Throughout their existence, all living beings need water in order to survive, so that all activities of theirs are, in relevant measure, determined by such a need. Meeting this need draws the ultimate line between their being and their being not. For Thales, water seems to have an analogous role to play in that world, which we would call today "inanimate", namely the world of geological, physical, and astronomical phenomena. Aëtius attributes to Thales the notion that "even the very fire of the sun and the stars, and indeed the cosmos itself is nourished by evaporation of the waters."[70] Most probably, to be truer to Thales' understanding of reality, we should avoid any talk of "animate" and "inanimate". We should avoid the temptation of breaking down the comprehensive unity of the universe in all of its manifestations implied by Thales' doctrine of the *arché*.[71] On the basis of the textual evidence available to us, it is plausible to assume that Thales conceived of all natural phenomena as forms of life. The primary principle is said by him to pervade entirely, and manifest itself throughout, the universe, cutting across physical, geological, and biological distinctions, which we now take for granted and which, in fact, hide from us the 'being-aliveness' of the universe as a whole. Famously, Thales taught "that everything is full of gods" and not just select parts.[72]

Thales' search for the primary principle, the life-centred character of the primary principle that he individuates, and the manifestation of the primary principle in a life-permeated and divine universe of living matter (i.e. Thales' hylozoism and pantheism) are to follow diverging paths with his disciples.[73] Anaximander claimed the primary principle to be "the qualitatively indefinite", or "the spatio-temporal boundless", or "the unperceived", depending on the translation of the Greek *"apeiron"*.[74] Anaximenes, one of Anaximander's pupils, maintained the primary principle to be air [*pneuma*], which determines all natural phenomena by rarefaction and condensation. Diogenes of Apollonia, probably a pupil of Anaximenes', spoke of an intelligent primary principle, which flows throughout, orders, and vivifies the universe. Anaxagoras similarly argued that a rational primary principle—the "Mind" [*Nous*]—flows throughout the universe and regulates its existence in an orderly fashion.[75] With these thinkers, Thales' search for the primary principle sub-divides into a number of sophisticated investigations, each of which approaching separately the 'brick', the 'paste' and the 'hand' that contribute to the constitution of the edifice of the universe and of its many details. In this manner will develop the many sub-branches of the Western intellectual endeavour, which, until the late 18th century, is to comprise most forms of scientific investigation under the label of "natural philosophy". More importantly, Thales' most immediate followers start to wonder about the 'mind' that has conceived and/or conceives of the universe's edifice, thus initiating a shift of focus from the material features of the existing universe and its ability to reproduce itself in ever-changing forms (i.e. by analogy to a living organism), to the regular ideal features that allow for its consistent organisation, for our grasp of it in spite of its inherent diversity, and for its unchanged core of continuity through time (i.e. by analogy to a geometrical theorem). From water, through air, to intelligence, the primary principle becomes more and more rarefied. As a result, Thales' original philosophical enterprise starts to lose its material life-centeredness, as the emphasis shifts from the embodied and dynamic features of natural life [*poiesis*] to its abstract and static principles of organisation [*mathesis*].

Pythagoras of Samos

Pythagoras, also a pupil of Anaximander's, illustrates this *mathesis*-driven trend most formidably. The fundamental structure of reality is understood by him to be numerical. The universe is transformed into a mathematically ordered organisation of the indefinite that the finely trained mind can grasp. With the Pythagorean school of Croton, the search for the primary principle grows more abstract and, interestingly, more elitist. The Pythagorean life was based on the exercise of the human faculties for abstract thinking, i.e. for mathematical and geometrical study and, more in general, for theoretical contemplation of the objects of the mind. Only select few could do it, by perfecting such faculties in the hope of purifying their soul not to reincarnate as lower animals. Pythagoras' doctrine blended new philosophical notions with older religious ideas, the origin of which is obscure. For instance, scholars still debate on whether the ideas of soul and reincarnation used by Pythagoras came from India, Egypt or from Hellenic Orphism.

With the Pythagoreans, the ultimate being of the universe came to be identified with the special mental products (e.g. lines, points, units) of that remarkable human faculty allowing the human being to entertain the representation of the universe in a clear, inter-subjectively compelling way: reason. No embodied environmental system promoting broader and deeper ranges of life in a plurality of individual forms was left on the scene. In its place emerged sets of mathematical uniformities pertaining to a domain of intangible objects that can be observed by a select group of leisure-granted individuals, who can afford to devote themselves to a life of theoretical contemplation [*theoria*]. Pythagoras' alleged motto "a figure and a platform, not a figure and a sixpence" is particularly telling, as it suggests that the study of geometry is a stand to reach the noble abstractions of the mind and not a tool to resolve petty practical problems.[76] Even Pythagoras' celebrated pacifism and vegetarianism can be ascribed to his *mathesis*-driven worldview, insofar as the murder of living beings is a source of disharmony in the cosmos, which Pythagoras conceived of as a perfectly structured geometrical figure.

Heraclitus of Ephesus

Heraclitus exemplifies further the growing theory-driven and elitist attitude of pre-Socratic philosophy. On the one hand, he conceives of the abstract logic of opposites of the ever-changing material universe (e.g. life-death, hot-cold, day-night) as the fundamental, unifying 'backbone' of reality. The world may ignite, flicker, die out and revamp ceaselessly, as though it were made of fire; yet there is logic behind its mutability. The existence and behaviour of fire follow precise rules. According to Heraclitus, there is an underlying 'Word' [*logos*] that gives unity to the plurality of unrepeatable phenomena of which nature seems to consist: "Listening not to me but to the Word it is wise to agree that all things are one."[77]

On the other hand, Heraclitus claims this abstract logic of opposites to be accessible solely to the enlightened minds of the few: "Of this Word's being forever do men prove to be uncomprehending, both before they hear and once they have heard it... Other men are unaware of what they do when they are awake just as they are forgetful of what they do when they are asleep."[78] Heraclitus' social division between the unenlightened and the enlightened, and the mounting division between the sense-experienced world of nature and its underlying reason-grasped world of principles, reflect each other. The fracture between humanity and nature is also a fracture within humanity.

Parmenides of Elea

Emblematic is also the case of Parmenides, founder of the Eleatic school. Parmenides argues that only the one, unchangeable world discovered by reason alone is: "For it is the same thing that can be thought and that can be."[79] The fleeting world of natural phenomena, of which we have sensuous experience, is not: it is mere appearance. With Parmenides, the primacy of rational abstraction becomes absolute: epistemologically, ontologically, axiologically, and socially. The world that matters is not the world of matter: it is the ideal world; it is the world to which Parmenides has privileged access by reason.

Thales' hylozoism is vanquished completely, as life cannot pertain to the world of matter, insofar as this world is illusory. On the contrary, a form of 'nous-zoism' takes its place, for life comes to be understood as, and reduced to, the mind's [*nous*] life of intellectual contemplation. Nothing of any relevance can be dug out of the lower material world of the senses, to which the ignorant person is enslaved. All that is relevant descends from the higher, ideal world of reason, which the philosopher strives to attain. Revealingly,

Thales' far too many and far too trivial gods of the biosphere disappear from the scene. Parmenides' *Poem* or *Proemium* portrays philosophical wisdom as the gift of a goddess from a higher, celestial sphere. The fracture between nature and the human being is already as wide as the space dividing the Earth from the starry heavens, which, for centuries onwards, will be believed to be qualitatively superior to the earthly world of matter and, rather often, considered as identical to, or as part of, the incorruptible divine themselves.

Socrates of, and versus, Athens

"In obedience to God's commands"[80] springs the philosophical wisdom of Socrates. It is said that Socrates was led to search for the true nature of wisdom by the Oracle of Apollo, who had appraised him to be the wisest of men. If Pythagoras and Heraclitus were elitist, Socrates was simply unique. While engaged in his search, Socrates came to realise that he ought not to live for the sake of material gain, but for the sake of pure rational inquiry: "life without this sort of examination is not worth living."[81] No major concern for basic environmental and social systems promoting broader or even just deeper ranges of life in a sustainable fashion animates Socrates' philosophy, not even those that allow him to have time and opportunities to engage in rational discussion (e.g. Athens' slave economy).

On the contrary, Socrates is willing to face the fatal wrath of his countrymen—who had condemned him to death for religious heterodoxy and corruption of the Athenian youth—rather than relinquishing his business of "talking and examining both myself and others."[82] Socrates regards such a business as "the very best thing that a man can do."[83] When presented with the opportunity to flee from prison and avoid death, Socrates reacts by examining the reasons in favour and against such an opportunity, which implies breaking the laws of Athens. By the end of his examination, the latter reasons are such that "the sound of their arguments rings so loudly in my head that I cannot hear the other side."[84] Hence, Socrates opts for death, "since God leads the way."[85] Socrates' martyrdom combines *libido sciendi* [desire for knowledge] and *cupio dissolvi* [desire for annihilation]. With it, Parmenides' 'nous-zoism' strikes a major victory. Life is understood as, and reduced to, the life of intellectual contemplation. That which does not compute within the coordinates of *theoria* has, ultimately, no significant weight. Death itself is welcome on the grounds of reason, the authority of which is depicted with the colours of utmost divinity. It is not important in the present chapter to determine the exact nature of the notion of divinity employed by Socrates, insofar as it is evident that it implies an otherworldly character, i.e. a character that is opposed to the embodied and worldly one of Thales'.

"Death" is, in Socrates' words, "one of two things. Either it is annihilation... or it is really a change: a migration of the soul from this place to another."[86] In both cases, Socrates argues death to be better than life. On the one hand, "if there is no consciousness but only a dreamless sleep, death must be a marvellous gain",[87] for it liberates us from the endless sorrows of existence. "If on the other hand death is a removal from here to some other place, and if what we are told is true, that all the dead are there, what greater blessing could there be than this?"[88] Were death such a "removal", then Socrates would have, again, reason to celebrate, for he would love "to spend my time there, as here, examining and searching people's minds, to find out who is really wise among them, and who only thinks that he is."[89]

Socrates' sustained examination of himself and of other people leaves us with no exact idea of what death actually consists in, nor does it produce a comprehensive system of philosophy. Yet, Socrates' influence was destined to be enormous, especially because it exemplifies the *a priori* deduction of value, truth, and reality by means of dialogical reasoning, which will dominate most Western philosophy to come. Socrates' approach makes the compelling force of logical consistency absolute and, at the same time, belittles material life concerns, including the instinct of self-preservation. This happens because and insofar as they cannot be grounded in reason. Furthermore, Socrates identifies the human soul with our rational abilities and glorifies it as the godlike part of our being. With Socrates, Thales' gods find a fracture in the universe, through which they are able to reach a 'higher' and sacred niche where to reside. It is not my task to determine the exact nature of the relationship, or the possibility itself of a relationship, between worldly being and otherworldly being. What matters is that it is evident that there is a fracture between the two.

As already observed, twenty-two centuries later, Friedrich Nietzsche will accuse Socrates' approach of being profoundly nihilistic, i.e. opposed to life. Nietzsche's 'life' refers to the contingent reality that we experience from the moment of our corporeal birth to that of our corporeal death. But that's no life for Socrates. He envisages instead an intimate *ménage à trois* amid the human soul, reason and divinity, which relies upon a dualistic picture of reality. Socrates sees a fracture between the material existence of natural bodies and the immaterial one of supernatural bodies. This fracture gives him so much hope for a true and fulfilling life that he actually dies for it.

Plato of, and versus, Athens

Plato believes Socrates' latter hypothesis on the nature of death to be the more plausible. Death is, for him, the "removal from here to some other place." Plato depicts the human being as split in two sharply distinct parts: the mortal body and the immortal soul. The soul alone is to be regarded as truly human, hence valuable, for it is capable of rational thought. The body, instead, and the related material life requirements are a disgraceful nuisance, which hampers the path to enlightenment. The body and all material life requirements play hardly any positive role in Plato's system of philosophy, as he teaches that "we must get rid of the body and contemplate things in isolation with the soul in isolation."[90] The goal of human life is "assimilation to god."[91]

This assimilation is possible because the universe itself is split in two parts—the mutable material world of sense-experience and the immutable ideal world of rational intellection—and only the latter is regarded as truly real, hence valuable. Society is also split in two parts—those who are dominated by the irrational cravings of the body and those who have absolute self-mastery by means of reason —and only the latter are regarded as truly human, hence valuable. Plato, man of noble birth, is true to the growing elitist spirit of much Greek philosophy. Moreover, by splitting the human being, the world and society in this manner, Plato's philosophy cannot but neglect the environmental and the human systems fostering life in the biosphere, whether in a sustainable fashion or not. With him, Parmenides' 'nous-zoism' continues its relentless march. The immaterial life of the rational soul is the actual centre of gravity of Plato's philosophy: "it appears that when death comes to a man, the mortal part of him dies, but the un-dying part retires at the approach of death and escapes unharmed and indestructible... and that our souls will really exist in the next world."[92] The mortal life of the body and of any 'lower' soul (or soul's sub-section) can only be instrumental to the achievement of the glorious life awaiting the 'higher' rational soul in the next world. What this next world may be like, however, Plato cannot tell. Concerning this *post-mortem* domain of being, Plato gives only mythical accounts, as he draws inspiration from the great poets of the Hellenic world. Plato himself regards these mythical accounts as nothing but inadequate "old wives' fable[s]".[93] The full picture of the next world will present itself to the exceptional person that, during its mortal existence, becomes "as good and wise as it possibly can".[94] Being bound by the body to the current world, Plato's philosophy reaches the utmost limit of our rational faculties.

It is because of the lack of better means that Plato engages in the poetical language of Hesiod, Homer, and their mysterious gods. Plato concludes his journey there, whence Parmenides had started his own: mythical divinity. Still, Plato is neither a visionary nor a poet. His incursions in the territory of oracles, myths, and ancient gods lay in the periphery of his system of philosophical thought. Plato resorts to 'unreason' rarely and unwillingly, i.e. if and only if reason can find no route of its own. His epistemic paradigm recalls Pythagoras', i.e. mathematical demonstration, not poetical metaphor or oracular revelation. The use of suggestive myths is secondary and far less satisfactory than the "wisdom" that can be reached by the rational soul that "investigates by itself... into the realm of the pure and everlasting and deathless and changeless".[95] The pursuit of such comprehensive understanding requires of us the kind of examined life that led Socrates to his death. Plato, like his mentor, is not afraid of death. On the contrary, the mortal body is a burden to be freed from, by "doing philosophy in the right way".[96] After all, it is the imperfect and contingent body that prevents us from attaining full enlightenment. Consequently, the task of philosophy consists in "getting used to facing death calmly", or "practicing death".[97]

With Plato, Thales' quest for the primary principle translates into the attainment of an integrated, comprehensive, abstract understanding of the fundamental structures unifying reality, to be developed at as many levels of analysis as possible: logical, linguistic, ontological, epistemological, physical, psychological, ethical, political, and aesthetic. By exploring reality at all such levels, Plato attempts to provide a rational account of the perfect Forms (e.g. the idea of cat, temple, courage) that give unity to the knowable things of the world (e.g. cats, temples, courage) and consistency to the terms (e.g. "cat", "temple", "courage") by which we refer to the instances of such things (e.g. my pet, the Parthenon, Leonidas' last stance). Though by no means simple and devoid of self-critical reconsiderations, Plato's Theory of Forms constitutes the first, most articulate system of philosophical explanation in the history of the Western world. Plato's Theory of Forms can then be said to contain within itself Thales' pursuit of the primary principle, though emptied of its empirical character, as Plato does not rely on the extensive observation of natural phenomena. Plato prefers to it the deductive articulation of the abstract, multifaceted and inherently rational structure of the universe, which presides to the ordinate existence of all things. Plato may have believed the universe itself to be "a living creature truly endowed with soul and intelligence",[98] but this soul is ultimately other than the material world itself. Certainly, it is not water. Similarly, Plato may be said to agree with Thales on the notion that "everything is full of gods".[99] Still, he rarefies these deities into the Forms, a "class of object, which is wholly imperceptible to sense... [i.e.] an object of reason alone".[100] With Plato, the primacy of *mathesis* blossoms most powerfully. Little or no room is left for the senses and the reality they seem to disclose, i.e. the ever-changing, self-reproducing, individualised material nature. As a scientist of the ancient days, Plato does not look down at the moist semina of particular plants to find gods there. Instead, he looks up at the celestial bodies, which he regards as " living creatures divine and eternal ".[101]

Death as Conclusion

Plato's gaze is fixed upon the Uranic vault, i.e. already one level above the transient world of material nature. Plato's final hope goes even higher, though. Plato aims "to get rid of the body" and conquer the hyper-Uranic world of perfect ideas. This world lies beyond the Uranic vault. True life resides up there. Such a life is to be conquered, though, and its precise nature is uncertain. As long as it is bound to the body, reason cannot overcome all obstacles and render an adequate description of it. Only few, blessed souls will ever attain this life fully and satisfactorily: philosophers, *bien sûr*. The elitist character of Plato's philosophy is most evident in the *Republic*, where he discusses the ideal State or, as many scholars have argued, the ideal *polis* of Athens reformed on the basis of philosophical wisdom. For Plato, justice will never reign in any State unless "there is a conjunction of these two things, political power and philosophic intelligence,".[102] In his *Republic*, philosophers are kings and kings are philosophers, and they alone are allowed to know the actual ways in which the State operates, for they alone can conceive of the Good and lead the whole State to it. All remaining citizens, instead, should be kept unaware of such ways and, if necessary for the good of the State, deceived. For instance, the Rulers of the *Republic* are said to have to fabricate a sophisticate "lie" or mythical "tale" about the origins of the State.[103] This is done in order to justify and maintain the hierarchical tripartition of the *polis* into Rulers (philosopher-kings), Auxiliaries (guardians or soldiers) and Craftsmen (producers of material goods). The Rulers also implement a system of eugenics by running cunningly fixed mating lotteries amongst the Auxiliaries, namely those better members of society who may, one day, aspire to the position of Rulers and care for the wellbeing of the State. As for what this wellbeing may actually consist in, it can be stated that it is seems to be the production and preservation of an elite of philosophers, who can devote themselves to a life of contemplation and, unwillingly but necessarily, of kingship.

It is not my intention to deny that some remarks about material life and LSS loom in the background of Plato's works. This is particularly true of his *Republic*, where Plato describes what a just State would look like; meaning with "just" a State that, unlike corrupt Athens, would never have the wisest of men executed. In Plato's ideal State, the unenlightened mass of "shepherds and other herders... farmers... builders... weavers and cobblers... traders... shopkeepers... merchants... other servitors... [and] wage-earners",[104] who are relegated to the bottom layer of society, see to the basic material necessities of everybody else. In effect, Plato acknowledges that there are "necessary and unnecessary appetites"[105] and that the crucial appetite is "the desire of eating to keep in health... [with] bread and relishes", considering also that "bread is necessary in both respects, in that it is beneficial and if it fails we die."[106] The lowest tier of Plato's just society is going to attend to such needs, so that the rest of society may develop, flourish, attain the heights of philosophical bliss, and rule over the lowest tier by philosophically justified deceptions. If Plato concedes any room to the consideration of basic environmental or social systems promoting broader and deeper ranges of life, it is because they allow for the possibility of enlightenment and, with enlightenment, for the conquest of that truer life, which awaits the select few beyond the present life. Death, as seen, is the gate toward this truer life. As a consequence, it can only be desired most ardently by the sage. Socrates, verily Plato's mentor, leads the way.

The fracture between humanity and nature might be necessary to proceed to a deeper understanding of reality. It is not my task to address this issue now. What matters here is that the fracture is visible and, as I hope to have shown, it descends to Socrates and Plato from previous thinkers.

Chapter 3
Mechanism, Galileo's *Animale* and Heidegger's *Gestell*: Reflections on the Lifelessness of Modern Science

Confronted with the most life-destructive manifestations of scientific knowledge, such as nuclear arsenals and carcinogenic power sources, a succinct genealogical outline of the birth of modern science may help to realise its deeply ingrained *lifeless* character. Thus, reflections are offered upon the combined influence of mechanism and *mathesis*-driven abstractedness, particularly *vis-à-vis* Galileo's scientific revolution, which is taken as emblematic of the modern mind-set.

Mechanism, or the explanation of natural phenomena solely by physical causes, has been present in Western philosophy since its Aegean inception. Several pre-Socratic theories about the primary principle of reality [*arché*] attempted to account for the existence and permutations of the whole universe by individuating its ultimate material constituent/s and the rules of composition and transformation allowing it/them to become all things conceivable and observable. Empedocles of Acragas, for example, spoke of four fundamental material "seeds" or "roots"—fire, earth, air and water—that unite or separate due to mutual love or hatred.[107] Anaximenes, on his part, deemed the primary principle to be air [*pneuma*], which causes all natural phenomena by processes of rarefaction and condensation.[108] Leucippus and Democritus of Abdera spoke instead of qualitatively identical but quantitatively and geometrically different indivisible atoms moving in the void. Their motion produces fleeting aggregates, namely all the objects that are given in nature, including the human being, its soul and the soul's functions. This, they added, happens in accordance to a strict rule of composition: "Everything is produced necessarily, because the cause of the formation of all things is the whirling motion... called necessity."[109] Epicureanism, the only Hellenistic and Roman school to endorse atomism, added to the theories of Leucippus and

Democritus the explanatory notion of *clinamen* [inclination] of the atoms, whereby atoms can escape necessity and allow for the rather peculiar natural phenomena commonly associated with the most impalpable and volatile human soul (e.g. purposeful life, intelligent thought, free will, creativity).[110]

In order to tackle these peculiar phenomena, the ancients introduced several alternative categories of explanation that the atomism of Leucippus and Democritus did not contemplate. Amongst them, Plato's and Aristotle's *forms* proved most enduring, as they permeated the universe with immaterial intelligence and goal-oriented vitality analogous to those of the human being. In connection with these forms, Plato's insistence on the rational order of the universe and Aristotle's attention to the Earth's living creatures became rapidly essential components of the Western intellectual inquiry.[111] Variously reinterpreted, their forms persisted as the mainstream explanatory paradigm until the revival of atomism during the Renaissance, the later growth of modern science, and their joint triumph in the following two centuries.[112] Nonetheless, mechanism was not completely extinct during this prolonged Platonic-Aristotelian *intermezzo*. Theophrastus, for example, was the successor of Aristotle at the Lyceum and is saluted as the father of botany. He appears to have endorsed mechanism. Porphyry recalls Theophrastus arguing that "all animals" have "affinity" and share the same "principle" or "genus".[113] As such, they all respond to the same principle of organization of the universe i.e. "the circular motion" of the heavens.[114] Although dubbing at times this very motion as "Mind" [*Nous*] (e.g. *Metaphysics* 7b22), Theophrastus' picture of the universe identifies this motion with living nature itself: "To be in motion is, in general, a character proper to nature... the circular motion of the heavens is... the life of the universe itself."[115] Along analogous lines followed also the picture of the universe given by Strato of Lampsacus, successor of Theophrastus at the Lyceum. As Cicero reports, Strato "teaches that all that is and is generated either is or has been produced by weights and motions."[116]

Similarly, the Aristotelian medieval debate on motion (also known as the theory of impetus) reveals distinct elements of mechanism.[117] The core issue of this debate concerned the effort often required to keep something moving. Aristotle claimed that a body in motion requires a constantly acting force to keep it in motion. If you are dragging a heavy box and, at a given point, you stop dragging it, the box will stop moving. Aristotle deduced from this observation that there could be no motion in a vacuum. However, John Philoponus, a 6th-century Aristotelian commentator in Alexandria converted to Christianity, argued that a body put into motion acquires an impetus, which keeps it moving until that impetus weakens and exhausts itself. His theory was revived in the 14th century by Jean Buridan, who drew the inference that this explanation removed the need for intelligences to move the celestial bodies and, more broadly, to permeate the universe. These ideas, he claimed, were a legacy of pagan Greek philosophy and not of the Holy Bible. In the 18th century, Voltaire will reiterate these considerations, with a much more polemical and anticlerical tone than Buridan. Some years before Buridan's reflections, instead, Nicholas of Oresme had already suggested that the proper understanding of impetus made it conceivable that God could have created a clock-like universe, set it running and left it to itself. These suggestions, typically known only to specialists in medieval studies and history of science, foreshadowed the picture of the universe embodied in the new science of the Modern Age, with which the term "mechanism" is commonly associated.

The Doctrine of the Double Truth

It must be noticed that the speculations of medieval Christianity about impetus would have been impossible without the important lessons in intellectual rigour, empirical method and Aristotelian scholarship that flourished in the Islamic world. In particular, the works of the 12th-century polymath Ibn Rushd, known to Christianity as Averroes, led to a renaissance and critical re-examination of Aristotle's philosophy, beginning in 13th-century Europe. As a result of this renaissance, Aristotle's status amongst the ensuing medieval intelligentsia will become paramount. For instance, Thomas Aquinas refers to Aristotle simply as "the philosopher",[118] and Dante Alighieri, in the fourth *canto* of the *Inferno*, calls him "the master of those who know" [*il maestro di color che sanno*].[119] Moreover, Averroes contributed to one of the most controversial doctrines of the medieval world, i.e. the doctrine of the double truth. This doctrine states that reason and faith have their own specific truths, which do not necessarily coincide. In different forms, this doctrine was upheld openly in the Middle Ages by few brave (or reckless) thinkers, such as Siger of Brabant, Boethius of Dacia and John of Jandun. In all of these forms, it posed a threat to religion, for it suggested that the human being could pursue a satisfactory investigation of reality without the aid of faith, inspired tradition or revelation. Indeed, this alternative investigation could lead to conclusions that were not consistent with the main tenets of given religious beliefs or of the official dogma. Unsurprisingly, the doctrine of the double truth was condemned and actively opposed by the religious authorities of both medieval Christianity and Islam. Averroes himself spent the last years of his life in exile and most of his work has not reached us because of official censorship. Revealingly, much of the work by Averroes that has reached us is in Hebrew and Latin translations, not in the original Arabic.

The negative assessment of intellectual pursuits that may contradict established religion can be still perceived in Pope Pius X's 20th-century condemnation of modernism. Acting as the head of the Catholic Church, Pius X issued several official documents (including an official encyclical and a compulsory *Oath Against Modernism* for clergymen, religious superiors, preachers and seminary professors) in order to discourage the application of non-scholastic, allegedly scientific, and generally unorthodox methods to religious matters.[120] The truth of such matters, in his opinion, could not be discovered by means that do not presuppose any enlightening role for faith, or do not try to mutually accommodate faith and reason, as done masterfully by Thomas Aquinas—philosopher of reference and honoured saint of the Catholic Church.[121] The 20th-century condemnation of modernism signifies that the doctrine of the double truth did not just survive, but even blossomed in the Modern Age, particularly with the birth of modern science and its emancipation from faith-centred and theological constraints. The term itself chosen by the Pope—i.e. "modernism"—reveals the unreligious *Zeitgeist* of the times that witnessed the end of the Church's hegemony over Western culture. Perhaps, the most powerful expression of this emancipation lies in the following, celebrated statement: "The intention of the Holy Spirit, when inspiring the Bible, was to teach us how to go to Heaven, and not how Heaven goes."

Galileo and the Birth of Modern Science

Commonly, in today's social consciousness, Galileo gets the credit for this celebrated statement which, however, he merely reported in one of his letters.[122] It belongs to Cesare Baronio, a member of Filippo Neri's Congregation of the Oratory—it belongs to a Catholic clergyman. This common mistake, which is said to have affected even Galileo's famous biographer Ludovico Geymonat, is due to the idea behind the statement, which implies a claim to the pursuit of independent scientific investigation by means of the inductive method: observation, formulation of hypotheses, and experimental testing. Since Galileo advanced this type of investigation both theoretically and practically, and not the Roman Church of his day, today we ascribe to him, and not to the Roman Church of his day, the celebrated statement at issue. Still, Galileo had the courage and the ability to separate the cosmos observed by the human eye—and his novel eye-aiding telescope—from the divine cosmos revealed by the Holy Scriptures. He encountered truths about the universe that did not fit the Aristotelian theories endorsed by the official scholastic theology of the Roman Church and he did not hide them.

Additionally, Galileo gave natural science the 'particular' character that, though regularly forgotten or betrayed, natural science still possesses. Galileo wanted to abandon any pretensions for 'higher' or 'deeper' knowledge of natural phenomena, which pertain to philosophy and religion: "to grasp the essence is, for me, an impossible endeavour."[123] According to Galileo, the science of "natural substances" is "to be content with information regarding some aspects [*affezioni*] of theirs".[124] In exchange for a more timid and self-limiting science, Galileo expected maximal autonomy of investigation. Henceforth, Galileo stands out in today's social consciousness as an icon for the autonomy of science and the free pursuit of knowledge—free from the cumbersome presence of divinity, if necessary. It should not be forgotten that, for his views and the success of his views, Galileo was tortured, tried and humiliated by the Pope's Inquisition. The friar, philosopher, poet and astronomer Giordano Bruno fared an even worse fate than Galileo, as he was burnt at the stake for heresy by the Pope's Inquisition on 17th February 1600. Galileo, instead, after a first ban from teaching in 1616, was condemned to house arrests in 1632 and his works remained in the *Index of Prohibited Books* until 1823 (Galileo's condemnation was revoked in 1822).

Whether Galileo should be regarded also as an adversary of Aristotle and Aristotelianism or, instead, as a truer disciple of the great Greek thinker, it is an issue that historians of science have not yet settled. Surely, many 16th- and 17th-century Aristotelians were not eager to accept Copernicus' recovery of pre-Aristotelian astronomical theories and Galileo's novel methodologies, which, it should be noted, involved the use of scarcely tested and sense-deforming instruments such as the telescope. Rather than attempting the pursuit of knowledge by new means, they preferred to rely— sometimes reasonably, sometimes blindly—on the words of their ancient mentor. Nevertheless, Aristotle had himself practiced the art of empirical investigation and of critical re-examination of hypotheses based on experience. With Galileo, however, scientific experimentation reached new heights, especially with the application of technologies never seen before. Still, the patient collection and creative interpretation of experimental data was not the revolutionary aspect of Galileo's new science. Inductive thinking and experimentation had already been theorised and practiced in the Middle Ages (e.g. the Franciscan School of Oxford). Yet, during the Renaissance, inductive thinking and experimentation found vocal 'PR persons' such as Francis Bacon. A fierce enemy of the

Aristotelian scholasticism of the European universities of his time, Bacon envisioned in a *New Atlantis* (published posthumously in 1627), a utopian society to come, erected upon the discoveries of experimental science.[125] It is under these changed conditions that Galileo, working upon Leonardo's intuitions on the same subject, added to the experimental method the careful and consistent use of mathematics.[126] His motto was: "the Book of Nature is written in the language of mathematics". So radical was the integration of observation, induction and mathematics that, in his view, anything that could not be treated mathematically had to be discarded from any serious scientific investigation. *In nuce* [in essence], the combination of inductive reasoning, experimentation *and* refined quantitative methodologies derived from mathematics is the actual scientific revolution initiated by Galileo.

Galileo and the Abstractedness of Modern Science

One aspect of this 'mathematicisation' of modern science goes often unnoticed: abstractedness. Modern science is often dubbed as more factual and less abstruse than the formulations of the Aristotelians who opposed Galileo. Yet, Galileo's new science was actually less factual than, and at least as abstruse as, the Aristotelians' physics (e.g. the absence of friction required by Galileo's constant acceleration).[127] This point may be difficult to realise today, for several elements of Galileo's approach have become the new common sense of the Western world—which, in turn, makes several aspects of 20th-century physics puzzling to today's layperson.[128] Let us consider, however, that experience counted, for Galileo, but only and insofar as it was quantifiable i.e. reducible to mathematics. Personal, qualitative experience, to which Aristotle's science granted much room, did not count. Smells, colours, and tactile perceptions were not to be considered: "once the animal has been removed, all these qualities are removed and annihilated."[129] For Galileo, there is no need of the living *"animale"* [animal] and of its particular experience of the world, even if it is constantly presupposed by the existence of the scientist, no less than it was also presupposed by the existence of the ancient mystic or of the medieval believer.[130] Galileo's new science assumes that "as the ears, tongues and noses are removed, figures, numbers and motions are left" i.e. the quantifiable aspects of reality with which natural science ought to deal.[131] His science is built *"ex suppositione* [by supposition]... and... my demonstration... loses nothing of its [i.e. the supposition's] strength and conclusiveness; just like the fact that in nature one cannot find any object moving in the spiral fashion does not jeopardise at all the conclusions about the spiral motion reached demonstratively by Archimedes."[132]

Yet, as Bergson pointed out much later in his *Time and Free Will*, experiments can give us a succession of results concerning a given phenomenon, none of which is equivalent to their arithmetical mean whereby we derive the diagram describing that phenomenon.[133] Also, the results obtained by experimentation have taken place in different moments in time, whilst the diagram describing the phenomenon assumes them as simultaneous—time gets 'spacialised' in the diagram, which is the fruit of the mathematical ingenuity of human consciousness. Nevertheless, to Galileo and to his heirs, the mean and the resulting diagram are, in the end, more real than any actual, particular result, for God's Creation speaks the language of mathematics. Since its birth, the modern science of nature has sought after necessary laws and universal constants, none of which is given as such in the contingent realm of material nature —outside the abstractions of our thinking minds. Nature's laws are claimed to lie 'beneath' or 'behind' natural 'phenomena', thus assuming, more or less implicitly, that: (a) what we observe immediately as animals investigating nature (e.g. other animals) is not as relevant as what we are going to discover; and (b) what we observe immediately is an 'appearance' to be overcome in order to retrieve the true 'substance' of the universe i.e. mathematically formulae-expressible abstract knowledge. In this way, the scientifically minded study of material reality resembles the otherworldly tradition of Western philosophy discussed in my previous two chapters.

It must be noted, however, that sometimes mathematics worked against mechanism. The 17th-century mathematician and philosopher Leibniz, for example, distinguished sharply between the "truths of reasoning" of logicians and mathematicians, based on self-evident intuition and deductive reasoning, and the "truths of fact" of natural scientists, based on intelligent observation and inductive reasoning.[134] Whereas the former allowed for no exceptions, the latter could always do—hence the fundamental possibility for our world to be different from what it is and its ultimate dependence upon God's will. Also, the ultimate reliance of any intellectual inquirer upon conceptual tools and her own willingness to inquire suggested to Leibniz the notion of an ultimately spiritual universe. Three centuries later, the mathematician and philosopher Bergson, reflecting upon Zeno's logical paradoxes and ordinary unrepeatable experiences such as muscular effort and hearing a musical phrase, concluded too that mechanism could not explain all phenomena and that it relied itself upon phenomena (e.g. life, perception, thought) that it could not explain by its own specific categories. In brief, despite of its focus on the material realm of being and its apparent detachment from the otherworldly preoccupations of religion, modern science reveals a Platonic rather than Aristotelian flavour, for it focuses on abstract, mathematically worded laws of nature, rather than on particular instances of natural being. Significantly, modern science developed as, and concentrated upon, physics, not biology, and led to the full development of the former centuries before any modern, 'un-Aristotelian' biology ever developed. Additionally, by application of physics' concepts and methodologies to biology, modern science contributed to the recovery of ancient mechanism. In this manner, it led to the generation of the widespread conception of an inanimate—i.e. soul-less, de-spirited, devoid of life —machine-like, necessity-regulated universe. This is the modern mind-set, or worldview, that is going to be clarified further in the following paragraphs.

Descartes and the De-Spirited Extended Universe

Galileo's new science was not the only factor in bringing forth the modern mind-set. René Descartes' dualism of qualitatively different substances—the *res cogitans* [literally "thinking thing" or "stuff"] and the *res extensa* ["extended thing" or "stuff"]—has much to do with the modern mind-set as well. This conception divides reality into two types of substance: mental, i.e. distinguished by thinking; and physical, i.e. distinguished by extension (instead of holding only to physical existence).[135] Though Descartes' dualism was not new to Western thought, its cross-fertilisation with Galilean science resulted most fruitful. By separating sharply between the immaterial realm of thought and the extended one, Descartes attempted to leave the former to theologians and the Church, whilst opening the latter to natural scientists. In this connection, it is probably worth recalling the fact that the age that saw Galileo and Newton developing modern physics was also the age that saw medical anatomy flourishing in Europe. During the Middle Ages, and still in the early Renaissance, anatomy was a taboo endeavour. In the Modern Age, human corpses, now mere extended stuff, were no longer revered as much. Leonardo, Michelangelo and other famous artists of the Italian Renaissance recurred often to illegal trafficking of corpses and body parts for their anatomical studies.[136]

In the latter part of the 17th century, the new picture of the universe matured in Galileo's physics displaced the medieval one. Any lingering elements of evaluative categories were removed, such as, amongst others, circles being the most perfect form of motion, hence the paths taken by heavenly bodies, and the use of 'final causes' in the explanation of motion. Once again, the universe was pictured as a mechanism, i.e. a system of interacting physical things transmitting and transforming energy from one to another. Descartes' studies on the preservation of motion in physical bodies, later ameliorated by successive studies on inertia, pushed forth in this direction.[137] No notion of '*anima*' [soul], hence of '*animale animato*' ["ensouled" or "spirited animal"], was regarded as necessary. Aristotle's four causes were replaced by one alone, i.e.

that of efficient causation, which itself was radically re-interpreted. In the Aristotelian system, efficient causes were individual beings bringing about changes in other individual beings. In the new science, causes are events and likewise their effects, mutually linked in chains of causes and effects of motion, just as the movements of a sequence of cogs or levers transmit and transform forces within a machine. Furthermore, causes and events are events to be understood as manifesting patterns or laws, which are to be put in the form of mathematical equations. These conceptions were applied, with manifest success, in astronomy, mechanics and optics, i.e. the sciences that led the way in the advent of modern science.

Furthering Galileo's momentous contribution, Isaac Newton's 1687 *Philosophiae Naturalis Principia Mathematica* unified these studies and laid down laws of motion governing the whole universe.[138] His book and his own name epitomised the new science, which had, and still has, impacts upon all intellectual life and the whole course of European and Western civilization, and now upon the whole world. In particular, Newtonian physics came to be regarded as the best and, more and more often, as the exclusive investigative tool to tackle the domain of the extended. This predilection for physics took place despite Galileo's own awareness of the timid and self-limiting character of his new science and despite Newton's own exemplary religious fervour, which found powerful expression in his commentaries to the Apocalypse and other Biblical prophecies. Once again, Descartes contributed decisively to this trend. In his consciously and cautiously posthumous *Treatise on Man*—clerical institutions still held some weight, as Bruno and Galileo experienced—he sketches a mechanistic explanation of human physiology.[139] Descartes' follower Nicolas Malebranche, a sickly-bodied priest, led this approach to the point of declaring all bodies, whether of planets, dogs and people, to be mechanisms, analogous to the technological paradigm of his day, i.e. the clockwork. Mechanical calculators, hydraulic systems, the steam engine and electronic computers will also follow in an uninterrupted series of successive technological paradigms employed to exemplify and understand the way the universe functions. In contemporary cognitive psychology, the distinction between 'hardware' and 'software' is often used to refer to, respectively, the human body, or the brain alone, and the human mind, thus reiterating Descartes' dualism.

Throughout the centuries, these paradigms have displayed one common feature: in the same *physis* whence Plato and Aristotle saw underlying intelligent and vital forms, modern science seeks for lifeless regularities, not unlike the ancient mechanism of Democritus and Strato of Lampsacus. The explanatory model is no longer the animal—e.g. the hylozoism of Thales and Aristotle—but the premeditated and predictable complex human artefact, whether epitomised by the clockwork or by the microchip. Only the late 20th century, characterised by increased awareness of the ecosphere's destruction, is to recover, in a few rare instances, the picture of the universe as a living being (e.g. the Gaia hypothesis by James Lovelock).[140] Generally, Galileo's mathematical abstractedness, the aversion to Aristotelian qualitative considerations and the attempt to abstain as much as possible from anything non-quantifiably spiritual have typically led modern scientists and science-inspired philosophers to lose touch with *poiesis*—creative, experienced, actual life. In this perspective, the 20th-century difficulties on part of the Catholic Church with modernism may become easier to grasp. The Christian faith relies on the fundamental assumption of a life-giving God, a 'poietic' Creator of the living universe. The Holy Spirit is said to pervade and participate in the making of historical reality, though it may not be easy to understand how exactly this happens. Machines, however, are not alive.[141]

The Lifelessness of Modern Science I: Scientism

It is rarely noticed that Descartes' dualism of mind and matter omits the intermediate realm of life. Descartes himself declared that animals could be regarded as mere 'automata'. Regularly, since the time of Descartes, life and organisms have often been omitted, whether people believed both matter and mind to be real ('dualists', like Descartes), only mind to be real ('idealists' in the strict sense, like Berkeley), or only matter to be real ('materialists', like Hobbes).

Physics has changed considerably since Galileo's times. Atomism has been turned into common sense and, at the same time, overhauled, for the indivisibility of the atom has become obsolete. Besides, the equation of matter with energy has made materialism nearly nonsensical. Still, lifeless abstractedness persists. Descartes' geometry-based characterisation of material reality as extended and Galileo's emphasis on "figures, numbers and motions" suggested already a very impalpable picture of nature. The successive discoveries of subatomic physics, which tarnished the total explanatory ability of Newtonian physics, relied even more starkly on the mathematical models used to design the instruments intended to discover the unobservable smallest 'bricks' of the universe's edifice. Overall, the modern physicist's universe is better expressed by the mathematical formula than by the actual running horse. In this, it is consistent with canonical Western philosophy, which Nietzsche described as "missing every drop of blood".[142] The great achievements of Galileo's new science carried with them, directly or indirectly, implications adverse to the proper understanding of, and attitudes towards, life and LSS. It is these implications that, combined with the effects of the science-induced revolutions in agriculture, industry, medicine and technology, have led to the current sense of environmental and ecological crisis. Because of the great success and thence prestige of the new mathematicised physics, it was widely concluded that all the other sciences of nature should adopt its assumptions and methods, and, indeed, that those of the human world should also do likewise.

In the Modern Age, mechanism reached its peak. Its affirmation is acknowledged also under different yet equally revealing notions, such as 'scientism' and 'reductionism'. 'Scientism' means, more or less, the same as 'methodological reductionism', i.e. that a given realm of being may have something distinctive about it but that nonetheless it should be investigated by using the same methods as those employed by the natural sciences. 'Ontological reductionism' denies that there is any distinctiveness in a given level or realm, and asserts that it is 'nothing but' a lower one. Both forms can each be more or less radical.[143] For example, methodological reductionism is more radical when only the methods of physics and chemistry, the 'exact sciences', are allowed to count, so that biology, as well as history and psychology are to use the same methods as chemistry and physics. Likewise, ontological reductionism becomes progressively more radical as human beings are said to be 'nothing but' animals, animals 'nothing but' organisms, and organisms 'nothing but' atoms in motion or patterns of mass-energy.[144] The ultimate implication of this movement of thought was given by Laplace, who asserted that, given the initial positions and velocities of all the atoms in the universe, a universal mind could compute the whole future course of the world and there know everything about it.[145] Today, the same idea is sometimes expressed in terms of a theory that would unite all the fundamental forces in the universe and therefore would be literally 'a theory of everything'. In other words, beyond complete knowledge of the physical structure (or physical and chemical structure) of the universe, there would be no need, and no possibility, of any other knowledge. Henceforth, there would be no distinctive and separate biological knowledge, nothing else to be known about plants and animals save their physical composition, or physical and chemical composition, and the laws common to it and to all other matter and motion or mass-energy.

The Lifelessness of Modern Science II: Biology

The general mechanistic picture of the natural world had, or has been thought to have, other implications for human life, some of which have had further and indirect effects upon people's conceptions of and attitudes towards the natural world and thus towards living beings and LSS within it. We saw that 'the Book of Nature', for Galileo 'is written in the language of mathematics'. This has been taken to mean not only that the scientific study of nature should be a mathematical and hence quantitative and computable one, but that all genuine knowledge of nature is mathematical, and *ergo* that what cannot be quantified is either unknowable or not worth knowing.

Hence, all the everyday and practical knowledge that we have of the world about us is written off as false and worthless. As for our knowledge of our fellows, it is often dismissed as 'folk psychology'. The only knowledge that should count is that of the natural sciences: that which is explicitly stated in quantified, hence exact, universal laws, formulae and equations.

In respect of physics and chemistry, this attitude was justified to some extent. As the debates about the Aristotelian account of motion had shown, what was needed was a radical shift away from everyday experience to imagining bodies, as Galileo was to do, freely moving in empty space or on frictionless surfaces, and to drawing out the consequences of such conceptions. Analogously, in the 18th century, John Dalton revived and reinterpreted the old theory of atoms, at that time objects only of theory and not of observation.[146] Modern chemistry was, in this sense, as abstract as modern physics. In contrast, ordinary people—e.g. gardeners, farmers, herders, hunters, fishermen—often had a rich but implicit and practical knowledge of plants and animals, but, in the perspective of methodological reductionism, such knowledge could not count as 'scientific' and therefore could have no value. The devaluation of practical and common-sense knowledge was not novel to the Modern Age. Plato's and Aristotle's elitist conception of theoretical knowledge as superior had already set a hierarchy of epistemic value and related social respectability, which was continued in the Middle Ages as the superiority of theology. Perhaps, it is only today's talk of 'knowledge economy' that manifests an utter and perplexingly imbalanced reversal of this well-established tradition, for it prioritises knowledge that contributes to augmented money-returns to investors—unaware of the in-built contradiction: knowledge, as the pursuit of truth, may contradict the pursuit of profit. Still, the rejection of 'final causes' was probably appropriate for physics and chemistry to advance to a proper and progressive study of the natural world. A global and compacted apprehension of it, as seen in the old cosmologies, should be differentiated into distinct but overlapping personal, animal, vegetative and simply physical regions and levels, perhaps with intermediary ones among them, such as that of bacteria. Yet then, to single out one such region and level, the merely physical, and to deny the reality or distinctiveness of the others, is itself to stultify and distort the study of the latter.

The focus for debate about this in relation to living beings has usually been the question of 'teleology' i.e. the goals or ends which natural phenomena may possess. This term can and has been applied in different ways, and failure to distinguish them has led to confusion. What matters for biology is 'teleonomy', the idea that organs have functions within the organism, that the organism itself has goals such as maintaining and reproducing itself, and that the study of organisms and organs needs to be conducted with reference to these goals. For example, a heart is essentially a mechanism for pumping blood and what it carries, such as oxygen, around the body of the animal, and it, its operations and its parts can be understood only by continual reference to this function. Paradoxically, the model of a mechanism, which was chosen for the new way of understanding the universe, includes reference to functions, the human use for which the mechanism has been designed and made, and the functions of each of its parts in contributing to that goal. That aspect was typically ignored, however, and attention was given only to the transfer and transformation of energy from one part to another. Immanuel Kant, for whom Newtonian natural science and Euclidian geometry were the models of all science, attempted to settle this question by making teleology into a "regulative principle".[147] By this notion, Kant acknowledged that biologists have to refer to functions and purposes, but they need not assume them to be real: they are to be adopted to guide investigation without assuming them to be true of the world. Nonetheless, to use them in the conduct of inquiry is to take them to be true and to be instantiated in what is being investigated, for one would not use principles one knew to be false and not to apply to the things studied.

The Lifelessness of Modern Science III: Ethics

The general picture of the world that the new natural science was widely assumed to entail has also indirectly affected human attitudes towards the natural world and the LSS within it, usually along with other changes of world-and-life-views. The new picture of the world, stripped of final causes, could appear to present a meaningless world, alien to humanity, especially when thought to be 'nothing but' matter in motion or, more recently, fluxes of energy. The reign of universal causal laws appeared to be absolute.

One theological reaction was Deism, the doctrine that God, having designed the universe and set it in motion, then left it to continue by itself, just as a clock-maker winds up a clock and leaves to carry on ticking. Yet, being God perfect, He (God being traditionally thought of as a father) has made a perfect world. Hence, He does not need to return to it and interfere with it. As Pascal noted about Descartes' understanding of the universe, God's presence was required only to give the universe the initial 'stroke' that set it in motion. There was no room for any other, more existentially relevant role.[148] Deism was a self-consciously 'rationalist' doctrine that sought to dispense with revelation, miracles and priestcraft, though it often held that God did act as judge and assign human beings to eternal rewards or punishments after death, a doctrine needed for the good of society in order to constrain those whom the law could not punish. As Voltaire cynically said, "If God did not exist, it would be necessary to invent him".[149] Still, even this tenuous theology was not needed by Laplace, who, in answer to Napoleon, said that he had no need of that hypothesis. Explicitly or implicitly, Laplace, like many others then and since, held the laws of nature to be necessary and all-sufficient explanations of everything, even though he had to engage in wilful observation and creative experiment in order to discover them. Galileo had already recognised the creative aspect of scientific activity, for he insisted in his writings upon the notion of '*levata d'ingegno*' [ingenuity leap] required for induction's repeated observations to transfigure into useful hypotheses. However, unable to speak 'scientifically' of personal existence, will and creativity, modern science often blindly presupposed and wilfully neglected these spheres, as though the actual living scientist did not exist.

Devoid of any meaning or purpose beyond themselves, the universe and human life within it came increasingly to be seen without any meaning or purpose whatsoever. Even whilst asserting a complete secularism in the name of the scientific investigation of material reality, Laplace lost sight of the living creatures that belong to that reality and of their needs. The 'other' world of human representation of natural laws operated like a screen between himself and the third realm. Analogously, contemporary neoclassical economics, by equating wants and needs, cannot distinguish between life-sustaining and life-destructive economic transactions. The third realm, which is presupposed throughout each transaction, is unseen by the discipline that studies them. These trends came together in the self-baptised 'Enlightenment' of the 18th century. Immanuel Kant, perhaps the most representative figure of this time, defined it as *"man's emergence from his self-imposed immaturity"*—"immaturity" being "the inability to use one's understanding without guidance from another".[150] A later version was 'man come of age', that is, wholly autonomous and without any superior in the form of God or a Natural Law to tell him what to do and what to become. The most thoroughgoing statement of this new conception of man was given by the French existentialist Jean-Paul Sartre. According to him, we are each "a fold" in being, "nothingness", existence "for itself" and without "essence", and "condemned only to choose".[151] Sartre believed that we have to choose everything we do, are and believe, including the very principles that we choose and live by. But how could humanity define herself without guidance? Attempts were made to answer that question.

For example, Kant sought to derive the generally accepted moral principles from a principle, the Categorical Imperative. This imperative defines the form of a rational will, i.e. not an arbitrary will, that legislates for itself: "Act only on that maxim through which you can at the same time will that it be universal law."[152] Yet that has been found to require a 'matter' i.e. specific principles of good and evil, right and wrong, which it cannot supply for itself and which Kant had simply assumed. Others filled that gap with 'obvious' human desires or 'drives', such as Hobbes' "restless desire of power after power that ceaseth only in death",[153] or pleasure, material comfort and the like, which also usually provide the substance of the

Utilitarian goal of "the greatest happiness of the greatest number".[154] Meaning could also be restored by secularising Christian hopes for the vision of God beyond death into an endless political, material and economic progress, or, more radically, into a final kingdom of man upon Earth. Modern culture started dreaming of a fully rational and 'unalienated' life, of freedom from oppression, of human-directed evolution, and, usually, of the 'conquest of nature' and, with it, disease and poverty by means of technologies based upon modern science. Russian Cosmism even envisioned the possibility of defying mortality by scientific-technological means. The belief in a human-made providential uni-directional universe, and not in a cyclical one, had become dominant, Nietzsche being possibly the only major modern thinker to have defended a cyclical conception of the universe. The result of these tendencies has been to view humankind, not as stewards, but as masters over the Earth.

Martin Heidegger and the Modern Mind-Set

Human mastery over the Earth has become an actual power because of modern technology and the natural science, upon which it is increasingly based and which it assists. Among the thinkers that, in the 20th century, observed and pondered upon this mastery, stands the controversial German existentialist Martin Heidegger. Heidegger observed how mathematical abstraction pervades the whole genetic process of modern scientific inquiry, in a late and generally unseen reiteration of Plato's detachment from the mundane. As he noted, physics cannot even talk of an empty jug as an empty jug, for there is no jug that does not contain at least some air. Scientific inquiry requires considerable mental gymnastics in order to be acquired, understood and applied, which he compares to the mental gymnastics through which children go when acquiring, understanding and applying their mother tongue. Approximation in measurements (e.g. the average curve upon which no actually observed instance is located) and generation of models (e.g. the ideal condition of equilibrium) exemplify abstraction from personally experienced reality. Heidegger coined the notion of

"Gestell" ["form" or "structure"] to indicate the peculiar moral attitudes and conceptual 'pigeonholes' that are acquired by scientifically and technologically trained individuals, who then lose sight of the immediate natural world by adoption and internalisation of the interpretative categories of science and technology.[155] These categories become their second nature and, progressively, turn into their only ones. Given a scientific-technological *Gestell*, a forest becomes an object of inquiry or an opportunity for logging, no longer a forest. Rather than being open to that which is and 'receive' the world, they reduce the world's scope to that which can be taken from it.

Heidegger was deeply aware of the fact that the scientific revolution of the Modern Age had not only created new encyclopaedias, the empirical tone of which sounded very different from the allegorical tone of the medieval ones, but also a new mind-set. Human beings felt disconnected from their natural environment, with total sovereignty over it and everything in it, to use as they saw fit for purposes, which they set for themselves. Already in the 19th century, this new mind-set had become so widespread and well-established that it led some major novelists to tackle it—some to ridicule it (e.g. the character of Mr. Thomas Gradgrind in *Hard Times* by Charles Dickens),[156] others to eulogise it (e.g. the character of Sherlock Holmes in the crime fiction by Sir Arthur Ignatius Conan Doyle, between 1887–1927). Necessary, universal, regular, predictable, quantifiable, translatable into mathematical formulae— any serious, scientific account of the world should possess these virtues. The world seen through the lenses of Galileo and Newton's physics displayed just such virtues, whereby life may disappear from view in lieu of its abstract representation. In one of history's many ironic twists, as Western intellectuals started to look at material reality more and more closely, liberated from the cumbersome medieval fetters of official dogma, their intellectual tools made it more and more difficult to observe life therein.

The scientific interest in the realm of this-worldly nature, understood geometrically as 'extended', does not imply necessarily interest in material life concerns, nor does it make it easy for the scientific mind-set to grasp them clearly. As recognised, among others, by Schrödinger,[157] M. Polanyi[158] and Jonas,[159] living beings have distinctive features that are not found in inanimate matter, hence the difficulty to reduce biology to physics and the prolonged historical survival of spiritual, vitalistic and variously Aristotelian categories in biology. For instance, do consider: growth (not mere aggregation); reproduction (not mere repetition); goal-directed processes and behaviour (not mere events); self-definition *via* the membrane, skin or shell separating from its surroundings the individual organism to which pertain mutually supporting functions in view of consistent self-maintenance (*ditto*). One feature expresses all of these: flexible adaptivity. In all respects of their growth and self-maintenance, organisms and the organs within them manifest direction towards goals (e.g. reaching towards light and water, maintaining a stable body-temperature, etc.), with a flexibility that cannot be captured in anything like the laws and formulae of physics and chemistry. Because of their goal-directedness, living beings either succeed or fail in achieving their goals. Hence, the study of living beings has also to employ categories of value and disvalue to recognize organisms, organs, environments and neighbouring organisms as positive or negative (e.g. alive or dead, whole or impaired, healthy and pathological, etc.), which physics and chemistry do not employ. 'Being alive' is not a predicate that mathematics, physics and chemistry can utilise *de iure*, as they are designed to talk of reality in other terms. They are neither biology nor medicine, both of which ought to consider material life concerns, respectively, by theoretical definition and by practical commitment. These disciplines themselves 'ought to' do so, for they do not always do. Modern biology has been capable of assisting in the production of biological weaponry, whereas medicine has contributed to increasing the profits of pharmaceutical conglomerates by official adoption of false pathologies.

Moreover, 'being alive' may not be an actual predicate in other sciences that deal supposedly with human beings and their LSS. For instance, classical and neoclassical economics do not utilise it *de facto*, as they reduce everything into money-equivalents (e.g. a forest is not a living ecosystem, but an asset to which a certain monetary value is attached; a living person cannot be computed, if she is too poor or isolated to be able to exercise any money-demand). For example, David Ricardo combined the most ingenuous study of material reality with the utter inability to appreciate the complexity and the value of the life ground. When addressing the human tragedy of the starving masses in nearby Ireland, Ricardo could speak coldly and without regret of the unavoidable destruction of human lives during periods of economic crisis. Similarly, he did not seem disturbed by the misery of the masses devoured by the factories of the booming Industrial Revolution. The famous motto of his 1820 volume *On Protection to Agriculture* could not be more explicit: "There is no way of keeping profits up but by keeping wages down".[160] For Ricardo, like for Margaret Thatcher one hundred and fifty years later, there was no alternative. Conscience could be appeased before the gruesome spectacle of poverty by the assumption that economic laws are as strict and as necessary as those of physics are. Choice, empathy, hope, charity, love, freedom and virtue do not apply. Human affairs are regulated by causal principles as certain as those regulating celestial motion—*dura lex sed lex*. In more recent times, Vladimir M. Bekhterev and Burrhus Frederic Skinner were to echo Ricardo's de-spirited necessity, as their psychologies attempted to explain human behaviour without any reference to internal motivation, creativity and free will.[161] Even Sigmund Freud, the revolutionary explorer of the unconscious, did describe the functioning of the human psyche like a hydraulic system, following rigid principles and ultimately casting doubts upon the individuality and the freedom of the living person. The modern scientific mind-set has been certainly most prone to treating living beings like automata.[162]

Concluding Remarks

Freud's case is perhaps the most revealing example of the intellectual appeal of, and technical adherence to, the modern *Gestell*. It teaches how, in order to grow indifferent to the life ground, one does not need to go as far as Malebranche and mechanise the whole universe, including its living parts. It is enough to grow insensitive to the aesthetic and moral value of the living, which resides also, if not primarily, in the individual living creatures and in their purposeful activities. Ancient and medieval thinkers had found their own path to disregard the natural world, although they could not but fear it, for its demands required a constant effort to be met. Lucretius' sense of fragility of all life, in his *De rerum natura,* portrays this fear most forcefully.[163] Modern thinkers, instead, have been able to proceed along a new path, though in the same direction. They have been able to do away with fear, as the world has fallen more and more into the grasp and control of the human will. This alternative path has been possible, at least, until the late 20th century, when the ecological threat represented by our species to the world's LSS, hence to our species itself, reached such levels of gravity that humility started to be regained. This humility has been limited, however, for science and technology are still regarded as the tools for salvation, i.e. the return to a pristine ecosphere.

Salvation is not, however, a matter of scientific-technological *Gestell*, for it requires a deeper change of aesthetic and ethical attitude—science and technology having been born insensitive to life, they give us means, not ends. The alleged 'savages' brutalised, amongst others, by the Spanish *conquistadores*, have protected their environment much more successfully than the self-proclaimed 'civilised' human being of the West, who have created the conditions for toying dangerously with the fate of the Earth's environment. Modern science is able to provide us with the most powerful tools to serve the goal of a pristine ecosphere as well as the opposite goal. The science that shows the risks of global warming is the same science that allows for the combustion of fossil oil. In this sense, a revealing duplicity lies behind the birth of Galileo's science itself, as he received financial support for his research from Italian princes, who were interested in the lethal military applications of his knowledge, especially with respect to ballistics and long-distance reconnaissance. The Modern Age succeeded in surpassing the Middle Ages by producing not only the possibility of an intellectual investigation of the world without divinity, but also that of a world without life, or, at least, a world where life could be eradicated more easily by better weapons.

PART II – Money

Chapter 4
Deadly Economics: Reflections on the Neoclassical Paradigm

When I started preparing this chapter, mainstream Italian newspapers issued articles on the following topics: a further draught-due reduction in the production of hydroelectric power by the *Ente Nazionale per l'Energia Elettrica* [hereafter ENEL], Italy's largest energy supplier;[164] renewed coverage by the *New York Times* of the professional footballer's suffering from a remarkably high rate of early dementia, which the National Football League [hereafter NFL] claims not to be directly linked to their profession;[165] the growing production of rare-woods-fitted private jets and super-yachts for the world's billionaires and of low-cost automobiles for the increasingly affluent lower-middle class of the developing world and the decreasingly affluent lower-middle class of the developed world.[166] From an axiological perspective, a common thread runs through each and every piece of news reported above: the priority of money-capital returns over life-capital resources.[167] Italy's recurring draughts are a fairly recent phenomenon, which scientists regard as the combined result of global-warming-induced climate change and untamed over-consumption of hydraulic resources for industrial use, particularly agribusiness. It should be noted that the increasing scarcity of water goes hand-in-hand with the increasing privatisation of water and water-related services across the globe. Scarcity of a fundamental life-resource is a potentially immense source of profit, for its value cannot but increase as its availability decreases, analogously to what repeatedly observed throughout human history, with food supplies being hoarded by producers and merchants in order to augment their profitability, thus causing or worsening famines.[168]

Contrarily to what neoclassical proponents have been arguing, privatisation does not imply a more successful management and distribution of this vital resource *vis-à-vis* populations' life-needs, for an increase in availability would reduce the margin of profit available. Indeed, even advocates of private management of water and water-related services, if not even their direct ownership, tend to agree on the fact that supervision by public authorities and regulation of the private companies managing water and water-related services are necessary.[169] Also, privatisation seems to occur most commonly wherever public authorities do not increase taxation or borrowing to maintain and improve the existing water utilities, i.e. where they behave in accordance with the 'minimal State' ideal of the neoclassical paradigm;[170] or where they collude with organised crime in exchange for money and/or political support to make water scarce, thus forcing the citizenry—those who can afford it—to rely on alternative, for-profit suppliers, i.e. where public officers behave in accordance with the self-maximising anthropological ideal of the neoclassical paradigm. The worldwide plethora of business-related illegality, from bribing to tax evasion and espionage, bear further and daily witness to the connection between crime and the same paradigm.[171]

Mental diseases in their 40's and 50's and a generally shorter life-expectancy rate await many professional footballers, most likely because of the amount, intensity and frequency of physical stress endured in their fairly short careers as well-paid sportsmen. Fast-pace, intense, even brutal games seem to be most popular amongst spectators, who are willing to pay for tickets, merchandise and TV subscriptions, whilst private sponsors pay the NFL large sums of money in order for their advertisements to reach these spectators.[172] Fossil-fuel-thirsty vehicles of all types and dimensions pour onto the world's seas and land as well as into the skies above, with rare woods made even rarer for the most expensive ones.[173] In the process, manufacturers secure returns for their investments. As for the lifestyle connected with these vehicles, the super-rich set the example, which the other classes emulate within the constraints of their position—and all participate in adding to the atmospheric pollution that scientists regard as a factor in Italy's depleted hydraulic resources. The circle is closing.[174]

Several other common elements can be observed from alternative perspectives. For example, from an ontological perspective, they all involve human beings. From an ethical perspective, instead, they all involve individual as well as institutional choices. However, in the following paragraphs, I focus exclusively on the axiological perspective, in order to highlight the fundamental blindness to life of the neoclassical paradigm. I use intentionally the term "paradigm" rather than "school" or "tradition", because I deal hereby with a set of politically significant, typically inter-connected ideas, which have generated an ideological framework that, born in the field of economics, informs nowadays the mind-set of the most influential policy- and decision-makers, both at the level of interpretation of world's affairs and at the level of institutional action. From Milton Friedman's 1962 *Capitalism and Freedom* to Morrison's and Wilhelm's 2006 *Investment Banking*, *via* the 1970s adoption by Margaret Thatcher of Friedrich Hayek's 1944 *Road to Serfdom* as the polar star of new conservatism, its main tenets have been reiterated in several forms throughout the 20th century, particularly in its closing three decades.[175] Some of these tenets, without any doubt, belong to the classical tradition as well, which was made famous by the likes of Jean-Baptiste Say and Adam Smith. Others, instead, pertain more fittingly, if not exclusively, to its 20th-century reformulation alone.

The differences between classical and neoclassical economics tend to be stressed by scholars less often than their similarities. And when they are stressed, the focus is posited mainly on methodological (e.g. the increased role of mathematical formalism and models) and historical-technological changes (e.g. the advent of trusts and corporate business over individual or family-based enterprises, the massive shift from secondary to tertiary sector in first-world countries, the informatisation and virtualisation of world trade). Little is said about the striking *contradictions* between the two and *vis-à-vis* the types of capitalist praxes that they have contributed to justifying. In this perspective, particularly interesting are those that emerge from comparing today's alleged free-market age *cum* its neoclassical theoretical apparatus and Adam Smith's celebrated 1776 'Bible' of capitalism—*An Inquiry into the Nature and Causes of the Wealth of Nations*[176]—*cum* the entrepreneurial reality of his times.

[a] First of all, Adam Smith opposed most vocally monopolies and oligopolies, which are the given of today's world trade, especially in strategic areas such as oil extraction and aerospace technologies. He admitted that "free trade" was as idealistic a goal as More's island of "Utopia" or Harrington's Commonwealth of "Oceana", for it conflicted with the interests of many private market actors, but he believed in trade as free as reasonably possible.[177]

[b] Secondly, Adam Smith spoke as vocally against joint-stock companies or corporations, i.e. today's dominant form of business, for he regarded the separation between ownership and management as detrimental to good business. In his view, the owner of such companies are content with dividends or short-term financial gains, caring little about what actually goes on within the company or even the company's long-term prospects, lest they move their capital elsewhere in the pursuit of higher profits. The "court of directors" (i.e. managers, CEOs, etc.), on the other hand, do not put heart and soul into running the company as efficiently as possible, for it is not theirs and, as common instead in smaller family-run businesses, it does not constitute an essential part of their personal identity and reasons for living.[178]

[c] Thirdly, Smith expected profits to be reinvested in productive national activities, i.e. manufacturing tangible goods in the entrepreneur's home country, thus creating employment, domestic consumption and demographic growth, i.e. generating the life-affirming conditions for the country's wealth, as the title of his work indicates.[179] However, economic virtualisation and capital migration have become standard realities of today's capitalism, reaching their most life-destructive, national-wealth-reducing expression in financial capital being siphoned to foreign fiscal havens and later utilised to speculate against the home country's currency or other national assets. Indeed, the very idea that money could become more than a means of exchange was alien to Smith, whereas currency speculation is nowadays the leading form of international trade. Not

to mention the notion of 'jobless recovery', born in the 1970s, whereby economic performance is evaluated positively for augmenting the value of financial assets *contra* steady or decreasing rates of employment.

[d] Finally, Adam Smith argued in favour of progressive income taxation in order to generate the public revenue required for the provision of public goods that he regarded as unlikely or inappropriate for the private sector to provide (e.g. law and order, national security, communication and transport infrastructures, primary education, government).[180] Yet, today's economic reality shows no area that is immune to privatisation, which the neoclassical paradigm commends as sole and absolute guarantor of efficiency, whilst at the same time decrying taxation as unfair appropriation of resources by the "rapacious state".[181]

[e] Also, in Smith's view, the separation between "merchants" and "the rulers of mankind" ought to be as rigorous as possible, in order to avoid corruption, unfair competition and *ad hoc* legislation. Today's world displays pervasive lobbying and funding of political parties by private business and corporate-lawyer-dictated State-binding regulations (e.g. regulation by the World Trade Organization [hereafter WTO]), not to mention the direct participation in politics of major capitalists (e.g. Italy's former Prime Minister, Silvio Berlusconi), whilst the neoclassical paradigm praises State intervention that is conducive to increased money returns. In fact, some of the most lucrative fields in today's free market are heavily dependent upon State subsidies, research-and-development grants, and tariff protection, e.g. agribusiness, armaments, oil extraction and refinement.

Contradictions with Adam Smith aside, the neoclassical paradigm does exist now, determining the life and death of entire communities, and must be acknowledged and understood. The following list tries to summarise its key tenets succinctly, highlighting when possible their continuity with classical economics:

- All value is ultimately understood as, or reducible to, money capital; hence the neoclassical equation between prices paid for commodities and satisfaction of preferences, whatever they may be. Pareto's ophelimity, a standard presupposition of the neoclassical paradigm, does not distinguish qualitatively between the want of golden toilet seats and the need for potable water.

- The maximisation of money-capital returns from invested money capital is regarded as natural (i.e. an anthropological *datum* already endorsed by Adam Smith), rational (i.e. not to follow this principle is insane) and it can even be normatively binding (e.g. corporate managers have a 'fiduciary duty' before shareholders to the maximisation of their returns).
- No limit to the maximisation of such returns is set, as revealed by the neoclassical principle of 'non-satiety'—a reformulation of Say's law in classical economics.
- This maximisation is believed to be accomplished most effectively through a system of free sale and purchase of commodities i.e. the 'free market' commended already by Adam Smith.
- The free market is believed to guarantee the fairest distribution of commodities, i.e. their 'optimal allocation', approaching an ideal balance between supply and demand, thanks to its alleged ability to self-adjust and regulate. Adam Smith regarded this ability as divine, for a Providential invisible hand was said to make it possible for the pursuit of individual self-interest to become the origin of collective well-being i.e. the wealth of nations.
- It is inferred from the previous point that the public authority should interfere as little as possible with the free market, whether by means of taxation, subsidy or public ownership of assets that could be privately owned.
- An exception is made for those interferences that are deemed to serve the free market, thus ultimately leading to the paramount goal, i.e. maximisation of money-capital returns. Adam Smith, for example, regarded progressive taxation of income and the public provision of both domestic and international security as necessary to the wealth of the nations.
- Since all value is ultimately understood as, or reducible to, money capital, then the free market is regarded as the source of all that is valuable hence good and desirable.

- Whenever undeniably negative effects are produced by the free market (e.g. carcinogenic pollution, life-threatening obesity, sexual exploitation), then these effects are either discarded as 'externalities' (i.e. the causal connection between the free market and its effects is nominally reduced) or accepted as 'unavoidable costs' that the alleged market's self-adjusting and regulating ability is bound to resolve.
- Since the free market is regarded as the source of all that is valuable hence good and desirable, those who criticise or threaten it are condemned as either irrational (e.g. incompetent, unscientific, ignorant) or evil (e.g. terrorist, communist, anarchist).[182]

It is my contention that, if the preservation and enhancement of life-capital resources is desired—the LSS discussed in my previous chapters—then criteria must be employed that are not those supplied by the neoclassical paradigm, despite their current and widespread popularity. Free markets, competition, deregulation, property rights, maximising stockholders' returns, monetary criteria for wealth-creation and faith in the invisible hand do not suffice. Glimpses of awareness about the life-disconnected character of the money-capital economy are rare in the works of mainstream economists, despite known facts such as the World Health Organization's [hereafter WHO] acknowledgment of the causal relationship between growing carcinogenic pathologies and human-made pollution.[183] For example, in a recent article, Ross M. Starr writes: "Like written language and the wheel, money is one of the fundamental discoveries of civilization. Financial markets for debt instruments (intertemporal contracts for money) and claims on capital, serve to implement an efficient allocation of consumption and capital across time. They rearrange the control of capital from those who have saved it (and retain their claim on it) to others who can make the most productive (or most profitable) use of it".[184] By disjoining "productive" and "profitable", the author, whether consciously or not, allows for conceiving of productive returns that are not money-capital returns.

In point fact, actual free-market policies (as opposed to theoretical models or ideal hypothetical instantiations of them) make things worse, generating insecurity in the name of security and paucity of vital resources in the name of prosperity. For instance, it has been observed that the increasing for-profit privatisation of the traditionally public, most evidently life-protecting institutions, i.e. domestic security (e.g. policing services) and international security (e.g. armed forces), has contributed to generate, on the one hand, a higher perception of personal insecurity and social division[185] and, on the other hand, a higher likelihood of warfare on the planet, i.e. the life-destructive activity *par excellence*.[186] Not to seek an alternative is tantamount to persevering in a systemic blindness to life, the final result of which can only be death. Emblematic is the Pasqua-Lama project, where the Barrick Gold Corporation has been physically uprooting and removing three millenary glaciers along the border with Argentina—Toro 1, Toro 2 and Huasco—in order to gain access to gold, silver and copper ores located underneath the ancient ice. Since the very beginning it was manifest that such a major operation would have affected negatively the already arid climate of the area and altered the fresh water aquifers of local populations and ecosystems, including the UNESCO-protected Biosphere Reserve of San Guillermo. Proprietary rights to those locations had been lawfully purchased by Barrick Gold from the Chilean authorities, whose assessment criteria had been directed towards the goal of money-capital returns, rather than life-capital ones.[187]

Death by Method

The neoclassical paradigm is blind to life because of its conceptual and methodological assumptions. By recovering part of 18th- and 19th-century classical economics *à la* Smith, Say and Ricardo, it reduces the room for conceiving of genuinely free and genuinely human agency, since it interprets what humans do as the instantiation of regular uniformities that are both describable and predictable in the light of necessary economic laws. It is generally forgotten that the methodological paradigm endorsed by the fathers of modern economics was mechanical—that is Newtonian—engineering. This paradigm was attractive because it allowed to conceive of complex, multi-causal phenomena along clear mathematical lines, thus permitting also the prediction of outcomes. Under the ensuing descriptive apparatus, complex human societies came to be seen as complex machines, whilst human beings became, consistently with this picture, cogs within such machines, responding to causal stimuli according to laws that, as Ricardo famously put, were as certain as those of physics.[188]

In the neoclassical version, the practical application of the science called "economics" has been seen as an obvious extension of this powerful, Newton-inspired source of knowledge. Economics can then serve the purpose of constructing highly efficient machines. Therefore, in recent decades, entire societies have been openly and extensively subjected to 're-engineering' or 'structural adjustment plans' whenever they did not prove efficient enough, i.e. whenever they did not generate sufficient money-capital returns, regardless of the life-capital that they might have been able to sustain. All this, it must be noted, through an ironic contradiction of the still-heralded principle of 'minimal State' or 'non-interference', which characterised the classical school. Governments sign binding agreements, the police force quench protests, and State armies surround and protect strategic locations. Indeed, it is public authorities that grant incorporation and other rights to private businesses, including the privilege of limited liability, analogous to pre-modern aristocratic privilege. In other words, State authorities legitimise and implement 're-engineering' and 'structural adjustment plans', which the IMF, amongst other international bodies and 'development' agencies (e.g. the World Bank), develop and promote, generally on behalf of corporate manufacturing giants and gargantuan merchant banks.[189]

Additionally, other mechanics-based notions have become so integral parts of the economist's lexicon that both their origin and their life-blind implications remain commonly unseen (e.g. 'equilibrium', 'inputs/outputs', 'overheating', 'cooling down', 'circular flow').[190] Mechanics is not bad *per se*, but it becomes troublesome when applied to realms of being for which it was not originally intended and for which its predicates are inadequate. Biology, not mechanics, deals with life. As discussed in my previous chapter, to be alive means to display rather peculiar attributes: growth (not mere aggregation), potential for reproduction (not mere repetition), goal-directedness (not mere involvement in causal chains of energy-transferring events), self-definition *via* membrane, skin or shell (i.e. separation of the individual organism from its surroundings), self-maintenance *via* mutually supporting functions (i.e. metabolism). All these attributes cannot be captured in anything like the laws and formulae of physics and chemistry. Besides, living beings either succeed or fail in achieving their goals; henceforth the study of living beings must employ categories of value and disvalue (e.g. alive or dead, whole or impaired, healthy and pathological, etc.), which physics and chemistry do not employ and, more worryingly, neoclassical economics, as this discipline is claimed to be 'factual' and 'value-free'. I say "more worryingly" because neoclassical economics does not merely describe certain aspects of human societies, but affects on a vast scale today's policy- and decision-making as a leading paradigm of interpretation and action. Therefore, whether through the diktats of the IMF or the profit-maximising strategies of multinational conglomerates, it affects the lives and livelihoods of millions.

Economics, like mechanics, is not bad *per se*. However, if unaware of its intrinsic conceptual limitations and of the consequent sphere of appropriate application, it becomes troublesome as well.[191] If one adds to the life-blind predicates of mechanics the abstractedness of mathematical instruments, originally favoured by the Lausanne school and today flourished in the field of economic modelling, then the detachment from the life-ground becomes even starker. Already in 1936, John Maynard Keynes lamented this formulaic drift:

[I]n ordinary discourse, where we are not blindly manipulating but know all the time what we are doing and what the words mean, we can keep 'at the back of our heads'

the necessary reserves and qualifications and the adjustments
which we shall have to make later on, in a way in which we
cannot keep complicated partial differentials 'at the back' of
several pages of algebra which assume that they all vanish.
Too large a proportion of recent 'mathematical' economics
are mere concoctions, as imprecise as the initial assumptions
they rest on, which allow the author to lose sight of the
complexities and interdependencies of the real world in a
maze of pretentious and unhelpful symptoms.[192]

Neoclassical economics steers away from inductive, *a posteriori* historical and sociological analysis, favouring deductive, *a priori* model-generation, heavily reliant upon mathematical instruments. This means that economic analysis becomes hermeneutically disconnected from the tangible historical conditions that have surrounded the definition of, and the control over, economic assets, including those that guarantee better chances to meet one's own life-needs. Indeed, a deep epistemological issue lurks behind the mathematical armour of mainstream economics, which the alternative "rhetorical economics" of Eszter Pethó, amongst others, reveals: "Let us take general equilibrium. *It is a perfectly consistent equation mathematically with poor economic significance, however.* The same can be said about several other rules of epistemology. Rhetorical economics offers the alternative of the rules of persuasiveness and plausibility instead of the perfect correspondence to the rules of epistemology for accepting an economic theory."[193]

An analogous disconnection between money- and life-capital takes place *vis-à-vis* the multiplicity of economic systems developed throughout human history and the life-needs-induced reasons of this multiplicity. In brief, what has actually happened in the living world becomes a paler and paler phantom lying behind mathematical formulations and persistent abstraction. Following the year 2000 protests of French students against the life-decoupling abstractedness of neoclassical economics, taught as mainstream if not exclusive in the universities of their country, the Austrian economist Kurt W. Rothschild stated:

Generally, I would agree. I think that a critical view of economics is missing. This is not necessarily true for neoclassical theory as such, but for the way is used to keep other approaches out of the economics profession. I also think that the way in which it is applied directly to practical affairs is—given its very strict assumptions—illegitimate. Sometimes it is also presented in its "vulgar" form just to exploit it for certain ideological and political purposes. The economy and the social system in general that comprise of course also politics and social factors and institutions are such a complex phenomena [sic] that you can't expect one single theory to provide a sufficient basis for studying it. So, economics like sociology is necessarily a multi-paradigmatic science. We need several theories to study these complex circumstances.[194]

This disconnection can happen to the point of forgetting that not all human beings, for example, can participate in the so-called market, for they may have no assets to trade. Or that ecosystems, rather than collections of potential assets, are the ground upon which any market whatsoever relies for its existence.[195]

To mathematics-related abstractedness one might also wish to add the ascription of human and other rights to non-human market agents, such as multinational corporations, for example. Perhaps, no more revealing indicator of life-decoupling can there be than attributing personality to entities that do not possess any of the relevant features of actual personhood but in the fictional realm of law. The spiritedness of the living creature is absent in chartered institutions or other collective bodies, whose members alone can be described as true persons.[196] Furthermore, as economic models are utilised by intergovernmental bodies, governments and multinationals, neoclassical economics turns from descriptive into prescriptive. In an often unrecognised conceptual and practical shift, that which does not conform to the economic models produced is selected out by enforcing onto the world's population the same models, whether the recipients like it or not, thus conflating scientific demonstration with eradication of falsifying factors.[197] Models are proven correct by preventing or smashing their factual negation, whereas humankind, treated like cogs in theory, are treated as cogs in practice.[198]

Death to Motility

The neoclassical paradigm is blind to motility or biological movement, which it presupposes throughout its enunciations.[199] The so-called "efficiency" of the global market is measured in terms of money-capital returns. Yet, this is neither the only nor the most important evaluative option available, at least *vis-à-vis* the human being *qua* living being, i.e. creatures endowed with motility or biological movement.[200] Life-capital efficiency, i.e. enabling wider and deeper ranges of life capabilities across time and space, is by far more essential to the survival and fulfilment of the human race—both individually and collectively—than the qualitatively distinct money-capital efficiency of an economic system that, according to its own proponents, has produced wealth to an unprecedented scale, whilst at the same time affecting negatively the Earth's most basic LSS at all levels. An economic system unable to secure, produce and distribute means of life otherwise in short supply is a failure, *not* a success.

Several existing standards can serve to the assessment of life-capital efficiency and inefficiency, e.g. the UN Human Development Index, the Genuine Progress Indicator, the Calvert-Henderson Quality of Life Indicators, the Ecological Footprint. However, the most comprehensive standard is likely to be John McMurtry's Basic Well-Being Index, first presented in *Value Wars* and comprising:

[A]ir quality... access to clean water... sufficient nourishing food... security of habitable housing... opportunity to perform meaningful service or work of value to others... learning opportunity to the level of qualification... healthcare when ill... temporally and physically available healthy

environmental space for leisure, social interaction and recreation.[201]

Taking stock of such standards, it is quite simply patent that there is no facet of the planetary life-ground that has not been depleted in the three centuries that have seen the affirmation of capitalism worldwide: the biosphere-protecting ozone-layer, breathable-air producing and reproducing pluvial forests and oceanic life-systems, self-regenerating water aquifers, nourishing-food-producing arable spaces, and natural-equilibrium-maintaining and science- and technology-inspiring biodiversity. Instead of providing means of life, i.e. actual goods enabling life abilities not possible without them, the worldwide affirmation of capitalism has crippled the planet's LSS, inundating it with commodities that disable or do not enable life abilities (e.g. junk food, addictive life-harming commodities). According to the 2006 *Living Planet Report* by the World Wildlife Foundation [hereafter WWF], there has been only one country in the world that has succeeded in developing in a sustainable manner between 1961 and 2003, i.e. Cuba. We should then worry when that country's controversial leader denounces the development of bio-fuels, which would likely shift part of the world's agricultural production from food to fuel, as a threat to human life.[202] Not all renewable energy sources have equal potential *vis-à-vis* life-enhancement, while Mexicans and Italians are paying already higher prices for tortillas and pasta than before.[203]

If neoclassical economists bother tackling this issue at all, they do it typically under the category of 'externalities' i.e. as non-essential to the computation of overall benefits and losses. As Lawrence 'Larry' Summers stated in 1992, then being Chief Economist of the World Bank: "the economic logic behind dumping a load of toxic waste in the lowest wage country is impeccable, and we should face up to that."[204] Life-sustaining concerns are *not* a significant element in the battery of technical predicates with which their discipline is endowed. From this fact alone should follow that governments and international bodies ought to rely on other sources of knowledge and interpretation than neoclassical economics and/or related conceptions when dealing with problems that they cannot tackle *de iure*, not just *de facto*, as they lack appropriate categories of thought. The most fundamental LSS lay outside the neoclassical paradigm, unless they are turned into life-indifferent commodities to be exploited for money-capital maximisation.[205] The neoclassical paradigm does not see the Earth's topsoil layer requiring a sustainable utilisation, but land onto which property rights can be established in order to generate profit, in a money-capital-driven *Gestell* that not even Heidegger had been able to identify as the force behind modern science and technology. Business opportunities are thus seen, not life-needs. One of the most startling cases of neoclassical thinking prevailing over life-concerns in recent times was the creation of a carbon trading market out of greenhouse gases reduction schemes such as the European Union's [hereafter EU] Emissions Trading Scheme [ETS] and the UN Kyoto Protocol agreement. By turning pollution into a commodity, this market did not counter it, but merely allowed for a for-profit redistribution of the same, in the kindest of possible interpretations.[206]

Besides, benefits and losses from the perspective of life-capital are too conspicuous to be regularly ignored. The stakes are simply too high. Unsurprisingly, critical voices have been heard. Initially, these voices were either dismissed or marginalised as those of radicals, nostalgic hippies, and imprudent non-economists:

> *The disappearance of alternative models of development provoked anguished reactions from the old anticapitalists of the postwar era, who ranged from socialists to revolutionaries and remained captive to a nostalgia for their vanished dreams... in fields other than economics. English, comparative literature, and sociology are all fertile breeding grounds for such dissent.*[207]

But as the voices became louder, originating unambiguously also from respected and recognised public health and safety institutions (e.g. the WHO and the U.S. Surgeon-General),[208] intergovernmental bodies and major international organisations (e.g. the UN), the problems, at least, could be ignored no longer.[209]   Indeed, even Joseph Ratzinger, the leading Catholic theologian of his generation and then Pope of the Church of Rome as Benedict XVI, stated:

> *A thick layer of dirt covers God's creation. The world must not be abused. We must regard the Creation as a gift given to us not to destroy it, but to let it blossom into God's garden, hence humankind's garden... Considering the many forms of abuse of the Earth that we are witnessing today, we can almost hear the Creation crying out. And both Creation and history await men and women who be truly God's children and behave accordingly... Committing themselves to take care of the Creation, without wasting its resources and sharing them amongst themselves equitably.*[210]

This mounting pressure on governments and public consciousness must be continued in order to obtain much-needed changes and monitor closely the positive steps already taken.[211] In this sense, educators and intellectuals can do much, *qua* public actors, in order to keep the level of awareness high and promote a culture of sustainability. The path along which the planet is moving is not positive and allows for limited optimism, as conflicts for basic life-resources are foreboded by eminent scientists and influential political advisers. A 2002 secret report by the Pentagon about climate change, later leaked to the press, even stated "that major European cities will be sunk beneath rising seas as Britain is plunged into a 'Siberian' climate by 2020. Nuclear conflict, mega-droughts, famine and widespread rioting will erupt across the world... Disruption and conflict will be endemic features of life... Once again, warfare would define human life."[212] The stakes are again too high to ignore what is going on. Life-destruction takes place simultaneously at the global level (i.e. planetary LSS) and at the individual level (i.e. life-functions of particular organisms). They are the two sides of one and the same coin. For example, skin cancer rates have been increasing in the Southern hemisphere due to the depletion of the Ozone layer.[213] The main cause of these problems, however, has been ignored, or left untouched, like some sort of political taboo, especially when the life-destructive causal mechanism at work is observed in the sphere of the individual consumer, i.e. the maximisation of money-capital returns.[214]

On the one hand, even the eminent UN IPCC does not link openly the current ecological degeneration to the causal mechanism that produces the greenhouse gases. On the contrary, as previously mentioned, new markets in carbon trading are prescribed. The life-blind market mechanism causing the problem is thus perpetuated, rather than extinguished. Even the politically cautious 2006 *Stern Review on the Economics of Climate Change* commissioned by the British Government implies that the ETS cap-and-trade scheme implemented by the EU as of January 2005 has not improved the situation *vis-à-vis* the overall emissions of greenhouse gases. Successful industrial lobbying, political-clientele- concerned lax allocation plans and inefficient enforcement praxes are highlighted as the reasons for the ETS failing to accomplish its goals. However, the causal mechanism underlying each of these phenomena, i.e. the maximisation of money-capital returns, is neither clearly acknowledged nor openly addressed.

On the other hand, the more the global market system produces and consumes, the more it impairs planetary LSS. Given its life-blindness, money-capital returns drive towards global ecological meltdown, as every form of life capital is factored out of for-profit decisions, and selected against whenever doing so may result profitable.[215] Yet, green taxes and preventive laws are rejected as too 'costly', i.e. limiting the maximisation of money-capital returns, or as undue interference in the free market, i.e. impeding the maximisation of money-capital returns. It may be worth recalling the Latin etymology of "capital" i.e. "head" or "commencement". If the LSS and/or the individual organism—actual bodies of actual people —are damaged, the head suffers too. Actual human beings, *qua* biological creatures, are the commencement of any human collective enterprise, and substantial health is required in order for them to unfold. Three centuries ago, Edmund Burke, though close to the classical school, recognised that: "Even commerce, and trade, and manufacture, the gods of our economical politicians, are themselves perhaps but creatures; are themselves but effects, which as first causes, we choose to worship... They too may decay with their natural protecting principles."[216] Burke referred to the venerable cultural, moral and religious traditions inherited from centuries of British history as the "natural protecting principles" of "the gods of our economical politicians", many of which were in fact not the result of prolonged adaptation to the environmental conditions of the country and successful provision to the ends of the population, but rather of prolonged oppression and exploitation by the British nobility. Still, some were, most notably the Poor Laws (significantly abolished by the free-market Liberals in 1834), aimed as they were at meeting at least some of the basic needs of the kingdom's indigents. In other words, another, more compelling level was acknowledged, prior to any interest of commerce, trade and manufacture: the level of life-needs.[217]

'Capital' cannot be reduced to money stocks. Real capital is life-relevant wealth that produces more life-relevant wealth, as with those natural and human-made LSS that generate ecological stability, social infrastructures and knowledge, i.e. life-enhancing goods. A successful economic order is therefore one that produces and distributes life-endorsing and life-enhancing goods through generations and across populations, while at the same time protecting the life-ground, i.e. those LSS upon which these goods rely for their coming and/or continuing into existence. The world is not at our complete disposal, unless we are planning to dispose of ourselves.[218] In this perspective, economic progress, and *a fortiori* adjudication of better and worse economic systems, ought to occur by reference to life-capital parameters such as, for example, nutritional intake, access to clean water, literacy rates, life expectancy rates, livelihood participation. The greater is their provision, the better is the system. And if money capital affects negatively life capital, even if at the same time it augments money-capital returns, then real capital is being lost, not gained, to false capital. Means of life, instead of becoming available to a greater extent, are being misallocated, by increasing scarcity and concentration in few hands. Even by adopting money-capital parameters the results of the worldwide application of the neoclassical paradigm has been far from positive. Between 1980 and 2000, i.e. after twenty years of neoclassical-inspired deregulation, the number of people living on less than $2.00 per day had risen by almost 50%,[219] while the share of the 49 poorest countries in the world had declined from 40% to 0.4%.[220] In the meantime, life-decoupled financial speculation and Foreign Direct Investment [hereafter FDI] grew enormously, mainly in the form of currency speculation and mergers-and-acquisitions, yet hardly contributing to any significant growth of GDP, which grew much faster in the golden age of Keynesianism (1950–1980).[221] All in all, about 1.6 billion people were worse off in the year 1999 than they were in the year 1980.[222] Organ trafficking, illegal drug tests and medical experiments, prostitution, sweatshops (manufacturing 'consumer goodies'), full-time employed households living below the poverty line exemplify just some of the implications for those whose money-power is inadequate *vis-à-vis* their life-needs.

Tragically, it is generally assumed that money capital is the only or the primary 'capital' by definition. In fact, it is money stocks seeking self-maximisation by continuous pressure upon real capital, i.e. life-capital (e.g. ecosystems' soundness, people's health, free access to cultural resources). As a result, LSS are sacrificed to the growth of money capital, from the carbon- and oxygen-crucial photosynthesising forests and oceanic phytoplankton to the planet's fresh waters. Amongst the criteria to assess the wealth of a nation, Adam Smith included "the populousness of every country", for that "must be in proportion to the degree of its improvement and cultivation".[223] With the shift from the classical perspective to the neoclassical one, which took place as humankind progressively abandoned *en masse* the countryside *in lieu* of urban centres, even Smith's marginal sensitivity for the life-ground was lost.[224]

The neoclassical paradigm is blind to life at another level, that of felt being or spiritual health. It is not enough for a living creature to enjoy adequate, free motility for its well-being: it must also be able to develop typically human faculties (e.g. rational thought, symbolic communication, creative self-expression, non-instrumental social interaction, meaningful work), so as to be positively open to further experience.[225] Without the opportunities required for meaningful social interaction and emotional self-expression, for example, human life turns into nightmare, even if the environmental surroundings and metabolic functions of the individual organism may be in good shape. Winston Smith, citizen of the totalitarian State of Oceania created by the literary genius of George Orwell, describes himself repeatedly as already dead, albeit physically alive. Things change when he develops a sense of self-worth by rebelling against the system and, overcoming his isolation, loving another citizen. Then, for the first time, he *feels alive*, hence exemplifying both the meaning and the meaningfulness of felt being for a proper understanding of 'life'. Also, Orwell's Winston Smith lives in an advanced industrial country that combines together the liberticidal features of Stalinist Russia, Nazi Germany and Imperial Britain, thus suggesting that, unfortunately, several avenues are open to the establishment of societies where life-capabilities are systemically hindered.[226] What can the neoclassical paradigm offer to us in this sense?[227]

Emblematically, *The Economist* identifies "happiness" with the free pursuit of "incomes" and "a plethora of consumer goodies making living easier and more enjoyable".[228] Certainly, "incomes" and "consumer goodies" may well count for something, yet one is left to ponder upon when, how and how much they count. Incomes are crucial *vis-à-vis* life-security, e.g. being well-nourished and keeping in good health so as to enjoy additional, wider ranges of life capability. Consumer goods may enhance one's opportunities in this sense, e.g. IT technologies can facilitate communication between friends.[229] This notion of happiness implies an axiological baseline that the paradigm does not account explicitly for, i.e. life itself, which *The Economist* reveals as "living easier and more enjoyable". Owing to this implication, it is tempting to conclude that self-maximisation and consumerist acquisition of priced goods work as long and insofar as they serve the purpose of life-enhancement, meeting human life-needs across populations and through time. John McMurtry argues himself for the possibility of a virtuous use of money that, variously regulated for the sake of serving life, follows the following sequence: "L $\rightarrow$ MofL $\rightarrow$ L^1" (L = life, MofL = means of life i.e. life-enhancing goods and services, L^1 = more life). Thus, it is possible to conceive of a virtuous capitalist economy, which generates profit insofar and inasmuch as it enhances life at the same time, i.e. "L $\rightarrow$ \$ $\rightarrow$ MofL $\rightarrow$ \$^{1} $\rightarrow$ L^1" (\$ = money, \$^{1} = more money i.e. profit).[230] However, things are not so benign.

The philosophical anthropology of the neoclassical paradigm says that the human being is a self-maximising, non-satiable consumer, taking part—as far as this is possible—in the operations of the free market. For one, millions of human beings have hardly any access to the free market, because they lack the resources required to exercise money-demand. When possible, faced with the lethal threat of undernourishment, they sell what is left of their labouring power and of their children's, prostitution being the exemplary option, or die in the attempt:

Official data on the number of fatal casualties resulting from unauthorized border crossings are not available. The figures concerning European borders are based on data collected by the UNITED for Intercultural Action NGO, which has been monitoring death tolls since 1993. The sum of documented cases of migrants' deaths attributed to border crossings mounts up to 5,785 between 1 January 1993 and 10 April 2005. These numbers can only be taken as an indication of real figures, since many deaths are never discovered.[231]

However:

[T]he obvious conclusion here seems to be that as long as the 'migratory pressure' in the countries of origin persists, and no or only very limited possibilities of legal immigration exist, any effort to render the EU's Mediterranean (or its other) borders more impermeable will mainly produce such undesirable side effects instead of limiting the overall volume of irregular immigration.[232]

Others, who cannot even do this, starve and eventually die.[233]

To a deeper level, the paradigm does not regard the human being as a living creature, a fact which instead it presupposes tacitly throughout its enunciations.[234] Consistently, this paradigm does not command us to live well or wisely, but to make money in order to consume insatiably the ever-growing priced goods newly available on the market. It therefore uses notions of 'preferences' or 'wants' to be satisfied, whatever they may be, not of 'needs' to be met, for that is what computes within the paradigm's coordinates. Given the unnatural character of this lifestyle, contemporary corporate business like Coca-Cola and Nike invest on average less money in manufacturing goods to be sold worldwide than in mass-conditioning human beings *via* military-inspired advertising campaigns aimed at seizing hold of the individual's subconscious drives, so as to instil artificial wants and turn them into perceived needs. Artistic creativity, psychological and sociological research, conscious and repeated lying are all employed to the utmost extent in these campaigns: what matters, in the end, is the return the investor gets on its marketing investment. Jon Steel, famous marketing strategist in the 1990s, provided an involuntary exposé of the utter life-blindness of the advertising business in *Truth, Lies, and Advertising: The Art of Account Planning* (Mississauga: John Wiley and Sons Canada, 1998), whereas the book's triumphal success in the business world has served as an example of the general life-blindness of the dominant neoclassical paradigm.

However, happiness research in psychology has rediscovered a long-known truth: happiness is not something that one can buy; indeed, consumerist self-maximisation by satisfaction of wants through acquisition of priced goods stands in the way of happiness. Consumerist self-maximisation is a source of continuous frustration, which reduces people's quality of life.[235] This type of self-maximisation posits as its cardinal foundation an individualistic notion of the self, yet it involves as well an unending process of wanting more things that are not the individual. Henceforth, apart from projecting *de facto* happiness outside oneself and into the future (i.e. never within oneself and in the present), happiness is also continuously postponed *de iure*, for wants are defined as non-satiable. Elaborating on classical and, in particular, Hellenistic philosophy, Michel de Montaigne thought of our inability to master our passions and, as far as possible, retire within ourselves as the fundamental source of human unhappiness. He thus expresses this secular wisdom in a powerful passage: "We are never at home: we are always outside ourselves. Fear, desire, hope, impel us towards the future; they rob us of feelings and concern for what now is, in order to spend time over what will be."[236] Preference satisfaction can never be complete: no matter how much one has got already, there are newer opportunities, better investments, chances to stay ahead of one's competitors, etc.[237]

In contrast with all this, life-needs are satiable. "Human [life] capabilities are diverse", writes Jeff Noonan in *Democratic Society and Human Needs*, probably the sharpest study of needs *contra* wants to date, "and a maximal cultivation of our defining capabilities demands that we alter our activities."[238] The same applies even when we consider life-needs that transcend motility: "One cannot be overeducated in the sense that one's finite mind could ever know too much… but one can hide in books from the other demands of a full and free existence. Likewise, one can have too much free time."[239] Life-needs require *balance* amidst one another, as the needs for biological movement must be satisfied in order to fulfil those for a truly human existence, i.e. being free to pursue one's life-plans by developing vital capabilities within and around oneself. Sensitive to the life-ground, the old philosophical ideals of eudemonia (i.e. the pursuit of happiness, or leading the good life) and cultivation of virtue had already captured respectively the requirement for balance amidst life-needs and the inter-subjective character of human life-fulfilment. Instead, were we even to consider the 'capital' at one's disposal one's share of valuable human relationships, the anthropological philosophy endorsed by the neoclassical paradigm would still be nonsensical. Should one maximise these relationships?

One cannot do it alone. Nor can these relationships be maximised, in the sense that there may be a deepening of the quality of certain relationships, while others must remain at a certain level of intensity and not beyond, in order for them to subsist for what they are. Not to mention those that cannot be increased without disrupting others. All this, while at the same time taking care of the many other spheres of existence in which one is involved: maximisation must be put to a halt or neglected if one wants to take care of them as well. The neoclassical paradigm does not make sense in human life, yet we are increasingly trained to think that it is the sole paradigm.[240] As for distinguishing between wants and needs, "No revision of my self-interpretation as living, human, and potentially free being can alter the needs that those elements of nature impose upon me". Needs, in other words, "are non-voluntary", whereas "Wants, by contrast, are subject to wilful change"; in other terms, "I can change my wants by changing my self-interpretation", whereas the needs I have cannot change, for I am a certain creature.[241] To be honest, to a trained philosopher, the connection between priced goods and happiness appears to be ridiculous, for it denies the wisdom of nearly all ancient, medieval and Renaissance philosophy.[242] In more or less forceful ways, all classical, Christian and neo-pagan schools but one, Aristippus' Cyrenaic hedonism, recognised that the multiplication of wants could only generate a multiplication of dissatisfactions and that to keep one's wants as close as possible to one's needs was the key to autarky, or self-sufficiency, hence to happiness. If anything, the ancient schools of Aristotle and Epicurus were considered mundane, because less austere than Cynicism or Stoicism, and the same can be said of Machiavelli, Alberti and Erasmus in the heyday of European humanism. Still, none of them did ever depart from the notion of seeking happiness through the selection and overall reduction of wants. Even Francis Bacon, who first theorised the full human mastery over nature by technological means, recommended the careful 'pruning' of one's wants in order to lead a happy life.

Although wants and needs have not to be mutually exclusive, focussing on the latter means focussing on what matters most, i.e. that which ought to be satisfied before a wise person or a just society reach the position in which they can choose rationally and maturely whether to want more and how to get that. And what matters most, in *all* these accounts, is invariably a set of life-enhancing attributes, including the anti-individualistic recognition of human sociability. For Aristotle, for example, the human being is a 'political animal', whereas for Epicurus friendship is a 'natural necessary desire' like eating nourishing food and drinking clean water. Self-sufficiency, in other words, is less inimical to human relations than self-maximisation. Nevertheless, the problem is ignored. Modern 'wisdom' proceeds in the opposite direction, even if consumers in the developed world are not made happier by ever more market commodities. The breakaway from the cultivation of autarky and, more broadly, from an ethics of personal virtue valuing moderation and self-restraint is a defining aspect of modernity, sharply revealed and discussed, amongst others, by F. M. Dostoyevsky, Max Weber and Alasdair MacIntyre. The selfish, self-serving, ever-wanting, lupine human being theorised by Thomas Hobbes in his *Leviathan* is probably the first full expression of a novel philosophical anthropology that began to turn into Western common sense during the 18th century and that is now taken as the sole paradigm of rationality *tout-court*. Paul Fairfield calls this human being "the appetitive machine", thus capturing its being both wants-enslaved and mechanised.[243]

Still, Hobbes hoped that the Sovereign could prevent its subjects from fighting like wolves against one another in a perpetual state of war. The 'state of nature' where competition reigns supreme was meant to terrify his contemporaries and convince them to prefer the existing 'state of civility', not to lead them to novel savagery.[244] A plethora of scientific studies like Barry Schwartz's *Paradox of Choice: Why More Is Less* show that satisfaction does not increase with yet more income and consumer goods.[245] The abundance of affordable consumer choice drowns people into the sea of hyper-stimulation, anxiety and inadequacy *vis-à-vis* those that can afford even more: "No man is rich who shakes and groans, convinced that he needs more".[246] All in all, the law of diminishing returns seems to hold true, as material affluence counts merely up to a certain level for people's well-being—a level that can be set and understood only by means of life-centred parameters.[247] Yet, economists and policy makers hardly seem to respond to this awareness, or actually cannot, for their paradigm is incapable of tackling this point. The neoclassical paradigm, imprisoned by its simplistic anthropological presumptions, assumes that market growth is the one and only path: The more is produced, the more is bought, and the more is bought, the happier we become.[248]

Supply takes care of itself: thus had prophesised Jean-Baptiste Say in the classical age of economics. The neoclassical paradigm reinterprets this idea as the key to the human search for happiness. Therefore, it inundates us with unnecessary gadgets, for the purchase of which we must work harder, whilst their production and consumption, in addition to falling short to delivering the promised happiness, typically contribute to further the ecological destruction of the planet. As highlighted before, demand needs a lot of artificial stimulation in order to meet supply, and the ultimate end of this process is the maximisation of money-capital returns. Praising fashion designer Giorgio Armani, Amy M. Spindler provides an unaware splendid display of modern anti-wisdom: "selling fashion means *creating new needs,* and most men do not need another classic jacket. Armani is an expert at creating new needs."[249] Yet, as foreboded by the likes of Antisthenes, Epictetus and Aquinas in pre-consumerist societies, non-satiety is a nightmare, for it expects the human being to strive endlessly for more, newer goods, hence implying that no amount of material affluence can quench the thirst for more and newer goods. Behind every TV commercial of today's corporate-controlled mass media lurks the tragedy of the modern consumer: buy x to be happy, but never be happy, for you must buy y next.[250] Also, self-maximisation is a source of worry: whatever one wishes to augment can be lost. Even large, well-established reserves of money-capital come at a cost: the fear of not having it any longer.[251]

Indeed, the consumerist culture promoted by today's advertising campaigns diverts people's lives from the actual search for happiness to the search for accumulation, for it is (wrongly) believed that it is only in the abundance of material wealth that happiness will be found—in *The Economist*'s "incomes" and "consumer goodies". Apart from the fact that only some will become actually richer, there will always be fewer that are better-off, and while this race to the top is pursued, the room for human relationships, free time and free self-expression is lost. The classical paradigm, which regarded most human beings as cheap means of production, sacrificed human relationships, free time and free self-expression to increasing industrial output, as denounced, amongst others, by Paul Lafargue's famous pamphlet *The Right to be Lazy*.[252] The neoclassical one, which regards most human beings as consumers, obtains similar results, for it sacrifices human relationships, free time and free self-expression to increasing mass consumption.[253] 19th-century novelists like Giovanni Verga (e.g. *Mastro Don Gesualdo*)[254] in Italy and Mikhail J. Saltykov-Shchedrin in Russia (e.g. *The Golovlyov Family*)[255] had already described this phenomenon as the growing anxiety for further material self-affirmation by individuals who own enough wealth not to have to worry about the life-needs that most other humans struggle to satisfy.[256] These individuals, who could afford to be participants in valuable human relationships, treat instead the persons surrounding them instrumentally. Everything and everyone is turned into means to the unattainable end of maximising one's own self-interest, which is understood as the ability to purchase priced commodities in order to fulfil one's whims, including expensive holydays in exotic resorts. Hans T. Blokland speaks aptly of "Machiavellian syndrome", whereby human relations are reverted from Kant's Kingdom of Ends into a nightmarish Kingdom of Means.[257]

Given the absence of alternative parameters (e.g. well-being, wisdom, saintliness), the only yardstick available to measure one's achievements is Veblen's money-capital-serving conspicuous consumption (to which conspicuous leisure is reducible as well). But money-capital does not capture being alive, and even less being human. Hence loneliness, hopelessness and an automaton-like inertial habit of existence-pro-accumulation takes the place of actual human life. The human being, under these conditions, is dead. Sometimes, the animal being dies too: *Karoshi*, a Japanese term describing death by overwork or 'occupational sudden death' due to stress.[258] In less dramatic cases, time vanishes nonetheless that could be devoted to oneself and others for the sake of being oneself and enjoying others' company and interaction. Opportunities for getting to know oneself and cultivating oneself freely as oneself are diminished. More and more time is put into increasing opportunities for augmenting "incomes" in view of "consumer goodies" marketed as the bearers of true happiness. Even the allegedly 'free' time left is invaded by another horde of leisure and entertainment commodities, aimed at the human being *qua* consumer only, but above all at maximising money-capital returns.[259] The path towards wisdom is closed. Roger Kimball, managing director of *The New Criterion*, writes on this issue:

> *This is a point that many commentators, including many putatively conservative ones, have had difficulty digesting. In their enthusiasm for free markets, they have elided the distinction between the market, where freedom encourages growth, and morals, where genuine freedom requires virtue. This is not a new idea, but it is one that seems to have been lost sight of. The one thing that everyone remembers about Adam Smith was his idea that the improvement of civil society was founded not on benevolence but on the "invisible hand" that directed the self-interest of individuals to a higher good. But Smith also argued that the worst form of government was one "directed chiefly by the ends of commerce." The disposition to improve oneself, so essential to economic health, Smith wrote, was at the same time "the great and most universal cause" of the "corruption of our moral sentiments."*[260]

Instead, the self-maximising individual is trapped within one Goffmanesque character and ceases to participate in social plays where improvisation is allowed, if not even welcome. A priest or a nun may be content with this one-sidedness of one's own life, given the original commitment that lies behind religious vocations, but it is far less likely to be a satisfactory situation for individuals in more prosaic professions, whether they are affluent managers or lawyers. As their higher intellectual and spiritual skills are directed and exploited by the process of money-capital accumulation, only fleeting, unreflective desires are left to oneself as the expression of one's own genuine selfhood, and the human being is reduced to a bundle of juvenile yens.[261]

Karl Marx and other 19th- and early-20th-century scholars and social commentators witnessed already the life-reducing, de-humanising effects of the then novel capitalist mode of production, from the brutal exploitation of the industrial worker to the frantic lifestyle unfolding in the sprawling urban centres of their time. The working class suffered from the physical destructiveness of prolonged hard toil, as well as from the spiritual annihilation caused by lack of sleep, education and free time, hunger-led resort to crime and prostitution, self-loathing-induced alcoholism and propensity to violence. The chapter entitled "Baal" contained in Fyodor M. Dostoyevsky's 1863 *Winter Notes on Summer Impressions* is one of the most powerful descriptions of working-class life-reduction in the history of 19th-century European literature.[262] The bourgeois class, on its part, experienced spiritual annihilation too, as those who could afford a life of leisure did so by promoting consciously or ignoring the deprivations of their less fortunate fellow human beings, or found themselves trapped within the sense of inadequacy due to their endless pursuit of additional wealth. Fyodor M. Dostoyevsky's *Winter Notes on Summer Impressions* illustrates also on the life-reduction typical of the French and British bourgeoisie.[263] New notions were then developed in order to describe this condition of reduction of life ranges. Marx's 'alienation' and 'estrangement', Durkheim's 'anomie', Weber's 'disenchantment', Baudelaire's 'ennui' and Simmel's 'blasé attitude', just to name the most famous, compose a lexicon of unhappiness. This lexicon used to be required by the classical paradigm in order to keep labour cheap and profits high. It is now required by the neoclassical paradigm, so that we may buy into the dreams of happiness prepared by market strategists—and continue to keep profits high.

Wants may be diverse and volatile, nihilism and relativism may be ascribed to post-modern, post-Fordist consumer societies, yet the hidden dogma of the worldwide-pervading neoclassical paradigm stands as the bedrock of the global new order: the priority of money-capital returns over life-capital resources.[264] Unhappiness itself, in the consumer society, becomes a source of revenue, whether actual or potential. A 'normal' level of unhappiness leads to standard consumer responses, i.e. harder labour,[265] the purchase of unneeded goods,[266] and escapism in artificial, for-sale 'second lives'.[267] An 'abnormal' level of unhappiness leads to the mass purchase of 'happy pills' or clinical therapy: research suggests that inhabitants of consumer societies develop anxiety, bipolar and obsessive-compulsive disorders younger and at higher rates,[268] and there appears to be a clear correlation not only between poor mental health and poverty, but also between poor mental health and time stress, perceived deprivation, and social exclusion, i.e. phenomena magnified by profit-driven consumer society.[269] Either way, money-capital returns are secured, while for-sale science prospers at both ends of the spectrum. On the one end, researchers provide their services to the advertising industry that promise happiness that never comes. On the other end, pharmacologists and therapists provide theirs to those who cannot stand any longer under the crushing weight of unhappiness, and can afford to pay for them.

Concluding Remarks

David Korten, Founder President of the People-Centred Development Forum, once stated:

> *The capitalist economy… has a potentially fatal ignorance of two subjects. One is the nature of money. The other is the*

nature of life. This ignorance leads us to trade away life for money, which is a bad bargain indeed. The real nature of money is obscured by the vocabulary of finance, which is doublespeak.... We use the terms "money", "capital", "assets" and "wealth" interchangeably—leaving no simple means to differentiate money from real wealth. Money is a number. Real wealth is food, fertile land, buildings or other things that sustain us. Lacking language to see this difference, we accept the speculator's claim to create wealth, when they expropriate it.... Squandering real wealth in the pursuit of numbers is ignorance of the worst kind. The potentially fatal kind.[270]

Life-blindness *imperat* [rules] and death accompanies today's globalisation. As States become unable to control the current economic development, pull out of coordinating and regulating it, or remain involved as mere instruments for money-capital maximisation, the neoclassical paradigm seems to meet no resistance but that of grassroots social movements, generally attempting to preserve sections of life-enhancing structures inherited from the past (e.g. public healthcare, free access to higher education) or, more rarely, to introduce new ones. In this perspective, this grassroots resistance connects with a long history of popular struggles for "the organized, unified, and community-funded capacity of universally accessible resources of society to protect and to enable the lives of its members as an end in itself."[271] This is what McMurtry calls the "civil commons", as distinguished from both Garrett Hardin's unregulated, tragic "commons" and the "life-ground" itself, which the civil commons develop upon and protect in socially conscious form.[272] Their appropriation for class or elite benefit and their conversion into means to a non-universal and/or non-life-enabling end has been resisted for centuries worldwide, from the English peasantry opposing 16th-century enclosures, to today's EU-wide protests against the Bolkenstein directive aimed at facilitating the privatisation of public services, through the Catholic-Communist Costa Rican social legislation of the 1940s-70s. Life-capital efficiency is the priority behind all these instances of popular action, which the neoclassical paradigm cannot but interpret as 'bad for business', for the parameters of its own notion of efficiency are life-disconnected.[273]

Naturally, there is no guarantee that communities or States may behave wisely, as the tragic Soviet record of ecological disasters or the widespread electoral support for life-destructive political programmes in Western countries have shown. Past civilizations disappeared because no longer able to connect with the life-ground, worshipping blindly their own life-blind systems. The 'divine' self-regulating free market of the dominant neoclassical paradigm moves along an analogous path, from which we can divert by recognising that we have the world itself to lose. Moreover, we already have the instruments to use internationally in order to counter the present state of planetary collapse (e.g. public infrastructures, life-protective laws and standards, green and social taxes, binding trade regulators). We do not have to invent anything new or revolutionary. Just apply that which is already in place and regularly neglected or misapplied, for 'too costly'.[274] Blinded by the miraculous attributes of the Providential "invisible hand", we are often incapable of realising that a sane economic order protects and develops further the Earth's LSS, favouring the provision of means of life through time. Life-needs must be at the core of any society that wishes to prosper. And we can know rather easily what truly constitutes a life-need: anything the deprivation of which causes our life capacities to be reduced. Nothing else counts.

Chapter 5
Life and Death Economics: A Dialogue

Hermes L.: How transient are these earthly masters of the universe! Lehman Brothers commercial bank has just collapsed, an event which is unprecedented, at least over the last eighty years, and which gives us an indication of just how serious is the crisis of capitalism through which we are passing. Therefore, this seems a good time to evaluate where we stand with regard to economics and the assumptions about human behaviour on which it is based. It seems to me that the sub-prime mortgage crisis in the USA that has led to today's problems, which incidentally do not just affect bankers and politicians but also the lives and livelihood of most citizens, throws up a number of issues which are explicitly or implicitly covered in the previous chapter of this book. Wouldn't you agree?

Athena B.: I do agree. The collapse of a major commercial bank is no small event. Yet, it is also an event that, quite frankly, could have been predicted. We might not have known which specific commercial bank was going to go bust, since we do not have access to their books, but we could have expected that one would fail, and that others would follow suit. The previous chapter does in fact discuss the dangers of today's deregulated quest for ever-growing profits by the world's financial 'juggernauts' and the ideological myopia underpinning it. This quest resembles very closely the path of action, and of self-destruction, followed by their 'ancestors' in the early 20th century. The spree of worldwide 'liberalisation' that we have witnessed in the last thirty years or so was meant to do away with institutional 'constrictions' that had been placed upon trade, including the trade in currency and financial commodities. Leading members of the American Republican party, for example, voiced repeatedly and loudly their desire to get rid of all the vestiges of Roosevelt's New Deal, hence of the capacity for State intervention that they required. It is a process begun in the USA with Nixon, I would argue, and later followed by many governments worldwide, whether right-wing or left-wing. Blinded by the neoclassical dogma that wants the freer pursuit of individual profits, if not sheer personal greed, to translate into collective wellbeing, these governments never paused to consider why certain 'constrictions' had been set up in first place. George Soros, Andrew Glyn and a few others have written and spoken about this folly; ten years ago, John McMurtry argued that capitalism had already reached its 'cancer stage', for the immune defences of the planetary social body were unable to recognise the biocide invasion and actively cooperated with it by massive doses of further liberalisation. Nevertheless, all these eminent critical voices were ignored, underplayed, or attacked. And if you stop taking your medication against a certain disease, you are much more likely to catch it again!

What is going to happen, I presume, is that we will rediscover the medication, or else the disease will eat much of the world's economy and, what is implied and never truly spelled out in the mainstream media, the actual lives of many. Millions' employment and livelihood are now at stake because of other people's decisions and errors—the educated, business-savvy elite of some still-then prosperous, 'glittering' country. At least, in the late 1920s, the Russian Bolsheviks had a powerful propaganda machine that kept some people in the West aware of who was responsible for the West's own faults. How difficult it is to do that in the days of Fox News and Berlusconi! Incidentally, I do not entertain the hope that we may learn the lesson once and for all, because humankind seems tragically prone to repeating the mistakes of previous generations. Rather, what worries me is that the medication the world's economy needs, a mix of socialism and effective political leadership, can be administered in various ways. In the 1930s, for example, the State intervened and, gradually, rescued the world's economy from its irresponsible 'champions'. However, in most of Europe, that recovery meant the affirmation of the fascist model of government and its bellicose forms of public spending. One thing is to cure a wounded limb with an antiseptic solution; another is to amputate the limb—it is a fairly simple comparison of life-value.

Hermes L.: It seems as if some of the lessons of the 1920s and 1930s have, to an extent, been learned. As far as macroeconomic management goes, the Fed cut interest rates repeatedly in early 2008, and the Bush administration showered the population with tax rebates in order to stimulate demand (which incidentally brings a wry smile to many economists, given that this is the sort of pure Keynesianism which the neo-cons have so ridiculed in the past...). And you are right, there is going to be a move towards more regulation in the future, and what is more some massive direct intervention by the US government in capital markets. The plan here is for the US government to buy up the bad securities which are at the basis of the so-called `credit crunch' and thereby re-capitalise the banking system, at a cost, it would seem, of some \$700billion. The plan, which needless to say is a controversial one, not least among US Conservatives, is to buy the debt at full rather than current market value, thereby effectively subsidising the banks and exposing taxpayers to considerable risk and possible big losses in the future. It is also important to understand the potentially inflationary effects of such a move. What about moral hazard one may ask? It seems to me this is a wonderful example of the old French saying 'privatisation of profit, nationalisation of risk'...

Nevertheless, there are undeniable similarities between the early-20th-century experience and today's. For example, we live once again in a world dominated by free market capitalism. Since the demise of central planning in the 1980s, the market has established a virtual monopoly (excuse the unintended pun!) across the world as a form of economic organisation. Economic activity, and in particular the financial aspect of free market capitalism, was substantially de-regulated over subsequent years, according to the neo-liberal economic principles that are exposed in the fourth chapter of this book. These principles have come to dominate thinking among academics and practitioners of the 'dismal science'. We have let the proverbial genie out of the bottle, and now it is difficult to see how it can be put back.

However, I do not think that history repeats itself in an identical manner. I believe today's world economy to be different in some fundamental respects from any previous age. And these different, fundamental respects are actually a further source of worry. First of all, economic activity has, over the last couple of decades, escaped from the boundaries of the nation state, where it had been essentially rooted since the days of Adam Smith, and moved to the supranational level. This phenomenon commonly referred to as 'globalisation' is of course due to a number of factors including improved technology, increased and unrestricted trade, the increased importance of Multinational Corporations, accumulations of petrodollars resulting from the balance of payments surpluses of the oil producing countries, and the increased privatisation of welfare and savings. The implication of this is that the world is now much more interdependent: what happens in one place affects everybody. To an extent this has always been the case. In the 1960s and 1970s it was commonly held that "when the USA sneezes Europe catches a cold". Today, however, the sneeze is much more infectious, as we have seen from the way in which the sub-prime crisis has spread across the Atlantic and beyond. In addition, nation states could, in earlier times, quarantine themselves and administer their own form of 'paracetamol' to mitigate the effects. Capitalism is now much more difficult, if not impossible, to regulate. When, in the 19th and most of the 20th century, capitalism was nationally based, it was relatively straight-forward for nation states to develop regulatory frameworks designed to alter the outcomes of the free market to the socially desirable. In principle, people voted for governments that promised them their preferred outcomes, and the governments legislated accordingly: economic democracy in action. Today, we live in a different paradigm: supranational economic activity is impossible to regulate and to police, since we do not have a world government or any other body which might be capable of regulation free market capitalism. In addition, it is clear that the operation of nationally based macroeconomic policies is much more problematic, as a number of local crisis have shown, from the ERM crisis of 1992 onwards.

Athena B.: But aren't we supposed to have international institutions, including non-governmental ones, that monitor and manage financial flows and banking practices? The Basel Committee, the Financial Stability Forum—not to mention the world's central banks, the Bank for International Settlements or the IMF—are at work to prevent massive crises like the one we are witnessing today; or are they not?

Hermes L.: We actually have an international free-for-all on our hands, the objectives of which are certainly not to protect the interests of the vulnerable, or even the majority, and the outcomes of which are probably de-stabilising and certainly unpredictable. Hence there was very little available to prevent the sub-prime crisis: the classic accident waiting to happen. One wonders how many more of these there are, and when the next one will come out of the woodwork. The development of the EU and other supranational organisations such as the Association of South-East Asian Nations can be viewed as an attempt to develop a competent authority capable of modifying the outcomes of the free market on a regional basis. However, such organisations are still a long way from being practically effective regulators of the free market. This is also an issue of democracy: the bankers and market operators that call the shots are not elected by anybody. Democratically elected governments are increasingly unable to control their own economies, which begs the question of why should people continue to vote for people who cannot deliver on the big issues.[275]

Athena B.: I believe their impotence to be due to the beliefs and behaviours of the actual individuals involved, rather than to the existing structures—personal, moral factors, rather than structural, organisational ones. The institutions needed for supervision and regulation are there, yet they are not used, or they are used inadequately. Often they even collude with the most blatantly reckless sources of the havoc that we are talking about—the failed response of the social immune system discussed by McMurtry, who thus compares the ongoing crisis to a cancer: it is much more serious than a cold that makes you sneeze... Sometimes, major world leaders and the directors of these institutions plead ignorance or impotence *vis-à-vis* the gargantuan market forces that they should be managing. Still, minor infringements of trade agreements are detected and punished across the planet, suggesting that we or, at least, the WTO, have both the technologies and the expertise to follow countless transactions taking place every month *via* telephone cables and the world-wide-web.

Hermes L.: I think it is a bit of both. Of course, the international structures you mention do exist, but their objective is usually to push the free market agenda on the international stage–certainly that has been one frequent criticism of the WTO. It is arguable that they are part of the problem. In addition, the existing institutions are not capable of regulating the type of corporate behaviours and international capital flows that we have experienced. As a minimum requirement, the role and power of existing institutions need to be re-visited, and arguably we need a 'new financial architecture' more capable of dealing with the issues we are discussing. Naturally, this requires political will and leadership.

Athena B.: As you know, in the book chapter you refer to, it is suggested that the neoclassical paradigm has become a *forma mentis* that prevents people from seeing that which is necessary for collective wellbeing and sustainable growth, and thus from behaving in a truly constructive manner. Within the myopic boundaries of this *forma mentis*, value is understood merely as money capital, not as life-enhancement. Moreover, it is assumed that this pecuniary value ought to be maximised always and anyway, as a sort of Kantian categorical imperative turned 'Rockfelleresque'. We are somehow 'designed' to increase whichever initial capital we are endowed with, says Smith. His disciples emphasise that we ought to do it, therefore leaping from a factual observation, whether correct or not, to an economic, moral, and political imperative. This logic of maximisation is further justified insofar as it is believed to be bound to guarantee 'optimal allocation' of resources and 'the wealth of nations' itself, as though Adam Smith's 'invisible hand' were out there for sure, which is far from ascertained and ultimately a matter of religious belief—an aspect of Smith's Protestant economics that contemporary economists seem to have forgotten completely. Thus, a debatable hypothesis about human nature, indeed a token of Smith's religiously inspired philosophical anthropology, becomes the cornerstone of individual and collective agency, indeed the paradigm of human rationality itself.

Hermes L.: I think you are spot on. The free market system is essentially based on self-interest and short-termism, or if we are to be ungenerous (and why not, given the mess we are in?), greed. Remember that famous quote from Keynes: "Capitalism is the extraordinary belief that the nastiest of men for the nastiest of motives will somehow work for the benefit of all." The sub-prime crisis is a classic example of this. Salespersons sold mortgages to people who could not afford them in order to rack up their own earnings. In this they were encouraged by managers who had their own careers and earnings in mind, in turn encouraged by shareholders who want maximum returns now in order to maximise their own wealth, or in order to keep their jobs if they are fund managers. They were all allowed to do this by a regulatory system which is essentially weak and turns a blind eye as long as returns are good and the major actors are happy. And what is more, this very system allowed the mortgage companies to then package these essentially unstable and unreliable loans into financial derivatives and products that were then sold around the world and used as collateral for other deals. A pyramid based on a deck of cards, the bottom layer of which was rotten. Of course the collapse of this deck affects us all in one way or other: we all by necessity have a stake in the system through our pensions, our savings and the like.

However, some have a much bigger stake than others, for the demise of national regulation has allowed the free market system to move towards an inevitably more unequal society in which wealth is concentrated in the hands of fewer and fewer people. This, of course, has many implications, but what interests me particularly is the motivation of the super-rich, many of whom dominate the international economic scene and are the driving force behind many of the developments we are experiencing. Why is it that people who have so much money they would need ten lifetimes to spend it, want to accumulate more and more? And indeed why are they prepared to exploit and endanger the interests of us all (and in particular the hundreds of millions who are living on the breadline and for whom economic crisis is not just an increase in mortgage payments, but the difference between life and death), in order to get enough money to last them twenty lifetimes? What motivates them? Why do they do this rather than concentrate on enjoying what they have got? How does this bring them happiness? It seems to me that until we understand more about this, we cannot begin to fathom the new international economic realities.

Athena B.: To date, I believe that the most insightful studies on the mentality of the rich are still Thorstein Veblen's, to which, perhaps, I would add some later reflections by John Kenneth 'Ken' Galbraith— two economists, hence colleagues of yours, as a matter of fact! Veblen observed the wealthy elites of the *belle époque*. He concluded that two patterns of behaviour seemed to characterise them, namely 'conspicuous leisure' and 'conspicuous consumption.' Typically, the rich spent more time in idleness or on vacation than the rest of the population and they threw their money around as much as possible and in as many ways as possible. In this perspective, as Galbraith noted seventy years after Veblen, the rich-filled casinos have served the peculiar end of allowing the rich to lose money in public. And why did they want, and still want, to do all this? Because conspicuous leisure and conspicuous consumption are the two main ways in which the rich can show the world that they are rich.

Hermes L.: Do you think they were suggesting that the pursuit of profit was an end-in-itself from a subjective point of view as well, in addition to being the defining element of capitalism as an economic system?

Athena B.: I believe they thought it could be so for many people. However, Veblen and Galbraith painted a more articulate picture of the wealthy individual's 'human condition under capitalism', if you allow a rather philosophical expression. Being rich meant then, and still means today, the certainty of gaining social status. Thus, what Veblen and Galbraith ultimately argued is that the pursuit of wealth is instrumental to the pursuit of status, which is something that the non-rich strive for too, and may even attain by virtue of, say, political power or cultural recognition. Yet, in their studies, Veblen and Galbraith maintained an unwavering emphasis on wealth. No other instrument seems to be as effective in obtaining and maintaining social status. The rich may be feared, hated, resented, envied or despised, but they are so by the multitude looking at them from the bottom of the pedestal upon which the rich stand.

In this light, political favours and careers, visible statements of cultural distinction, and all the rest that the rich may have bought with their money, are aimed at securing their status, whether directly or indirectly. Ministries, party leaderships, seats at the House of Lords, foundations, art galleries, villas in Sardinia or the Bahamas are status symbols. Certainly, as Galbraith observed, the typology of status symbols may vary as often and as quickly as the weather, although there tends to be always a rough distinction between the 'tasteless' and 'flashy' symbols of the parvenu, i.e. the new rich, and the 'sophisticated' and 'subtle' ones of 'old money', i.e. the well-established elite. At times, this distinction is unintended. More often, however, it is the result of an ongoing competition between two or more groups within the larger family of a society's wealthiest members. Should I go for a big, polluting, uneconomical monster-limousine or a smaller, green, fuel-efficient hybrid car? By opting for either path of conspicuous consumption you side with a certain 'party' within the elite, while at the same time showing that you are well above the *hoi polloi*.

Hermes L.: It is true that riches are a tool for social advancement and social recognition but, as an economist, I cannot avoid seeing how social advancement and recognition, and the status symbols you are speaking of, are often also a tool for gaining or retaining riches. They can be publicity stunts, long-term investments, or ways to humiliate and destroy one's competitors. For example, recently there have been a spate of rich individuals using their enormous wealth to buy football clubs in the United Kingdom [hereafter UK]. An example would be Abramovich at Chelsea, but I believe there is also an Icelandic example at West Ham. It doesn't matter how much money you've got, nobody might have heard of you, but if you own a football club you are on the back pages all the time and you become a public figure. Plus, there is the added attraction of possible capital gains. Also, wealth seems to me to be much more stable in time than the various status symbols it can buy. If you like, it is the best status symbol there can be. Nothing beats a hefty bank account —as long as people know that you have it, of course. Yet, what interests me, is that there must be some deeper psychological drive at work here, which explains why money, *qua* 'king' status symbol, and its 'vassals', things like yachts and private jets, are accumulated by people who have already enough of them.

Athena B.: Status symbols are a matter of fashion, a dimension of social existence that is always characterised by a tension, a contradiction, between conformity and distinction. As the sociologist Georg Simmel argued, an individual follows fashion to fit within a special group of people, yet she wants also to stand out, hence she introduces an element of variation in the existing fashion, which may become eventually a new trend altogether, to which people conform and modify for the sake of distinction, and so on. If Simmel is correct, and I believe he is correct, this means also that even the wealthiest few are never entirely pleased with their immense fortunes and what they can buy with it, if there are other very rich persons that can do the same, or even outdo them, which sooner or later is likely to happen. There may be exceptions, of course, but even if only a minority of the world's most affluent individuals play this game, then they can affect the lives of millions who, either directly or indirectly, depend on the factories, enterprises, capitals and speculations manoeuvred by this minority.

Hermes L.: I doubt that we are talking of a minority: look at the size of the worldwide trade in luxury goods, works of art, and top-level real estate, or at the glossy magazines targeted at the super-rich and 'wonna-be-rich'… As for the majority of the population, the irony of course is that the pursuit of individualism seems not bring happiness. Some economists, for example Andrew Oswald at Warwick University, have begun to take an interest in this, and surveys on both sides of the Atlantic suggest that people are no happier now than they were fifty years ago, despite huge increases in National Income. Interestingly enough, reported happiness is highest among the highly educated, women, the young and old (not middle aged people who are directly involved in the 'rat race'), people who are married and retired, those staying at home and those who are self-employed. Material prosperity clearly comes at a cost. It is certainly true that 'it is better to be rich and unhappy than poor and unhappy' (an old Italian lady I knew well), but the 'those who say money can't buy happiness don't know where to shop' (anonymous) brigade don't quite get the whole picture, it seems.

Athena B.: Indeed. It is also ironic that the logic of the struggle with one's peers for status is the same amongst the super-rich as it is amongst the kids in a Brazilian favela or a Nigerian *bidonville*. As the poor kid steals to have the fanciest Nike trainers in her group, so does the rich banker crave for more, and sometimes steal, in order to display her supreme luxury item of the moment that the others can't buy, whether it is a Picasso, a football team, a younger trophy-husband or trophy-wife, or a mega-yacht. This logic is reproduced at all the levels of the social hierarchy: employers and employees, CEOs and part-time cleaners, aristocrats and plebeians. Yet, instead of wearing an overpriced, mass-produced, coloured plastic wristwatch, the very rich are to boost an outrageously expensive, custom-made, gold-and-diamonds watch. Besides, in this circus, the very rich set the tone of the whole show. They are the role-models for everybody else in the capitalist society, since no alternative economic order is either praised or permitted (see what has happened to the communist bloc or to socialist economies in the Middle East). And to make sure that the tone is heard and followed, this form of gluttony is fuelled and refuelled ceaselessly by scientifically crafted advertising. It is even theorised and justified by neoclassical economists as a natural and good disposition of the human being, just like Adam Smith's presumption concerning the human being's natural and laudable tendency to augment the initial capital available. They dub it the 'non-satiety principle' and that is why I find the word 'gluttony' very appropriate.

Hermes L.: This is all very interesting and important, and it may explain the motivations of some of the people we are discussing, although I still find it unfathomable how intelligent people can have so little self-analysis and self-awareness. I guess these kinds of attitudes are ingrained in our societies, and have been increasingly so since the demise of the post-World-War-II settlement, which in Europe at least had emphasised the 'social market' and a degree of collective consciousness and responsibilities. One of Thatcher's most significant sayings was "there is no such thing as society", for example. The attitude right now seems to be that the market has seen off the competition, and cannot be challenged. Former Labour government minister and now European Commissioner (for trade!) Peter Mandelson, Blair's adviser and confidant, is quoted as saying that he was "immensely relaxed" at the prospect of the emergence a class of super-rich people in the UK–if you can't beat them, join them! These people clearly set the societal moral and philosophical agenda, which since the 1980s has been firmly based on self-interest. In terms of the analysis of individual behaviour, historically economists have attempted to analyse behaviour and social phenomena, but have not really managed to escape the straightjacket of an economic rationality based on self-interest. The Nobel prize-winning economist Garry Becker is a good example of this. More recently, some economists have toyed with the idea of analysing happiness, but the numbers that are interested in this is very limited, and their work is firmly outside of the mainstream. Having said that, it is one thing understanding why people behave as they do, and quite another to tolerate the essentially anti-social implications of this kind of behaviour, and so we return to the issue of regulation…

Athena B.: Regulation and culture or, if you like, moral education. The mind is the place where we turn modifiable human arrangements into dogmas, cages and straightjackets; but it is also the place where we can be freed from them. You mention the analysis of happiness. Much of the horror and folly that we have been eviscerating is due to a largely mistaken notion of happiness, which characterises modernity. This is particularly blatant to a person like me, trained in ancient and medieval philosophy. Back then, as savage and 'unscientific' those times may have been, the mainstream notion of wisdom was tied to the idea of reducing needs, not satisfying wants. 'Non-satiety' was a nightmarish option, which only the child, the hedonist and, in essence, the unwise, would choose.

Hermes L.: Yes, in the UK and some parts of northern Europe we have the Puritan tradition, which incidentally is still strongly present in some of the green and alternative schools of thought. I do have a problem with aspects of this approach, however, as it seems to me that some people seem to revel in tokenism, depriving themselves and others seemingly for its own sake.

Athena B.: Certainly, these ideas were the offspring of ages in which extreme misery was much more common than today, and consolation could be found in sharing poverty rather than in generating more wealth for all. Mass cynicism, early Christianity and many medieval 'heresies' exemplify it. Still, I believe they teach us something of fundamental importance. Material affluence may be important, but it is neither the only nor the most important dimension of human existence, individual and collective. Aristotle and Epicurus, for instance, were regarded as rather relaxed *vis-à-vis* material goods: they were not ascetic enough for many of their colleagues. They nevertheless lived and preached a mantra of moderation, reduction of needs and focus on what truly matters in life: peace, health, friendship and the cultivation of spiritual abilities.

German historian Markus Meckl claims that capitalist societies are characterised in late modernity by a depressing lack of higher ideals, which we face most brutally when we want to tell our children how they should lead their lives. Be successful? Make a lot of money? Become a professional footballer or a TV starlet? Our forefathers had a much more interesting set of things to say: be virtuous and save your soul, serve your God and your country, be a good example. Today, we have all these beautiful material goodies and yet even the super-rich flock into rehab clinics or get caught with crack and heroin in their purse while entering the American Embassy in London. They reflect on the grand scale the far-too-common condition of meaninglessness that pervades modern societies. The loss of religious belief, but perhaps the unseen faith in Smith's 'invisible hand', has been seen as a sign of emancipation from superstition and oppression, but it came at a cost. 'Rationalisation', as Weber called the modern liberation from ignorance and superstition, brought the whole universe within reach of the calculating human intellect—scientific and economic—thus depriving it of mystery, beauty, and of the awe-inspiring 'otherness' that was commonplace in previous ages. 'Disenchantment', he dubbed it; to the point that we have been trying to re-enchant it with things like scientology and Star Trek's unknown alien species to be discovered!

But there is another aspect that I find most troubling and that connects with the issue of economic rationality that you have just mentioned. What sort of rationality can this be, I wonder, that is leading the world to the brink of ecological collapse? How shallow is this reason that treats the damage done to the very basic environmental structures that sustain life as 'externalities', as though those structures were not in fact the most 'internal' dimension imaginable? Without those structures, life would not be possible; and without life, your clever rational agents would never be able to trade freely whichever goods may lead them to be mutually satisfied and bring about optimal allocation. It is a rationality that seems to favour the short-term gratification of whichever immature yen one may have and be willing to pay for, rather than the long-term satisfaction of well-established needs of human communities across generations. It is a rationality that seems unable to see and deal with life and its essential requirements; and whenever it stumbles into these, it sacrifices them to the interests of balance sheets and higher rates of return. I must confess that this rationality looks rather like a grand-scale Freudian 'rationalisation' of base instincts. As for the super-rich, they operate as role-models of life-destructive consumption. Their private jets, big cars, expensive furs, rare-woods furniture, blood-covered diamonds and many and often empty villas are the ideal horizon towards which the non-rich direct their gaze and, as far as possible, imitate.

Hermes L.: I share yours views regarding economic rationality, and I am also painfully aware of the number of people out there who 'know the price of everything and the value of nothing'. I was also wondering when we would arrive at the issue of the environment and its compatibility with capitalism. This is clearly the issue of the day since, as you mention, it is pointless to argue the toss about philosophy or economics if there is no planet! Now it seems to me that the problem here is that most economists have been either in denial about climate change, or alternatively have no real answers to the problem. Denial has been increasingly difficult recently, in the face of pretty overwhelming scientific evidence, although enough economists still cling on to the opinion that 'it isn't happening' (the Bush administration), or, if it is, then the market and technology will automatically solve the problem, so why worry.

The emphasis of the non-deniers has therefore turned, sometimes reluctantly it would seem, to possible solutions. The suggested way forward has in one way or other involved the market and the price mechanism, in the tradition of the theory of State intervention in the market in the presence of the 'market failure' and the 'externalities' to which you have referred. The approach has been to advocate price increases to reduce the demand for car use, air travel, and other activities which are likely to have a negative effect on the environment (although some other activities like road haulage and even military activity seem mysteriously to have been ignored; one wonders what the carbon footprint of the wars in Iraq and Afghanistan might be…). A variant of this has been the introduction of carbon trading, which in principle attempts to reduce carbon emissions by pricing them–economic agents are given permission to emit carbon, and these permits can then be traded. The problems with carbon trading are both practical and philosophical: firstly, the permits so far assigned have been far too liberal to have any effect on the environment. More centrally, this is an attempt to solve problems by using the very mechanisms which, as we have discussed, have been partly responsible for creating many of the problems in the first place. In fact, a result of carbon trading is that it has spawned yet another way for wheelers and dealers to make more money. Putting economists in charge of tackling climate change is tantamount to putting Dracula in charge of a blood-bank, or Tony Blair in charge of peace in the Middle East!

Even if the use of markets to tackle climate change did have an effect, it is important to note that the 'burden of adjustment', as economists refer to the pain that results from change, would fall almost exclusively on the shoulders of those least able to bear it. The poor would be effectively excluded from activities such as flying and driving, while the rich of course would continue merrily along their trajectory of conspicuous consumption. The good news, such as it is, is that there are some economists, such as the New Economics Foundation in the UK, who seem to be aware of the issues that we have been discussing and are actively involved in seeking alternative solutions. These must inevitably involve a combination of: (1) stricter and more effective regulation; (2) changes in the fundamental way in which we approach life and the planet, which brings us back to the basic issues we have been discussing: everything is connected; (3) international co-operation.

The third point applies to the first two. The environment is the classic example of a global issue: it is pointless for countries to act in isolation over global warming. In this the developed countries find themselves in a moral dilemma: how can we ask China and India to approach growth in a different way, when it is us in the developed world that have caused the problem over the last century or two? Of course it is in the interest of the developing world as well to tackle climate change, since they too will have their lives and their livelihoods disrupted (more so in the case of the poorest countries in Africa, which are likely to be worst affected). So the way forward is fraught with difficulty. An example of this is the shenanigans over Kyoto, which have clearly demonstrated the difficulties of acting in concert in this area. Nevertheless, there are some encouraging signs emerging, many to do with the election of Obama as President of the USA.

Athena B.: I share your worries, and your hopes. And more than anything, I believe this chapter—our dialogue—should serve as a sign of how relevant insights on contemporary issues can transmigrate from a given area of inquiry to another, across disciplinary boundaries. As I stated before, the mind is the place where we turn modifiable human arrangements into dogmas, cages and straightjackets; but it is also the place where we can be freed from them—disciplinary fields, turfs and fences included.

Chapter 6
Life and Death Economics Revisited: One Year On

Some time has passed since the collapse of Lehman Brothers, so it seems a good time to review the 2008 crisis of finance capital, albeit with the benefit of a little hindsight, and to take stock of what we have learned since then. In particular, as foreboded in the previous chapter, the international economic crisis unleashed by the infamous 'credit crunch' is generating conspicuous harm to life, both strictly human and environmental at large.

Economics Can Kill

The United Nations' Food and Agriculture Organization and the IMF's Managing Director Dominique Strauss-Kahn have denounced the increasing number of people who, especially in sub-Saharan Africa, are facing starvation due to growing unemployment, contraction of trade, declining remittances, freezing of aid and dwindling foreign investment. Not to mention the minimal or absent welfare remedies available that, *inter alia* [among other things], IMF- and World-Bank-dictated neoliberal policies have caused to shrink dramatically in the recent past. More affluent countries are experiencing less visibly life-threatening problems, yet they are pregnant with examples of crisis-induced life-reduction: public education, culture and healthcare are being further sacrificed after several years of cuts for 'efficiency' and 'rationalisation'; unemployment is soaring; depression and anxiety-related pathologies are on the rise; poverty, homelessness and malnourishment are becoming more conspicuous. As a symbol of human and environmental suffering, international media have reported that Kenya's authorities are planning to build thousands of miles of high fences to protect their strategic assets, namely foreign-tourist-visited national parks, because impoverished and famished Kenyans are plundering them for timber, game and pastures. Analogously, in the attempt to retrieve ways to counter the crisis, Peru's government has declared that most of their rainforest-covered areas are to be opened to oil- and gas-drilling operations, despite the opposition of local indigenous populations. Similar steps are being taken in the East–i.e. in Indonesia's rainforests–and in the North–i.e. in the Arctic region– as though fossil-fuel-induced global warming were not an issue. All this might have happened anyway, given the nature of the economic regime in question, but the crisis has certainly not helped.

The steps that the world's nations are taking in order to cope with the crisis further reveal the life-blindness of dominant economics denounced by Canadian scholar John McMurtry, whom has been discussed extensively in the previous chapters. Possibly, a notable exception is USA President Barack Obama, who has promised to deliver a "green New Deal": history will tell whether it was an election promise or a major success.[276] Indeed, the recent award of the Nobel peace prize to Barak Obama, before achieving anything concrete, testifies to the hope that has been vested in him, that he might indeed be the harbinger of a new order. As for the current order, one point must be emphasised: mistaken conceptions of economics can be deadly. They can guide the economic policy of entire countries and bring them to disastrous consequences. Look, for instance, at those African nations that, in the past twenty years or so, turned their arable spaces from subsistence crops to cash crops, as recommended by major international cheerleaders of 'development': the current collapse of imports in rich countries means their inability to feed adequately their own citizens. Or look at fairly affluent countries, like Argentina. In the 1990s, it impoverished itself by pursuing growth according to so-called "free trade" principles: the middle class was wiped out; the country became a net importer though it used to be an exporter; unemployment soared and all life-indicators (child mortality, violent crime rates, nutritional standards, etc.) signalled a worsening of the situation. Only equally 'free-market' post-communist Russia and unfortunate war-torn African countries fared worse. As for more recent cases, the issue of "national food security" was addressed last year in a speech by the President of Iceland, which one would not immediately think of as a country unable to feed its own citizens.[277]

The 'free trade' policies of the 1990s and early 2000s are described as "so-called" tokens of free trade because the experience of Argentina might suggest another, less straightforward way in which mistaken conceptions of economics can be deadly, namely the ideological use of a certain well-established academic jargon, which in fact hides a web of corruption, nepotism, bribery, quasi-monopoly and unfair competition. On the other hand, it is also true that the free-trade-sponsoring oligopolies of today's corporate world have hardly anything to share with the freely trading small businesses envisioned by Adam Smith in *The Wealth of Nations*. Perhaps the gap between theory and practice is not that wide… Whichever be the case, it is nevertheless a given that mistaken conceptions of economics can kill. For one, economics kills by leading people to identify themselves with their status as affluent members of society: when their wealth vanishes, they believe they are worthless and they opt out of life. A spike in suicides followed Iceland's sudden financial collapse in 2008.[278] On a different level, Italy's news agencies have reported of entrepreneurs who committed suicide because they could not bear the fact of having to fire their employees–in the only Western country devoid of any substantive and extensive system of unemployment benefits, one should add. Strict economic logic can contradict fundamental moral principles. When this happens, it would seem reasonable for the former to subside, not to prevail. Or are we to replicate classical economists like Ricardo and Smith, for whom the starvation and death of labourers and their children were as necessary as gravitation itself? [279] Rather, we would look at the age of Keynesianism as a plausible alternative, when 'full employment' was the main target, above strict profitability.

General Lesson #1: Old Debates Need Re-Opened

This, then, is the first thing that we have learned: that the arguments over the various forms of economic organisation and their consequences are still with us and are as relevant as they ever were. Capitalism is severely flawed, particularly in its extreme neoliberal or neo-conservative form. The pursuit of Hayek's and Nozick's utopia has shown disastrous limitations. Therefore, confronted with today's collapse, it is possible once again to air criticism *and* be heard. Until October 2008, when the magnitude of Lehman Brothers' collapse started sinking in, any critical view, especially from outside the field of standard economics, was dismissed as uninformed, unscientific, pessimistic, radical or nostalgic. Non-mainstream economists and informed non-economists who did not buy into the Chicago mantra were largely ignored, ridiculed if capable of some success, attacked if capable of more. The list is long and the origins are old. Galbraith as of the 1960s, Hobsbawm as of the 1970s, Castoriadis as of the 1980s, and McMurtry as of the 1990s: they were not listened to and the results of such an obtuseness are before us today.[280] And yet today, as it often happens to those who pursue the truth rather than conformity, yesterday's critical views have become something of an obvious given, the causal import of which is not fully disclosed though. The time should be ripening for radically new thought and radical reform, or so one would think. However, as we speak, history is being re-written and the intellectual fight-back by neoliberals has begun. Recent publications from the UK Institute for Economic Affairs, for example, would have us believe that the recent problems had nothing to do with the decades of deregulation pursued across the globe.

General Lesson #2: The Emperor Has No Clothes

A further important lesson is that it was false that Central Banks could not pump more money into the economy, which is what citizens all over the planet have been told for twenty years whenever they asked their State to pay better wages, support education, promote culture and strengthen healthcare provision. Nonetheless, as of 2008, in an attempt to prevent more private banks from going bust, ways have been found worldwide to 'inject liquidity', if not printing money altogether. Fascinating. Inflation is no longer their main concern, evidently... Many people may not have seen this happening, but the financial-capital-serving nature of the modern liberal State has been revealed most blatantly. Huge amounts of public money, accompanied by further cuts to social spending, have been transferred to private entities, some of which directly responsible for the 'credit crunch', so that they may keep lending, for profit, to enterprises and households. In other words, I, the citizen, threatened by debt, unemployment and reduced public services, give my tax money to the State, so that the State may give it to the banks, which have sold debt, forced newly acquired firms to lay off workers and pressured the State by treasury-bonds ownership to adopt "austerity" measures. Then, the banks come to my door or to my employer's and tell us that they can help us by letting us borrow from them... our money. What is more, worse, tragic paradoxes may be yet to come. The big debate in the lead up to next year's UK general election has seen the main parties vying with each other over who will cut public expenditure, and in particular public services, most aggressively. Whatever happened, the UK citizens will all be paying the costs of the bailouts with their jobs, health and standards of living for years to come. We use the word "all" loosely– some of them will be paying more than others; that is for sure. The possible future Conservative Chancellor of the Exchequer in the UK utters the mantra "we're all in this together". Is it really so? Will he or his family, for a start, endure worse healthcare or increased pension insecurity?

What the vicious circularity of tax money and bailed-out private banks also reveals is the redundancy of private banks, or at least of those that needed bailed out by public money in the first place. If they needed public assistance to keep afloat, then they should be owned by the public, whether as State banks, regional authorities' banks or else. Back in the 1970s, John Kenneth Galbraith made similar considerations with regard to any company that is labelled "too big to fail": if they are not able to compete in the allegedly free market, then they are not capitalist enterprises any longer and, as such, they should be owned by the public. The alternative is to privatise profit and socialise losses, thus flagging the disappearance of 'moral hazard', which is fundamental to the functioning of capitalism. Certainly, public ownership has its flaws, as also seen in the pre-neoliberal age. After all, new trends in economics do not flourish unless there is some concrete economic problem to be tackled. Nevertheless, at least within most Western constitutional frameworks, it would be much easier–and desirable–for the public to control, reward, and punish publicly elected officials by means of active political participation, than it is to do the same and by analogous means to corporate managers and shareholders. Analogously, it would be much easier to reinvest within the nations whatever profits the publicly owned companies may have. If anything, the G20 leaders' recent outrage at the prosperity of tax havens in times of crisis shows how difficult it is to prevent private firms from siphoning large amounts of taxable income to Monaco, San Marino, the Channel Islands, Panama or the Caribbean. Moreover, as the State-funded bailout of large banks today reveals, public companies may offer advantages in coping with crises and fostering development. The State is the only institution that, say, can run a steel factory unprofitably, yet providing the nation's industry with cheap steel.

In this connection, after the 2009 London G20 meeting, it was tragically ironic to see the IMF becoming even stronger, indeed a potential international lender of last resort. Such a renewed IMF would be nowhere near to being a democratic institution bound to respond to the world's ordinary citizen. Moreover, amongst other expressions of the 'Washington consensus', the IMF has promoted relentlessly international deregulation, privatisation of public assets and free capital trade. It is amongst the culprits of the present crisis. Sure, as Larry Elliott has observed on several occasions, in the IMF official statements you can find sparse recommendations to be vigilant, careful and prevent abuse.[281] Still, as he remarks, if you have been telling me to make money at all costs twenty times, and then you say once "be nice", what do you think I shall do, especially if I need your approval to attract investments? If truth be told, IMF Managing Director Strauss-Kahn himself has admitted that "mistakes" were made in the past. It should be enough to consider the IMF's nefarious impact upon the populations of, say, former Yugoslavia in the 1980s and Argentina in the 1990s. Even so, the Fund is hailed as the "new" and indeed sole saviour of us all. Of late, IMF officials say that they have changed their views and methods. And yet, not long ago, as soon as they stepped into Iceland, they recommended the privatisation of the State-run national mortgage fund, the *Íbúðalánasjóður*, which made a little profit every year and allowed most Icelandic citizens to purchase a first home at a fairly convenient interest rate. Somehow, that did not make sense to the IMF officials.[282] Again, life-blind criteria can make it impossible for intelligent people to perceive that less profit–and we are not even saying no profit altogether!–is desirable if it produces life-value gains, such as the security of a home for the citizens; whereas more profit–even outrageous amounts of it–may be undesirable, if it produces life-value losses. In short, here is another example of the re-writing of history and of the fight-back by the proponents of 'free market' solutions to the economic problem.

General Lesson #3: Regulation, Checks and Balances

There is another thing that we have learned. If the intellectual arguments persist, then the proponents of change have not won them, at least not yet. One is tempted to conclude that a big chance is being missed to make important changes to the structures of capitalism. As things stand right now worldwide, no adequate steps have been taken to address the roots of the systemic collapse. Strict regulations for international finance are not being deployed and the main tenets of the reckless 'development' pursued in the past two decades are not being challenged openly. Even the OECD's unprecedented blacklisting of tax havens has been little more than a sheer expression of good intent. Shall we plunge into the depths of despair of the 1930s to witness renewed policies resembling F.D. Roosevelt's? We sincerely hope that we do not need that sort of eye-opener. Indeed, F.D. Roosevelt's case illustrates one path of action that has not even been discussed by contemporary world leaders. He, amongst other things, promoted the trade unions as a counterbalance to private enterprises. In this manner, wealth had to be redistributed more fairly and the middle class could grow in size. As Castoriadis observed already in the 1990s, the general decline of trade unions and left-wing parties has meant the disintegration of an important barrier that prevented capitalism from being utterly destructive and, ultimately, self-destructive. According to Castoriadis, as it was already for Marx and Weber, the constitutive relentless pursuit of profit is what turns capitalism into a major source of instability, for itself and everything that orbits around it. By a painful process of trial and error, our forefathers had little by little learned to acknowledge capitalism's self-undermining drive and to rein it in. Neoliberalism, devoid of this wisdom, on the one hand created a novel financial reign of seemingly endless profits and, on the other hand, brought down the dam that fear of communism, socially aware conservatism, Keynesianism, and social and Christian democracy had slowly built during part of the 20th century. The flood ensued, like a derivative one could say...

In the light of the ongoing crisis, it should seem obvious that international capital and currency trade be thwarted and intelligently selected in view of life-sustaining development and long-term stability. Countries may make good use of FDI, but to do so capital flows must be regulated according to life-enhancing principles. A first step in this direction would be to oblige foreign investors to have their money, above a certain amount, kept in the receiving country for a fixed minimum number of years. Another step would be to guarantee that incoming capitals have some clear relation to underlying trade in actual life-serving goods and services, e.g. foodstuff and pharmaceutical research. Possessing no such relation, currency speculation should be strangled mercilessly, e.g. by a heavy Tobin tax. So far, none of these remedies has been implemented on any significant scale. On this subject, the works by Joseph Stiglitz and John McMurtry should be read and pondered upon by the world's central bankers who wish to contribute to the wellbeing of their fellow nationals, rather than to the wellbeing of their international fellow bankers.[283] In the past twenty years, thanks to the privatisation of many banks and to the reduction of controls and regulations, oceans of liquid capital have far too often flooded entire nations, inflating giant speculative bubbles in real estate, local shares and currency. Then, these oceans have suddenly dried up, as soon as rumours of a burst were heard and/or cunningly spread around. As a result, dry countries drifted away with no foreign currency reserves, a plummeting currency, rising unemployment and worthless national enterprises. Who could survive in a desert like that?

Luckily, the IMF and the World Bank were always ready to come to the rescue. Their generosity meant increasing interest rates to attract foreign capital, slashing social expenditures, and privatising whatever national assets remained after the ideologically motivated or bribe-induced privatisations of the previous years. In the process, the poor got poorer, the middle class waned, the rich got richer, and national sovereignty was surrendered to the "financial markets" that the former director of the Central Bank of Federal Germany Hans Tietmeyer, as quoted in Galeano's 1998 *Upside Down*, described as "the new gendarmes" of the international order, to whom governments have to respond.[284]

General Lesson #4: Monetary Policy Matters

We do not know whether Tietmeyer, former head of the Central Bank of Germany, ever thought deeply of the implications of the terms he used, "the new gendarmes". "Gendarmes" mean the army; and if an army controls elected governments, then either the country has been occupied by a foreign invader or it has experienced a military coup. Either way, democracy has ceased to be. Whenever treasury bonds markets, foreign creditors, or the stock exchange market have more influence upon a government's decisions than the citizens who elected them, then democracy becomes nothing but a travesty. Therefore, if we wish democracy to have any meaning, these gendarmes must be stopped.

Besides, independent central banks and the private banking sector have failed to promote enduring wellbeing. In twenty years of neoliberal policies, affluent Western countries themselves have witnessed little genuine growth. And even that little, as Russian

President Vladimir Putin and Nobel-prize winner Paul Krugman have recently observed, has been annihilated anyway by the ongoing international crisis.[285] In the same period, the same countries have witnessed the erosion of public healthcare, subsidised cultural events, State pensions, job security, egalitarian policies, and the very notion of public spaces, interests and cooperation. Whenever money was needed to sustain these activities and institutions, it was not available. Yet money was available to subsidise private enterprises by tax rebates, research and development grants, dedicated infrastructures, or public commissions. Last and most gargantuan in this list of subsidies, trillions of taxpayers' money are now being thrown at the banks that have contributed to the 'credit crunch' crisis. Not to mention the trillions that are being routinely spent fighting wars in the Middle East. Money is all around, but it eludes most citizens. Therefore, it seems to us that some way should be found to return monetary sovereignty to the people. The creation of money is a privilege of the sovereign, yet, as Italy's Minister of Finance has recently stated, it has been surrendered to private banks.[286] By fractional banking, banks can create money, simply by lending much more than they actually own. In his famous book *Money: Whence It Came, Where It Went*, Galbraith described this system as "so simple that it repels the mind". Also, as a matter of institutional practice and inversion of sovereignty, private banks have become the creditors of the State, e.g. by purchasing treasury bonds. For the sake of nations' independence, this bondage must end. In the process, as higher education is concerned, one or two generations of MBA students will have to be retrained into some useful occupation, analogously to the way in which post-WWII France and Italy retrained millions of agricultural workers into industrial workers.

Specific Lesson #1: Memories of the 1920s and 30s

Having considered these general lessons, it is also interesting to focus on some specifics which might help us to frame and inform the debate more fully. For a start there are many similarities between the current crisis and what has happened in the past, particularly with reference to the Great Depression of the 1920s and 1930s. If history is about learning from previous mistakes, we have clearly not taken heed. Both the Great Depression and the current crisis have occurred following periods of laissez-faire ascendancy. This is no coincidence–there is a link between crisis and ideology. Free markets and lax regulation ultimately beget problems, and we have very much taken our eye off the ball over this. Markets overshoot, and the mechanisms through which this happens involve issues of confidence and sentiment that create bubbles that eventually burst– social psychology if one likes. It is for this reason that markets need to be regulated and policed. We forgot this basic fact. As we did the fact that the 'something for nothing' mentality, the casino economy which unregulated capitalism begets, needs to be reined in too. At the heart of this issue are human behaviour and its vagaries. Maximising personal welfare does not necessarily lead to good outcomes on the community level. Simple, no–Keynes himself made the point in no uncertain terms often enough. Obviously, not.

What we did remember from the past was the link between the finance economy and the real economy, as well the international nature of these issues–if this was true in the 1920s, it is totally evident now. The specifics of the link between real and monetary economies were different—in the 1930s the problem started in stock markets and then spread to banks, agriculture and industry, whereas the current crisis started in the USA housing market and spread to the finance sector and now to real production–but the essentials are the same. This has led to better policy responses in the form of the tax stimulus which has been given to the world economy, and the monetary easing which have occurred, particularly in Europe and the USA. There has also been lip service, at least, paid to the global nature of the crisis, in the form of calls to avoid the wrong sort of competitive protectionism and promote co-operative and concerted international responses. We should not forget that in the 1920s the US government actually increased taxes and cut spending in the early part of the crisis, and there was a long delay before Hoover changed policy tack, to be followed by Roosevelt and the New Deal.

Also, during the 1920s, central banks were very slow in cutting interest rates, and there was a knee-jerk descent into protectionism, typified by the Smoot-Hawley Tariff Act in 1930's America.

For all the reservations that we expressed above, there is a small ray of hope, much of which can be traced back to the fact that we have a new president of the USA, and some relatively aware European leaders, although the latter might be about to change, as far as the UK is concerned. Therefore, some of the measures we outline are somewhat vaguely on the international agenda, awaiting implementation.

Specific Lesson #2: Today Is Not the 1930s

A further fact we need to bear in mind, and which should inform our views and responses, is that the world in the early part of the 21st century is a very different place from that of the inter-war years:

- The world is much richer than a hundred years ago. This should in principle allow us the possibility of protecting the innocent and most vulnerable from the worst effects of the recession. In the West, we may even be confident that nobody will die of hunger; but will the pain be fairly distributed? How even will be any life-reduction imposed upon us?

- We have the issue of ecology to contend with. Our responses to the crisis must be made in the knowledge that, in a nutshell, we have to save the planet from overheating. This offers some possibilities: new economic activity and employment resulting from the development of sustainable energy and production. It also offers challenges and threats, since such developments are likely to reduce our real incomes, at least in the short term. Survival may be worth it.

- The finance sector is infinitely more important and more complex than it was in the 1920s and 1930s. The recycling of the balance of payments surpluses of the oil producing countries into capital investments in the oil consuming countries and the rapid advances in technology have seen to that. In many ways, finance has taken on a life of its own, albeit quite a sinister one. It has been generating money and bubbles using financial products that are so complicated that only a few insiders actually understand them. So the key is to regulate even more closely this part of the economy, which will require political will and no small amount of dexterity and expertise on the part of the State.

- Globalisation. In the 1920s, the depression in the USA spread to the rest of the world, but at a much slower pace. With the greatly increased interdependence that exists in today's world, the international transmission processes are more rapid and more all-encompassing. The health worker in Greece loses rapidly his/her job because of bad loans made in the USA. We have less time to react to crises and the solutions must even more emphatically be international. This is a quintessential global problem that requires global solutions. Thus far the omens have been mixed.

- Finally, we have a different international monetary system to the one that existed in the pre-war days. Then we had to cope with the inflexibilities of the gold standard. Now we have more a more flexible system of exchange rates, even though this has gone hand-in-hand with the emergence of powerful new currencies such as the EURO and the Yen to counterbalance the domination of the USA dollar. This may afford us the benefit of more rapid adjustment, but it also means greater volatility and an excessive reliance on the markets. This, as we have seen, particularly in the case of Iceland, can be extremely painful.

These, then, are the issues as they stand after the crisis. A few things we have done better than in the past, many more lessons we have ignored, others are being buried in the ideological reaffirmation of the neoliberal dogma. Meaningful progress towards a more human interpretation of capitalism is still required, possibly as never before. Above all, there is a historical opportunity to achieve something.

Life is at stake–of the individuals left without any livelihood by the crisis and of our species as a whole on an overheating planet. Will we achieve something? We shall see.

Chapter 7
Cruelty and Austerity: Philip Hallie's Categories of Ethical Thought and Today's Greek Tragedy

In this chapter, 20th-century ethicist Philip Hallie's research on cruelty is outlined and explained in order to determine and discuss categories of thought that make cruelty attributable to social forms of agency. The semantic ambiguity of "cruelty" and its cognate "cruel" are acknowledged and also discussed, but Hallie's understanding is upheld nonetheless as technically articulate and, above all, as reasonable. As such, his understanding can be utilised to interpret and assess in ethical terms the recent austerity policies pursued in many countries of the world after the 2008 economic crash, which was induced by unsustainable deregulated trade of financial assets, particularly of toxic assets. The case of Greece is examined as exemplary, referring especially to the *Loan Agreements* of May 2010 between the representatives of the Greek State and those of the Euro-area Member States under the aegis of the IMF.

Cruelty

As 20th-century scholarship about cruelty is concerned, Philip Hallie's research is possibly the most extensive. Working for many years as an ethicist at Wesleyan University, Hallie wrote no less than three books on this largely neglected topic, the most famous of which being *Lest Innocent Blood Be Shed*, published in 1979. In this book, Hallie recounts and discusses how the inhabitants of Le-Chambon-sur-Lignon, a small village in South-eastern France, protected more than six thousand Jewish refugees from fascist persecution during the 1940s. The inhabitants were led by the local Protestant pastor, André Trocmé, who believed firmly that, albeit extremely risky, such a line of conduct was the only justifiable one, i.e. in line with the morals dictated by the Christian faith.

In his many works on cruelty, Hallie defines this term in somewhat different ways, such as "the infliction of ruin, whatever the motives"[287], "the slow crushing and grinding of a human being by other human beings"[288] and "the activity of hurting sentient beings"[289]. Besides, echoing Saint Augustine's classical distinction between natural and human evil, Hallie distinguishes between the "fatal cruelties" caused by nature and the "violent cruelty" caused by humans.[290] Violent human cruelty is distinguished further into "sadistic" and "practical": the former is "self-gratifying"; the latter is instrumental, i.e. cruelty *qua* means to ulterior ends.[291] Concerning "practical" cruelty, Hallie adds to the picture the subtler form of "implicit" or "indirect" cruelty, which arises because of sheer "indifference or distraction" to the pain that has been caused, rather than because of any explicit violence or direct "intention to hurt".[292] "Implicit" and "indirect" cruelty can grow in time and mutate into "institutionalized cruelty", i.e. a persistent pattern of humiliation that can often endure over many years or generations, and yet is downplayed by the perpetrator as well as the victim, both of whom take it for granted and may even justify it by appealing to the laws of science, the natural order, or religiously sanctioned traditions.[293]

In addition to these distinctions among different forms of cruelty, all of which would appear to be evil, Hallie's 1969 book *The Paradox of Cruelty* offers a puzzling reflection on some types of cruelty that might be better not to avoid altogether, for their disappearance could generate more harm than their continuation. For one, the processes of individual "growth" and maturation can be horribly painful and, in all honesty, "cruel", but Hallie thinks that they are a most valuable component of the long and tortuous road that leads to higher human fulfilment.[294] Then he considers the artistic insights and particularly the disclosure of sorrowful truths that can be obtained through *in terrorem* [terrifying] techniques, as well as many other aesthetic forms of elation, including "sexual" ones, that cruelty is capable of bringing about.[295] On top of that, Hallie admits that cruelty may be a necessary evil in the public sphere, since "responsive" cruelty is entailed by the national and international systems of law and order; although such a "responsive cruelty" can be mitigated, it cannot be avoided entirely.[296] Finally, Hallie notes how cruelty can be brought about in the name of altruism, happiness and justice, since "substantial maiming" can derive from "wanting the best and doing the worst".[297] For all these reasons, he deems cruelty to constitute a "paradox" (as of the book's very title): we may well regard cruelty as one of the most horrible things in life, perhaps even the worst thing we can do, yet we cannot and may not want to rid ourselves of it completely.

Hallie offers us what is to date the richest philosophical study on the paradoxical character of cruelty. As I discussed years ago, this is one of the five broad conceptions of cruelty that can be retrieved in the history of Western thought, the other four being:

- "Cruelty… as a quintessentially human vice affecting specific individuals" such as "persons involved in punitive contexts, e.g. courtrooms, schools, armies", that show no propensity for "clemency";
- "Cruelty" as "sadism", namely "a malaise of the soul", possibly "the result of a poor, incompetent or broken mind, which reduces the humanity of its carrier and makes her closer to wild animals";
- "Cruelty as harm to be avoided", as exemplified most notably by "[t]he champions of the European Enlightenment" and a long string of successive "political and legal reformers"; and
- Cruelty as something good, whether instrumentally or intrinsically, as exemplified respectively by Machiavelli's acceptance of extremely evil means (e.g. war) for good ends (e.g. the State's stability) and Sade's glorification of our natural propensity to violence.[298]

No univocal interpretation of 'cruel' and 'cruelty' applies to the five conceptions listed above, especially if we consider the fact that they are themselves only broad categories applicable to a large variety of more or less refined reflections on cruelty that started with Seneca's *De clementia* and have continued up to Michael Trice's 2011 theological work entitled *Encountering Cruelty* (the present chapter originates from a preparatory work for a larger reflection on the unacceptable cruelty of austerity from a Christian perspective).[299] In my past research, I identify seven frequent connoting elements for what is deemed 'cruel', which amount to little else than family resemblances among usages of a term that is deployed very frequently, defined very rarely and, even so, conceived of in different ways, as the five broad conceptions just mentioned bear witness to. Still, taken together, these connoting elements and broad conceptions chart a vast realm of linguistic expressions located *inter alia* in the fields of philosophy, theology, politics, economics, social theory, psychology, jurisprudence and literature. Referring to my own 2010 work, the seven connoting elements are:

1. "Pain": Whether only physical or also psychological, serious or minimal, justified or unjustified, cruelty implies pain.
2. "Excess": Whether of pain as such or of its usages to acceptable ends (e.g. penal sanctions), or of our hopes in a tolerable life, or of our abilities to understand reality, cruelty eventually steps "beyond"—acceptability, tolerability, comprehensibility.
3. "Roles": Whether directly or indirectly established, cruelty requires the roles of victim and perpetrator, even when the latter is institutional, impersonal or unknown.
4. "Power": It is only by means of power differential that the roles of victim and perpetrator can be established.
5. "*Mens rea*": Whether delighted in or indifferent to the pain inflicted, the perpetrator possesses a culpable mental attitude. Interestingly, when tackling impersonal and institutional perpetrators, several thinkers have personified the universe or the State.
6. "Evil": Cruelty is a species of evil. Even when conceived of as good, it is either an instrumental evil or an apparent evil, the goodness of which must be revealed and justified.
7. "Paradox": Cruelty horrifies and, at the same time, fascinates. This is just one of the many contradictions contained within cruelty, which can be aptly described as paradoxical. The array of diverse conceptions collected below further substantiates this point.[300]

Keeping cruelty's shifting semantic area in mind, let us focus nonetheless upon Hallie's claim that cruelty can be: (A) practical, in the sense of being a means to an end and not an end in itself; (B) implicit, in the sense that it is not a manifest attribute of the end being pursued; and (C) indirect, in the sense that it results from the choice of means by which the end at hand is pursued.[301] As such, cruelty can inform complex forms of social agency in which much dread, destruction, deprivation, loss of dignity and life are visible, and yet in which no explicit violence, no patent intention to hurt, no delight in other people's misery and no non-human constriction can be discerned.

Austerity

The austerity policies that have been implemented in a number of countries since the collapse of deregulated private finance in the year 2008 can be regarded as contemporary examples of practical, implicit and indirect cruelty. I believe that this can be shown by addressing a representative case, namely that of Greece, where leading constitutional lawyer Georgios Kassimatis writes:

> *The Loan Agreements (the Loan Facility Agreement; the Memorandum of Understanding between Greece and the Euro-area Member States and the agreement with the IMF for the Participation of Greece in the European Financial Stabilization Mechanism to the purpose of obtaining the approval of a Stand-by arrangement by the International Monetary Fund) form a system of international treaties the likes of which... the cruelty of the terms and the extent of breach of fundamental legal rights and principles... have never been enacted in the heart of Europe and the European completion; not since the World War II.[302]*

Constitutional lawyers are not renowned for their rhetorical flamboyancy or heated prose. So, where does Kassimatis' "cruelty" come from? In the 100 pages of the *Loan Agreements* of May 2010, annexes included, no mention whatsoever is made of cruelty, death, pain or suffering as the stated aims of the signed agreement, not even as a salient characteristic of the chosen means of implementation. Any possible ruin, crushing, killing, grinding and hurting of victims is nowhere remarked upon in the document, although it is conceded that provisions must be made to protect "the minimum earners" and compensate "the most vulnerable… for possible adverse impact of policies" that include, *inter alia*: layoffs of public employees; "pension" and "wage bill reductions"; decreased job security; and lessened provision of public services and "social security benefits" —i.e. policies that, combined together, are liable to weaken "social cohesion", cause "poverty" and shrink "employment".[303] The intermediate and ultimate aims stated in the agreements are the granting of loans "in conjunction with the funding from the International Monetary Fund",[304] to be duly repaid according to the schedule specified in the document, so as to "correct fiscal and external imbalances and [therefore] restore *confidence"* that alone is said to make "growth… buoyant" and let "the economy… emerge… in better shape than before [i.e.] with higher growth and employment."[305]

These three ultimate aims—buoyant growth, an economy in better shape and a higher rate of employment—are said to be the expected and projected result of the "economic and financial policies" listed in the agreements, which express grave concern for "the recent deterioration in market sentiment" and recommend ways to re-hearten it, such as: "fiscal adjustment" by novel and "special taxes"; reducing "incomes and social security" provision—old-age pensions included—so as to make them "sustainable" *vis-à-vis* the new debt obligations of the State; increased supervision over the banking system during a forecast "period of lower growth"; reforming "ambitious[ly]" the Greek "public sector" to "modernize" it by reducing its size and funding though "oriented to providing better services to its citizens"; making local "labor markets more efficient and flexible"; withdrawing the public role "in domestic industries" and managing or owning a large variety of "assets";

reforming the "health sector"; sustaining a "safety net for the financial system"; reducing "minimum entry level wages" and "employment protection" levels; and "facilitate greater use of part-time work".[306] The details for the implementation of these policies are spelled out *qua* "specific economic policy conditionality" for the disbursement of funds and make it clear that "elderly people", "workers in heavy and arduous professions", recipients of "disability pensions", "social security, hospitals", "existing social programmes" and the recipients of "unemployment benefits" are to bear a share of the burden towards debt repayment.[307]

Given the conditionality and the policies specified in the agreements, it does not take much to infer that much *pain*, both physical and psychological, has been bestowed upon the Greek population or a conspicuous portion of it. The signatories themselves admit in the documents that the immediate effects of the measures specified therein are likely to be a "growth" that is *not* "buoyant" and that the expected and projected positive outcomes would take place in the "future", though nowhere it is said when exactly that will take place.[308] Similarly, it does not require much imagination to realise that all this pain has *exceeded* the pain that most Greek citizens would have been likely to encounter in their life under normal circumstances. In point of fact, these policies have been implemented within the context of considerable diplomatic and economic pressure both at the international level (e.g. public indictments of the Greek government and citizens at large by representatives of the French and German governments, the European Commission and the International Monetary Fund);[309] and at the national level (e.g. street riots, general strikes and public demonstrations quenched by police force).[310] There have been, in other words, *perpetrators*, both at the national and international levels, who have used their *power* in order to have these policies and conditionality implemented despite popular protests and, above all, the visible ruin, crushing, killing, grinding and hurting of *victims* leading to these protests. The perpetrators have *intended* to pursue the policies listed in the agreements in spite of all this ruin, crushing, killing, grinding and hurting. Evidently, such a cruelty was either not their main concern, or not sufficient enough a concern to stop them in their pursuit.

It can be argued whether the ruin, crushing, killing, grinding and hurting, in short, the cruelty of these policies was a necessary, bitter medicine; or a deserved punishment for prior errors (i.e. a form of "responsive" cruelty); or a failed attempt to do good. What cannot be argued, however, is that there was no cruelty. That is where Kassimatis' "cruelty" comes from. As the italicised words in the comments above flag out, *all* the connoting elements are at play here, including that of *paradox*, for the declared ends of these policies have not only failed to materialise, but have been made more difficult to achieve, as the successive amendments to the agreements of 2010 have eventually revealed.[311] Today, the Greek economy shows no sign of buoyancy, the shape of its economy is among the worst in the EU and the rate of unemployment among the highest.[312] The bitter medicine has sorted no positive effect, at least as the declared aims of the May 2010 *Loan Agreements* are concerned. On the contrary, there has been a plethora of nefarious side-effects, such as: a sudden suicide spike, especially amongst men;[313] a considerable increase in mental illnesses[314] and infectious diseases like HIV, TB and malaria; and higher infant mortality.[315] If it ever was a form of "responsive" cruelty, the punishment has indeed reached "the most vulnerable", i.e. children, who cannot be deemed responsible for any pre-crisis errors made by the adults, of whom only some could be regarded as legally, politically or morally guilty. In essence, were we even to admit the possibility of this cruelty being "responsive", it would constitute nonetheless a case of collective punishment. In short, if any genuine good was ever intended as the main aim, such a good has become harder and harder to come by, to the point that leading IMF economists have admitted that, not unlike former experiences in the developing world,[316] the austerity policies originally recommended for Greece have failed the test of reality.[317]

Paradoxical is also the fact that, while such dramatic side-effects materialised, special credit lines and liquidity injections have been operated repeatedly by the European Central Bank [hereafter ECB] in order to safeguard the viability of the Continent's largest private banks, while no special intervention of this kind has been made in order to sustain, say, healthcare provision to Greek children.[318] As the language of the 2010 *Loan Agreements* would read, the ECB has provided funds for the "safety net of the financial system", which feeds on money that is not spent on meeting genuine life needs,[319] but has provided none earmarked for the safety net of the Greek children, whose life needs are being met less and less.[320] "Lifelines", as they are called in the financial world, have been thrown to private banks, their managers and shareholders; nothing comparable has been done for the Greek children, who needed them in no metaphorical way, i.e. in order to live.

Concluding Remarks

Given the evidence above, I believe that it can be reasonably stated that austerity policies like those witnessed in Greece constitute a token of cruelty in its social manifestation, as this can be conceived of thanks to Hallie's categories of ethical thought. There have been the infliction of ruin, *de facto* killings, the slow crushing and grinding of human beings, the hurting of sentient beings—all as a means to an end that does not focus upon the ruin, the killing, the crushing, the grinding and the hurting as such, and yet brings them about inevitably and remains in effective practice indifferent to them, for the ruin, the killing, the crushing, the grinding and the hurting are allowed to continue and the end is not abandoned or the means revised.

PART III – Masters of Thought

Chapter 8
Montaigne and Nietzsche: Ancient and Future Wisdom

The influence of Michel de Montaigne on Friedrich Nietzsche has been widely recognized by scholars for a few decades already, and the name of the former has been added to those of Thucydides, Machiavelli, La Rochefoucauld, Voltaire, and Dostoyevsky within Nietzsche's pantheon of intellectual heroes. Montaigne has been regarded as an important point of reference particularly for Nietzsche's writings of the 1870s and early 1880s. Such themes as solitude, the free spirit, the decentring of humankind and sceptical doubt are each clearly reminiscent of Montaigne.[321] Graham Parkes has been first among Nietzsche's commentators to investigate a fascinating dimension of their intellectual relationship, i.e. concerning the issue of death.[322] As part of a larger study in the philosophy of death, Graham Parkes argues that Montaigne's view of death is astonishingly similar to several German and Japanese authors of disparate historical periods:

> [N]amely... Nietzsche and Heidegger... Dogen, Shosan, and Nishitani... Comparisons admittedly lose some of their force when the thinkers and ideas are abstracted from their historical contexts, and scepticism is generally justified in cases where disparate philosophers are said to be "saying the same things about the same things". But even though death can be regarded as a cultural construct, the similarities in attitude and response to the prospect of death are striking. There is a sense in which the engagement with death as what Jaspers called a "limit situation" reaches something basic in human existence.[323]

Examining the relationship between Montaigne and Nietzsche, Parkes argues that with respect to death the philosophical approach of these two thinkers is remarkably similar. Both authors, Parkes claims, conceive of death as an ongoing process accompanying the human being along the entire life-path, the recognition of which constitutes the basis of a common philosophical illumination leading to freedom, happiness, and wisdom. Death is not an impending menace intervening *ab externo* [from the outside], but is unveiled *ex interno* [from the inside], as a way to better understand the course of the life-path itself. This knowledge, Montaigne argues, distinguishes the sage from the crowd who are condemned to encounter death unprepared:

> *They go, they come, they trot, they dance—of death no news. All that is fine. But when it comes, either to them or to their wives, children, or friends, surprising them unprepared and defenseless, what torments, what cries, what frenzy, what despair overwhelms them! Did you ever see anything so dejected, so changed, so upset? We must provide for this earlier... Let us rid it of its strangeness, come to know it, get used to it. Let us have nothing on our minds as often as death.*[324]

Three centuries later, Nietzsche writes: "How strange that this sole certainty and commonality barely makes an impression on people and that they are farthest removed from feeling like a brotherhood of death!"[325] Only the understanding of death can bring about life's most profound transformation, since only this higher form of awareness helps the sage to discharge false idols and useless concerns. Montaigne writes: "[A]ll the wisdom and reasoning in the world boils down finally to this point: to teach us not to be afraid to die."[326]

Parkes claims that Montaigne and Nietzsche are likewise accepting of human finitude and cultivate practical wisdom under its light. They step out of the long Platonic and Christian line that sharply dichotomizes life and death and offers an "evasion from life" *in nomine mortis*.[327] Against Montaigne's and Nietzsche's acceptance of human limitations, this line sees mundane existence as of little value, intrinsically unstable, and ultimately doomed:

"[D]ying to the world in advance, dissociating myself from the body, so that when the physical death arrives I am no longer home to receive it... [T]he idea is to die away from the world and detach from the body in order to identify with the ultimate, transcendent Reality."[328]   Montaigne and Nietzsche resist "these modes of transcendence", which Parkes identifies also in several Eastern approaches.[329]   Challenging these tragic, anti-mundane, psyche/atman-centred traditions, Montaigne and Nietzsche understand death "as an integral part of life, an ever-present aspect that is normally kept hidden. What is recommended is a detachment from life that somehow reverses itself, such that one re-enters life with heightened vitality—as in the Zen master's exhortation to 'live having let go of life".[330]   In sum, Parkes finds Montaigne and Nietzsche alike in conceiving death as something essentially intertwined with life, the philosophical scrutiny of which ensures a form of existential liberation, and consequently something to be accepted as a positive fact of human experience.

Undoubtedly, a number of similarities can be identified between Montaigne and Nietzsche. The historical and intellectual bond they share is unmistakable. However, I would argue that Parkes overstates their similarities with respect to the philosophy of death, betraying the true spirit of Montaigne's and Nietzsche's philosophical enterprises. First, Parkes' account oversimplifies their interpretations of death. Second, it understates their differences with respect to existential perspectives and cosmological assumptions. The existential liberation connected with Montaigne's and Nietzsche's philosophical understandings of death is fundamentally dissimilar. For Nietzsche, certain conceptions of death bring about a condition of slavery, while Montaigne's end is to soothe the fear of death. Nietzsche's aim it not to reduce suffering at all. The acceptance of death that Montaigne recommends is fundamentally a variation of Stoic and Epicurean doctrines, both of which deeply influenced Montaigne's intellectual education. Montaigne understands the intertwining of life and death in a strictly individualist fashion: we all must die; how, then, can I cope with this awareness? We must not worry about death, Montaigne argues, but concentrate on our mortal life instead. Nietzsche's account of death is located within a different cosmological framework. Ontologically speaking, life is regarded as a species of death. Not only must we die, we must do so again and again, in the endless circle of the eternal recurrence of the same. Moreover, we must be capable of not wishing it otherwise, thus expressing a heroic approach to death.

Montaigne vs. Nietzsche: On Reason and Passion

Montaigne regards death as a moment of liberation for the human being: "[P]remeditation of death is premeditation of freedom... He who has learned how to die has unlearned how to be a slave. Knowing how to die frees us from all subjection and constraint."[331] But who is subjecting us to this rule? From what or whom are we freed? Montaigne teaches us not to be afraid of death: "For as it is impossible for the soul to be at rest while she fears death, so, if she can gain assurance against it, she can boast of a thing as it were beyond man's estate: that it is impossible for worry, torment, fear, or even the slightest displeasure to dwell in her."[332] Fear is what has to be discharged. Montaigne laments fear's power to disrupt reason and lead the soul astray, depriving it of self-control. Fear is the most treacherous of passions, "penetrat[ing] right to the seat of reason, infecting and corrupting it."[333] Consequently, all passions, and fear in particular, must be purged as thoroughly as possible, and when they cannot be expunged, then they may be allowed "provided that [one's] judgment remains sound and entire."[334]

The freedom that philosophizing on death can grant, then, is the liberation from a particular passion. This is, however, only one step toward the goal of philosophical wisdom. As we read in several of Montaigne's *Essays*, the sage liberates herself from enslavement to the passions: "While our pulse beats and we feel emotion, let us put off the business. Things will truly seem different to us when we have quieted and cooled down. It is passion that is in command at first, it is passion that speaks, it is not ourselves."[335] Montaigne condemns anything that can challenge rational self-mastery. Since, for Montaigne, passions are not the real self, they cannot provide guidance. The "commonest of human errors", he writes, is that "we are never at home, we are always beyond. Fear, desire, hope, project us toward the future and steal from us the feeling and consideration of what is, to busy us with what will be, even when we shall no longer be."[336] Accordingly, "the wise man should withdraw his soul within, out of the crowd, and keep it in freedom and power to judge things freely."[337]

By contrast, the goal of Nietzsche's work is "to give men back the courage to their natural drives—To check their self-underestimation (not that of man as an individual but that of man as nature)—To remove antitheses from things after comprehending that we have projected them there."[338] His "revaluation of all values" includes a reconsideration of passions as the fundamental source of human action. Such drives are the expression of a more fundamental conatus that characterizes all life: the will to power. Nietzsche hardly shares Montaigne's ideal of liberation *via philosophica* [by way of philosophy]:

> *Excess is a reproach only against those who have no right to it; and almost all the passions have been brought into ill repute on account of those who were not sufficiently strong to employ them. One must understand that the same objections can be made to the passions as are made to sickness: nonetheless—we cannot do without sickness, and even less without the passions. We need the abnormal, we give life a tremendous choc by these great sicknesses.*[339]

Nor does Nietzsche hold much admiration for the "moderate" and "temperate" individual: "The 'great man' is great owing to the free play and scope of his desires and to the yet greater power that knows how to press these magnificent monsters into service."[340] Moreover, Nietzsche's wisdom does not call for the preservation of what is good in the present human being, or what was good in Montaigne's Roman and Greek spiritual mentors. Nietzsche wants to move beyond: "What is great in man is that he is a bridge and not a goal: what is lovable in man is that he is an over-going and an undergoing."[341] In spite of his deep admiration for the classics, and in spite of an equal respect for the French author, Nietzsche rejects Montaigne's opposition of reason and passion, breaking down the distinction itself, together with other traditional distinctions or antitheses such as good and evil, appearance and reality, compassion and selfishness. Nietzsche wishes to rewrite the lexicon of morality itself, including that on which Montaigne's wisdom is based.

Montaigne's references to the traditional moral lexicon and to the concept of existential pressure express the very conception of enslavement that Nietzsche condemns. In fact, they represent the heritage of negative nihilism. For Nietzsche, *ressentiment* lies at the core of many a religion and philosophy. The feelings of powerlessness, limitation, and the suffering of radical contingency are three enslaving structures of self-preservation, including the Christian religion, Hegel's Idealism, and so on. The realization of life's frailty makes the human being desire, create, and ultimately believe in the caging dreams of such structures:

Religion, and the meaning religion gives to life, spreads sunshine over such eternally tormented people and makes them bearable even to themselves. It has the same effect that an Epicurean philosophy usually has on the suffering of higher ranks: it refreshes, refines, and makes the most of suffering, as it were. In the end it even sanctifies and justifies.[342]

The most ubiquitous form of authority—spiritual authority—draws its force from the human being's incapacity to accept existential limits. "Faith", says Nietzsche, emerges from the "fear of a general 'in vain.'"[343] Religious casts of all times have known this truth very well. Their distinctive mark is to have "granted man an absolute value, as opposed to his smallness and accidental occurrence in the flux of becoming and passing away... [and] prevented man from despising himself."[344] Not everyone can tolerate the self-loathing that stems from the recognition of one's own contingency. Only a few pessimists have proven themselves capable of enduring it;

superior intellects such as the Buddha, Leopardi, and Schopenhauer, whom Nietzsche respects because they refused the consolatory dreams of any enslaving *Hinterwelt*, even as they themselves were incapable of accepting contingency in the serene, joyful way that Nietzsche does. Against both "preachers of the *Hinterwelt*" and pessimists, Nietzsche offers his own positive nihilism. Rather than despair at the fact of one's own contingency and finitude, the sage, or in Nietzsche's words, "the strong", "the noble", "the healthy", celebrates: this too is life.

> *[T]he ideal of the most high-spirited, vital, world-affirming individual, who has learned not just to accept and go along with what was and what is, but who wants it again just as it was and is through all eternity, insatiably shouting* da capo. *The religious character da capo not just to himself but to the whole play and performance, and not just to a performance, but rather, fundamentally, to the one who needs precisely this performance–and makes it necessary: because again and again he needs himself–and makes himself necessary.*[345]

Nietzsche's noble type dares to face her own mortality, wants all to be as it is and, purged of *ressentiment*, achieves real freedom. No longer does she perpetuate her enslavement to absolute values and to those who dispense them. Against Montaigne's claim that "to philosophize is [*per se*] to learn to die", and that "dissensions of the philosophical sects in, this matter [death] are merely verbal", for Nietzsche, philosophers are far from comprehending death in the same way.[346] For Nietzsche, philosophy's response to death entails neither the same doctrinal conclusion nor the same liberation. Indeed, many philosophies teach precisely how to become, or remain, a slave. Moreover, Nietzsche is far from believing that philosophy as such can help one to attain freedom—the *fullness* of life. The conquest of this goal has less to do with the philosophy one espouses, or with any artefact of consciousness, than with one's dominating passions, one's instincts and inclinations *pro* life:

Consciousness... is the latest development of the organic, and hence also its most unfinished and unrobust feature. Consciousness gives rise to countless mistakes that lead an animal or human being to perish sooner than necessary, "beyond destiny", as Homer puts it. If the preserving alliance of the instincts were not so much more powerful, if it did not serve on the whole as a regulator, humanity would have to perish with open eyes of its misjudging and its fantasizing, of its lack of thoroughness and its incredulity[.][347]

Montaigne vs. Nietzsche: On Pain and Pleasure

Life has many faces, and Nietzsche's noble individual experiences them all, rather than, in the manner of Montaigne, "call[ing] madness any transport, however laudable, that transcends our own judgment and reason."[348] Life in general, and the individual in particular, benefits from the many diverse possibilities that the "magnificent monsters" of our soul can produce-in -spite of, or even thanks to, the suffering they may involve. Nietzsche does not condemn excess, infelicity and pain *a priori*. Errors, even sickness, are among the many faces of life: "Pain does not count as an objection to life: 'If you have no more happiness left to give me, well then! you still have your pain...'."[349] Nietzsche condemns philosophers who "are prejudiced against appearance, change, pain, death, the corporeal, the senses, fate and bondage, the aimless... They are led by instinctive moral definitions in which former cultural conditions are reflected (more dangerous ones)."[350] Montaigne is among them, his main concern being the liberation of human beings from suffering. Both death and suffering more generally are constant themes of his *Essays* from the early 1570s to the late 1580s.

Indeed, Montaigne's entire wisdom orbits around the attainment of a quiet, serene life. Even the Stoics, so often at the centre of his teaching, become immoderate when calling forth difficult trials of virtue. Why should the sage undergo such trials when existence is so generous in misfortunes? "There is too much effort and harshness in that... We little men must flee the storm from further away; we must try to avoid feeling it, not try to endure it, and dodge the blows we cannot parry."[351] In Nietzsche's terms, Montaigne represents hardly more than Zarathustra's "spirit of gravity", since he derives from the contemplation of our finitude a "temperate" and "moderate" attitude toward life. One wonders whether Montaigne attains any genuine wisdom (in Nietzsche's sense) at all, or whether he is merely another of the nihilists at whom Zarathustra's invective is directed. Not *amor fati*, of which Zarathustra is the prophet, but fatalism pervades Montaigne's *Essays*. The latter affirms, "it will happen", and recommends indifference to the thought that one day all shall end. The former replies, "I will it to happen", teaching us to love it even "in its most terrible form: existence as it is, without meaning or aim, yet recurring inevitably without any finale of nothingness: 'the eternal recurrence'."[352]

Montaigne, however, is neither a pessimist nor a "preacher of the *Hinterwelt*'; he is neither Schopenhauer nor Luther. Still, the wisdom he imparts throughout his *Essays* is not Zarathustra's either. While Nietzsche shares with Montaigne a profound awareness of the inescapable finitude of all things human, he deduces from this awareness a joyful affirmation of contingency rather than a detached acceptance. Montaigne's wisdom is contained in Zarathustra's, but Zarathustra-Nietzsche has moved beyond this. Whereas Montaigne preaches indifference to unhappiness in view of happiness, Nietzsche counsels equanimity before happiness and unhappiness:

"The sum of displeasure outweighs the sum of pleasure; consequently it would be better if the world did not exist"—
"The world is something that rationally should not exist because it causes the feeling subject more displeasure than pleasure"—chatter of this sort calls itself pessimism today! Pleasure and displeasure are accidentals, not causes; they are value judgments of the second rank, derived from a ruling value— "useful", "harmful", speaking in the form of feelings, and consequently absolutely sketchy and dependent.

For with every "useful", "harmful", one still has to ask in a hundred different ways: "for what?" I despise this pessimism... [I]t is itself a sign of deeply impoverished life.[353]

Montaigne's response to death is life-affirming only insofar as life is capable of granting happiness, which Montaigne identifies with a Hellenistic, virtuous, rational life. By contrast, Nietzsche proffers life-affirmation *per se*, independent of happiness or suffering. Placing no limit upon life-affirmation, any determination of existence—death included—is, for Nietzsche, a function of life. True to the spirit of much Hellenistic quietism, Montaigne's wisdom aims at the attainment of all that tends to improve life: "the security, the freedom from pain and suffering, the exemption from the ills of this life."[354] Facing death helps the wise re-enter life with a precise goal firmly in view: the attainment of a "beautiful life... The most beautiful lives, to my mind, are those that conform to the common human pattern, with order, but without miracle and without eccentricity."[355] What could be further from the Nietzschean spirit of creation, from the heroic "attitude and response" to death, celebrating life for its own sake?

Some historical context can help us understand this divergence. Montaigne lives in the battlefield that is 16th-century Europe. He seeks an ivory tower where the sage can contemplate the discovery that the Platonic and Aristotelian dogmas of the past are not as solid as had been imagined, that his Christian quasi-divine status is not as assured as he had believed. Montaigne's philosophy is the first psychotherapy of the Renaissance, one dwelling in a novel secular dimension. Montaigne contemplates the challenges of his times: Copernicus is challenging the pompous *cathedras* [lecture halls] of traditional scholastics; Florentine philology and Neo-Platonism have crossed the Alps and are actively cultivating the art of critical inquiry; Pyrrhonism returns in vogue as the best alternative to both papist and protestant fanaticism; and conventional anthropological views are questioned by the encounter with the savage New World. Montaigne, *qua* psychotherapist, holds out the ideal of human happiness. Nietzsche lives in the century of progressive history, objective idealism and positive science. Absolute knowledge is proclaimed capable of comprehending all that is real. On the one hand, optimism pervades the corridors of European universities. Every phenomenon can be explained as the effect of causes and, more profoundly, as an epiphenomenon of the Absolute Spirit. The Prussian and British academies own the keys to life's secrets. On the other hand, boredom due to an unprecedented period of peace pervades many hearts on the continent. 19th-century Europe seems to have lost its original Romantic impetus. Instead of poets and visionaries, the continent is spawning hordes of wealthy bourgeois bellies and hungry proletarians. Nietzsche has stolen the fire of the gods; what he wishes for Europe is a new life, or better, and more radically, a new type of European person. Zarathustra, one should never forget, is searching for the *Übermensch*.

Montaigne vs. Nietzsche: On Nothingness and Selfhood

Both Montaigne and Nietzsche regard death as essentially interwoven with life itself. Montaigne writes: "Death is the condition of your creation, it is a part of you... The constant work of your life is to build death. You are in death while you are in life... [D]uring life you are dying."[356] Nietzsche reverberates: "Let us be wary of saying that death is opposed to life. The living is merely a species of the dead."[357] Their characterizations, however, of the interweaving of life and death are decidedly different. Montaigne's view aims at allowing the living and dying individual to become optimally aware of death and to liberate herself from the fear of it. Death is a problem for the self, and Montaigne provides the self with an opportune therapy: one who wants to reduce suffering and live a worthy life till the end must "familiarize [herself] with death",[358] realizing that being conscious of one's own mortality constitutes the basic step toward a wiser life. Only then, no turbulence of the spirit, no panic, no *terror vacui* [fear of the void] shall remain within the spirit. On the contrary, serene, detached self-control will lead the soul to its proper fulfilment and eventual annihilation. The sage learns to tolerate her finitude so deeply that she can even call death upon herself. On this point, Montaigne quotes the Greek gnomic poets: *"Either a painless life, or else a happy death. / To die is good for those whom life brings misery. / 'Tis better not to live than live in wretchedness."*[359]

In Nietzsche's terms, the interrelation of life and death is expressed at different ontological levels. Not only the existential sphere, but also cosmology is at the centre of his reflections on death. His cosmological assumptions are more articulated than Montaigne's. Destruction, creation, birth, and annihilation are seen within a broad frame of universal, all-encompassing *Werden*. The basic ontological notion upon which Montaigne fashions his wisdom —the individual self or ego to which happiness, pain, and pleasure are attributed—is fundamentally recast:

> *We set up a word at the point at which our ignorance begins, at which we can see no further, e.g. the word "I", the word "do", the word "suffer": these are perhaps the horizons of our knowledge, but not the "truths." Through thought the ego is posited; but hitherto one believed as ordinary people do, that in "I think" there was something of immediate certainty, and that this "I" was the given cause of thought, from which by analogy we understood all other causal relationships. However habitual and indispensable this fiction may have become by now-that in itself proves nothing against its imaginary origin: a belief can be a condition of life and nevertheless be false... The assumption of one single subject is perhaps unnecessary; perhaps it is just as permissible to assume a multiplicity of subjects... My hypothesis: The subject as multiplicity.*[360]

Not even Montaigne, master sceptic that he was, had dared so much. For Nietzsche, the very 'I' dissolves into that multiplicity of selves that has become a *Leitmotiv* of postmodernism. The individual presupposed by Montaigne is deconstructed, while her own reason— the starting point, for Montaigne, of the response to death and the path to wisdom—is reduced to a ghostly construction. The world itself, as Montaigne conceives it, vanishes along with the traditional notion of the I. Into this seemingly chaotic flux comes a provocative *Einsicht*: "The phenomenon of the body is the richer, clearer, more tangible phenomenon: to be discussed first."[361] Not even Montaigne, whose illnesses constantly reminded him of the relevance of the body, had gone so far. For Nietzsche, the body becomes that upon which all else is founded. The "tremendous blunder" of the metaphysical tradition is precisely the "absurd overestimation of consciousness, the transformation of it into a unity... something that feels, thinks, wills."[362]

Even more radical is Nietzsche's view that no life or death is definitive, insofar as the fate of the living and dying individual is to repeat her existence again and again, with no change or variation. While for Montaigne death, in a sense, stabilizes human existence, Nietzsche's eternal recurrence achieves the very opposite, i.e. a profoundly destabilizing perspective which denies sense to the category of Being itself. Nietzsche therefore recovers in his own way a feature of Stoicism that Montaigne did not consider in his *Essays*: the circularity of time. Yet he does not limit himself to this, or he would fall into a renewed form of nihilism. The Stoic view recommends passive acceptance of a law-like flowing of the same, whereas Nietzsche calls for an active participation in the flow, transforming the law itself into an act of one's will. The Nietzschean individual accepts her limited, ephemeral condition, not merely to endure it, but also and eventually to rejoice in it. Diving into the chaotic stream of the will in its eternal recurrence, the shattered self is regained to reality. Nietzsche, instead of falling into despair, as Schopenhauer or Leopardi had done, invites us to accept and rejoice in the chaotic flux of contingency. From a strictly cosmological point of view, the notion of the eternal recurrence makes the distinction between life and death puzzling, if not meaningless. It is on the existential level that the distinction retains meaning, for the awareness of death should make the subject more aware of life; on this, Nietzsche and Montaigne are in agreement. Yet, going beyond Montaigne, Nietzsche's life-affirmation becomes so radical as to make death a sublime moment of life. The subject can avoid a nihilistic fear of contingency, which death eminently symbolizes, by affirming contingency, or indeed by making death itself one's own wish for life. For without death no life would have value. Nietzsche's "death of God" subverts traditional theological perceptions of the real: in the place of a religion of immortality is a religion of mortality. Groundlessness and chance become the new frame within which human life is understood and experienced.

Chapter 9
Homer, Heroes and Humanity: Vico's *New Science* on Death and Mortality

The past decades have witnessed a renewed and growing scholarly interest in the thought of Neapolitan philosopher Giambattista Vico (1668–1744), particularly with regard to the third edition of his most famous work, *The New Science*.[363] Perhaps entangled in the loops of recurring history or in the book's obscure prose, fame took a long time to catch up with it. In Vico's lifetime, *The New Science* was received, reviewed and circulated poorly, not to mention that Vico himself paid for the publication of its first edition in 1725.[364] Even in Italy, any major acclaim, if not the widespread knowledge of Vico's main work, remained limited for longer than a century and a half, i.e. until Benedetto Croce initiated a substantial revival of Vichian studies in the 20th century.[365] In this perspective, just as much is owed to Croce's close associate and friend, Fausto Nicolini, whose lifelong laborious recovery of archival materials, sources and historical information has allowed for an articulate and deeper understanding of Vico's personal vicissitudes, intellectual formation and socio-cultural milieu.[366]

As far as the Anglophone academe is concerned, Collingwood's 1913 translation of Croce's study on Vico,[367] Adams' *Life and Writings of Giambattista Vico*[368] and the 1948 English translation of the third edition of Vico's *New Science* by Thomas Goddard Bergin and Max Harold Fisch constitute the three crucial steps in the 20th-century renaissance of Vichian studies in the British Isles and North America. The recognition of Vico's originality by liberal icon Isaiah Berlin was also important,[369] and so was the use that James Joyce made of Vico's ideas in designing his most experimental literary works.[370] Moreover, as of the 1980s, new translations and essays were written and promoted by Giorgio Tagliacozzo and Donald Phillip Verene, editors of *New Vico Studies*, which by now have succeeded in presenting to the English-speaking academic community the majority of Vico's works,[371] letting him become "the buzzword of a thousand academics".[372]

This is not to imply that Vico had been ignored during the 19th century. Italian scholarship was neither oblivious nor indifferent to him.[373] Indeed, after testifying to the oblivion of Vico's work in 18th-century Italy, Marini tries ardently to show how nearly all major philosophical systems of the first half of the 19th century are indebted to Vico's *New Science*.[374] The results of his efforts are perplexing, to say the least, for they are marred by the jingoistic presumption that nearly all valuable modern Western philosophy and historiography is somehow a variation on tunes played by "the great solitary of Vatolla, the immortal genius of the Italian peninsula".[375] Marini does identify a few tokens of actual knowledge of Vico's theories in non-Italian authors such as Condorcet, Michelet, De Maistre and Chateaubriand, which however fall short of proving his much more ambitious point. Rather, it can be evinced from Marini's book that Vico's focus on the theoretical discernment of human history had been a precursor of a philosophical trend that emerged forcefully only in the 19th century, well after Vico's death. Outside Italy, occasional references can be retrieved in the works of leading French and German intellectuals. For instance, Auguste Comte praised Vico for his insights in the stages of human progress and dedicated to him a day in his positivist calendar,[376] i.e. the 17th of the 11th month or "Descartes".[377] Karl Marx cited Vico while discussing the historical nature of man and the human nature of history.[378] Jules Michelet saluted Vico as a distant prophet of "the terrible creative power of ordinary people".[379]

Most 19th-century admirers of Vico commended specific notions of his *New Science* (e.g. the empathetic understanding of other nations, the popular nature of Homeric poetry). However, none of them seemed to adhere to the *New Science* as a project. Even less did they seem to grasp or care about the Catholic, conservative spirit of Vico's enterprise. His *New Science* included significant innovation as to the means of investigation that it employed, but it had also deeply anti-modern ends. Rejecting abstract ideals of social reform and Cartesian rationalism, Vico's work wished to show how Divine

Providence had been guiding human history since its remotest origins and how reason, left to its own devices, hence deprived of the aid of tradition, is bound to fall into scepticism and relativism.[380] On the one hand, Vico claims: "To be useful to the human race, philosophy must raise and direct weak and fallen man, not rend his nature or abandon him in his corruption."[381] On the other hand, philosophers have often displayed too proud an over-reliance upon reason and consequently forgotten about the religious truths that lie at the foundation of any cohesive human community. Thus, Vico "dismisses from the school of our Science the Stoics who seek to mortify the senses and the Epicureans who make them the criterion. For both deny providence, the former chaining themselves to fate, the latter abandoning themselves to chance… Both should be called monastic or solitary philosophers."[382]

Despite the recent wealth of Vichian studies, as far as I can discover, Vico's comprehension of death and mortality in *The New Science* has not been yet the subject of any scholarly study (I should emphasise that this chapter is not dealing with the related but distinct topic of immortality in Vico's *New Science*). Allusions to the metaphorical "death of a nation" appear in works dealing with Vico's theory of historical cycles, but not to death and mortality as such.[383] It is the aim of the present chapter to provide one, revealing how the topics of death and mortality recur in, and allow for the explanation of, three essential themes of Vico's philosophy, i.e. poetic wisdom, the providential unfolding of ever-changing civilisations, and the universal unchanging hallmarks of actual humanity. This chapter assumes no previous knowledge of Vico's work on the reader's part. Therefore, I endeavour to explain succinctly the main issues pertaining to *The New Science*, while addressing the three key-themes highlighted *via* death and mortality. Hopefully, the reader who does not have any previous knowledge of Vico will find this book chapter a useful introduction to *The New Science*; whilst the reader who does have some previous knowledge will deepen it with regard to Vico's understanding of death and mortality.

Death pervades the works of Homer. References to, and discussions of, Homer pervade Vico's *New Science*. As a result, death pervades Vico's *New Science*. But why was Vico interested in Homer? As he set out to review as much ancient material evidence as possible—the activity of "philology"—and extract from it the providential logic of the course of human history—the activity of "philosophy"—Vico could not avoid referring to the Homeric poems, which are the founding stone of Greek culture and, arguably, Western culture at large.[384] Vico's *New Science* offers a chronology of world's history and discusses it.[385] This way, Vico does address prehistory and several ancient civilisations, but eventually *The New Science* focuses on the Greek, Roman and, to a lesser extent, Israelite civilisations. This is due first of all to the limitations of his personal knowledge and competences, but also to the material available to him and to 18th-century Western scholars in general. Besides, he could have never managed to provide as exhaustive an account of the history of all cultures, nor even of just all the Mediterranean cultures. Focussing upon two well-known and reasonably evidence-endowed cases was a much more realistic strategy. Furthermore, Vico and his Baroque colleagues were bound to literary documents to a higher extent than today's historians and social scientists, who have benefitted enormously from the widespread technological application of scientific knowledge to the investigation of the remote past of humankind.[386]

Concerning the received view of Homer in the times of Vico, there was a widespread belief that both the *Iliad* and the *Odyssey* displayed a profound philosophical character. As Plato himself had argued, these poems were supposed to be the work of a true philosophical genius, who had cast profound metaphysical thoughts in marvellous poetic formulations.[387] Vico took issue with this belief, and death played a role in leading him to do so. According to Vico, no philosopher would have ever been so complacent *vis-à-vis*, not to say keen on, the "cruel and fearful... battles and deaths" with which Homer's poems are rife, and the *Iliad* in particular.[388] Similarly, the leading character of this poem, the fearless demigod Achilles, is far too merciless, vindictive and self-indulgently fickle to be regarded as a model of virtue under whatever philosophical perspective one may opt for. For instance, Vico observes that Achilles "is pleased—he who carries with him the fate of Troy—to see all the Greeks fall to ruin and suffer miserable defeat at Hector's hands."[389] As morally disturbing as it may sound, Achilles is so obdurate and self-centred that "not even in death is he placated for the loss of his Briseis until the unhappy beautiful royal maiden Polyxena… has been sacrificed before his tomb".[390] Vico's measure is not full though, given that "what is really past understanding" for him is "that a philosopher's gravity and propriety of thought could have been possessed by a man who amused himself by inventing so many fables worthy of old women entertaining children, as those with which Homer stuffed his other poem, the *Odyssey*".[391] Homer's delight in portraying repeatedly and unashamedly "[s]uch crude, coarse, wild, savage, volatile, unreasonable or unreasonably obstinate, frivolous and foolish customs" does not suit mature intellects that are capable of philosophising, but "men who are like children in the weakness of their minds, like women in the vigor of their imaginations and like violent youths in the turbulence of their passions".[392] Consequently, Vico's conclusion is unequivocal: "we must deny to Homer any kind of esoteric wisdom" and rather step up to "seeking out the true Homer."[393]

This is not to say that there is no genius in Homer's epic. Vico did believe the *Iliad* and the *Odyssey* to be magnificent poems. He praises openly Homer's inventiveness and, as further explained in the next subsection ("Heroes"), there is more to Vico's appreciation of poetry than sheer style.[394] For him, Homer's poems were genial works, but of the literary sort; hence they had to be grasped in their own terms, i.e. *qua* tokens of "poetic wisdom".[395] In them lurks no hidden form of "sublime" theoretical knowledge that can be excavated by some subtle application of philosophical reasoning.[396] Uniquely for his time, Vico thought the *Iliad* and the *Odyssey* to be highly imaginative, synthetic depictions of reality that were produced—indeed the only ones producible—by a fascinating primitive civilisation, somehow closer to the "American Indians" of his day than to him.[397] For Vico, Homer's Greece was an archipelago of order-conscious, slave-owning societies, which were headed by verse-reciting murderous warriors.[398] They were not the home of long-bearded, toga-robed sages surrounded by respectful disciples and sun-basked white colonnades.[399] What is more, the two Homeric poems seemed so dissimilar to Vico, as well as the tales and stylistic devices deployed in each of them, that *The New Science* posits the audacious and still-debated claim that they were composed by two distinct authors, if not even by a multitude of 'Homers'.[400] Vico's "true Homer" is finally revealed to be an "idea or a heroic character of Grecian men insofar as they told their histories in song."[401] In other words, the legendary blind poet is actually the *a posteriori* personification of the "history of the natural law of the gentes of Greece"[402]—an original interpretation of Homer that found positive acceptance amongst Europe's Romantics and their glorification of Europe's 'peoples' and 'nations'.[403]

Homer's works are not the only ancient literary sources of Vico's *New Science* that are redolent with death. A plethora of dramatic, gruesome, and sometimes morbid myths are cited throughout his book. For example, we read of: "modest maiden Daphnes", whom Apollo "pursues to the point of death";[404] Cadmus' slaying of the dragon and the fight of his ghost-soldiers;[405] Aeneas' murder of "his *socius* Misenus when it is needful for a sacrifice";[406] "Hercules [who], stained by the blood of the ugly centaur Nessus... go[es] forth in madness and die[s]";[407] and the cruel flaying of Marsyas by Apollo.[408] Death lies all around the gods and the mythical heroes of old.

Heroes

Death informs and surrounds the other major body of "philological" references harvested in Vico's *New Science* for the "philosophical" understanding of history: Roman law. The *New Science* focuses especially upon the early stages of the Roman republic. Contrary to its common albeit misleading representation as a precocious experiment in democratic self-rule, Vico describes Rome's senatorial republic as a harsh oligarchic regime: "forty years after the expulsion of Tarquinius Superbus, in the comfortable assurance of his death, the nobility had again begun to be insolent toward the unhappy plebs."[409] Seen from the side of Rome's *populus*, the republic was no better than the previous tyrannical regime: "the liberty instituted by Brutus was not popular (the freedom of the people from their lords) but aristocratic (the freedom of the lords from the Tarquin tyrants)".[410] The celebrated leaders of the young Roman republic, its "heroes", are depicted as intense, ruthless, and unyieldingly elitist. "Brutus… Scaevola… Manlius… Curtius… Fabricius and Curius… Atilius Regulus" either faced a brutal death or brought it onto others, sometimes even onto their own children.[411] Still, "what did any of them do for the poor and unhappy Roman plebs? Assuredly they did but increase their burdens by war, plunge them deeper in the sea of usury, in order to bury them to a greater depth in the private prisons of the nobles, where they were beaten with rods on their bare backs like abject slaves."[412] Furthermore, "if anyone in this period of Roman virtue attempted to relieve the lot of the plebs with some sort of agrarian or grain law, he was accused of treason and sent to his death."[413]

As a matter of "philological" fact, Vico notes that in republican Rome the death penalty was a standard feature of the judicial system.[414] The deadly severity of the republic's aristocracy is, in Vico's view, just another instance of a recurrent historical phenomenon, to which Greek myths and Homeric poems had given ample though unnoticed testimony. The recurrent historical phenomenon, which applies equally to "Assyrians, Chaldeans, Phoenicians and Egyptians",[415] is the creation of oligarchies by "heroic fathers" or "heroes".[416] These were men who had overcome the earliest condition of quasi-animal life in the wildernesses of the world (e.g. Vico's "Patagonian giants" or Homer's "cyclopes")[417] and the successive family-wide farming gatherings,[418] so as to establish the first real civil communities or "first cities".[419] They were heroic examples of *pater familias* ["family father" aka "patriarch"], who were thought of initially as "mortal gods",[420] then as priests[421] and eventually as monarchs.[422] Death, once more, is a crucial element in the picture. The *pater familias* was the one who had the supreme right of life and death (*ius vitae necisque*) over his children, wives, slaves and animals, i.e. all of his animate possessions.[423] Ancient oligarchies extended the deadly power of the "heroic fathers" onto larger and larger populations. Even so, the fundamental social criterion remained analogous to that between father and child, i.e. master and slave or, in the early days of Rome, patrician and "plebeians" or "plebs".[424] These two groups' mutual relations were forged upon acts of supreme domination and abject submission, which *The New Science* collects and examines extensively. Again, these acts of domination and submission were reflected not solely in Roman religious and legal formulations, but also and most originally in much older myths, e.g. the "Herculean knot by which clients were said to be *nexi* or tied to the lands they had to cultivate for the nobles... [or] how Ulysses is on the point of cutting off the head of Antinous [i.e. Eurylochus], the chief of his *socii*, just for a word which, though well meant, does not please him".[425]

Clarifying further the notion of "poetic wisdom" addressed in the previous subsection ("Homer"), Vico's "philosophical" interpretation of the ancient myths reveals itself as being socio-political. As he writes: although "philosophers later found all these fables convenient for the meditation and exposition of their moral and metaphysical doctrines... poets had... political ideas" in mind.[426] Equipped with this novel hermeneutical perspective, Vico could explain the tragic death of Orpheus as follows: "the founder of Greece, with his lyre or cord or force, which signify the same thing as the knot of Hercules (the knot with which the Petelian law was concerned), met his death at the hands of the Bacchantes (the infuriated plebs), who broke his lyre to pieces (the lyre being the law...)...so that already in Homer's time the heroes were taking foreign women to wife, and bastards were coming into royal successions".[427] Today, Vico's novel hermeneutical perspective is part of anthropology's methodological armoury. In his day, it allowed *The New Science* to make sense of a vast number of myths, thus engendering an inventive historical consciousness and, as I shall explain, to regard humanity as unfolding in stages according to an unfaltering inner criterion.[428] The very deadly time of the "heroic fathers" was not the end of history, as the mythical end of Orpheus implies. It was a step in a divinely inspired chain of events that, *mutatis mutandis* [changing what has to be changed], are to take place in all civilisation.[429] In the case at hand, the oligarchs' subjects, whether *qua* "citizens" of Pericles' Athens[430] or "plebs" of Quintus Publilius Philo's Rome, did eventually break free from the chains of slavery.[431] They established a "commonwealth" of "popular liberty."[432] As tokens of the changed humanity of these novel, free communities, habits and institutions became milder, and the death penalty far less common than before.[433]

Vico's *New Science* embraces an enormous array of sources and historical events. Human civilisations have been many and they have been changing all the time. Nonetheless, the logic according to which human civilisations have been unfolding can be described as a consistent triadic process. This process manifests itself in all civilisations, in a contextually particular and never identical fashion. Henceforth, according to Vico, no historiography had been able to grasp it fully before his "new science", which he defined as "a rational civil theology of divine providence".[434] Specifically, after God's providence allowed humankind to overcome an otherwise insuperable animal-like condition, societies are to advance through three stages: an "age of the gods" (i.e. rural theocratic gatherings), an "age of the heroes" (i.e. civil oligarchic regimes), and an "age of men" (i.e. "popular commonwealths" and related anarchy-correcting humane "monarchies").[435] From the peaks of refinement of the third stage, societies can relapse subsequently into a novel form of "barbarian times" and refuel another cycle of stages, thus instantiating "the recourse the nations take in natures and customs."[436] This "recourse" preserves however some of the wisdom accumulated up to that point, so that the new barbaric times are shorter and somewhat less barbarous.[437] Towards the end of the returned barbaric times of Medieval Europe, a new heroic poet appears, i.e. the Florentine Dante Alighieri, who collects the wisdom of the age like Homer did before him.[438] Still, hence indicating the reduced savagery of the recourse of history, Medieval Europe was capable of producing also tokens of masterly philosophical reflection such as "Peter Lombard" in Paris and his "subtlest scholastic theology".[439] This imperfect cyclicality is probably Vico's most original take on a notion of development in three stages that he claims to derive from archaic "Egyptian" wisdom and Roman historian Marcus Terentius "Varro".[440] Although he does address to some extent metaphysical issues, Vico's focus is social and historical. Perhaps he was afraid of getting in trouble with Naples' very active Inquisition, or more simply he wished to show that history does not make anything; we, with God's help, do.

Vico scholar Leon Pompa calls the recurrence of barbarism the "death of a nation".[441] Yet, for Vico, this "death" was literally a godsend, for it guarantees that history may move forward in spite of human errors. Vico's "recourse" of natures and customs is not the eternal recurrence of the same. Falling back into "primitive simplicity" is a "last remedy of providence", which rescues ungodly populations from the socially devastating evils of selfish "premeditated malice" and proud scepticism, i.e. the two causes of falsely civilised "liv[ing] like... beasts in... solitude of spirit and will, scarcely any two being able to agree since each follows his own pleasure or caprice." [442] Such are the bitter fruits of the irreligious and over-refined "barbarism of reflection", which lets the human being lose touch with its natural, corporeal and imaginative faculties and with each society's particular forms of traditional wisdom, including the poetic one.[443] Therefore, for Vico, returning to a novel form of "primitive simplicity" means that human beings are able to regain "piety, faith and truth".[444] Simon rightly dubs this point of Vico's thought a "phoenix-like rejuvenation."[445] All aspects of human civilisations are guided by this triadic providential logic, e.g. the notions of quantity ("weight... measure... number"),[446] the main psychological dispositions or "customs" of the age,[447] the graphic signs or "characters" standardly utilised,[448] the valid sources of legal "authority",[449] the penal chastisements ordinarily employed,[450] the spirit of the times or "sects of time" ("fashion"),[451] and even the rhetorical "tropes" that make conceptualisation and comprehension possible.[452]

Vico taught rhetoric for many years and his *New Science* does not reduce it to style, as it is still widely done today.[453] Instead, Vico takes rhetorical tropes to be the mental-linguistic "poetic logic" enabling us to conceive of reality and try to grasp it.[454] The originally mute "savages" were led by providence into gesturing[455] and then into communicating by few, simple, sung words prompted by "violent passions".[456] Afterwards, slowly, they progressed into "univocal", true poetry.[457] Prose, or "articulate speech", with its armoury of synonyms, analogies and even means of deception, came last.[458] In this linguistic context, Vico refers to "mortality",[459] which was conceptualised initially by "metonymy of cause for effect", such as the "little fable" of a female "pale Death" that seized human beings.[460] It was only later, "as particulars were elevated into universals or parts united… [to] make up… wholes" by increasingly evolved human intellects, that the poetic founders of civilisation stepped to the more abstract trope of "metaphor", such as "mortals" for "men".[461] Needless to say, "irony" was amongst the last tropes to be developed, for it requires a high degree of "reflection" to be understood, since "it is fashioned of falsehood"—try saying that rhetoric is, at least for Vico, nothing but empty talk.[462]

Humanity

Vico's *New Science* accounts for both diversity and similarity in human history. On the one hand, his work amasses an incredible amount of incredibly detailed—and sometimes blatantly incredible —information dealing with specific events and specific moments of specific human civilisations. On the other hand, *The New Science* detects consistent trends and patterns across this variety of phenomena, but without positing them as though they were devoid of unique circumstances of manifestation. An admirer and, at times, a devoted misinterpreter of Plato, Vico sought for the unifying harmony that could be discerned behind a vast tapestry of intimately particular historical events.[463] Once again, death is relevant, also in connection with this Platonic aim. Amongst the consistent trends and patterns across historical phenomena, Vico selects funerary rites or "burial" as a universal indication of civilisation as such.[464] This is another discovery that Vico claims to have derived from the proper interpretation of ancient poetic wisdom, as in the following example:

> *Aeneas... proceeds through the underworld to the Elysian fields (for the heroes, having settled in the cultivated fields, enjoyed eternal peace in death if they had proper burial). Here he beholds his ancestors and those who are to come after him (for on the religion of the graves, called the underworld by the poets, were founded the first genealogies, from which history took its beginning).*[465]

Vico claims that "among all peoples the civil world began with religion",[466] which sanctions the institutions of "marriage"[467] and "burial".[468] In this manner, death lies at the heart of humanity's establishment *qua* humanity: "Indeed *humanitas* in Latin comes first and properly from *humando*, burying."[469] Vico employs vivid images to make his point:

> *[To realize] what a great principle of humanity burial is, imagine a feral state in which human bodies remain unburied on the surface of the earth as food for crows and dogs. Certainly this bestial custom will be accompanied by uncultivated fields and uninhabited cities. Men will go about like swine eating the acorns found amidst the putrefaction of their dead.*[470]

Religion, marriage and burial are for Vico the principles upon which humanity was established and, even in the case of recurrence of barbarism, preserved, for: "all nations, barbarous as well as civilized, though separately founded because remote from each other in time and space, keep these three human customs: all have some religion, all contract solemn marriages, all bury their dead."[471] Significantly, "burial grounds were called by the Latins religious places par excellence."[472] As the dramatic event that it undoubtedly is in human affairs, remote as much as present, death is at the heart of civilisation in another way, since: "by the graves of their buried dead the giants showed their dominion over their lands, and Roman law called for burial of the dead in a proper place to make it religious".[473] Notions of territory, borders, property, ethnic identity, even statehood, emerge from sacred graveyards.[474]

Additionally, poetic wisdom suggests that death informs religion and *a fortiori* civilisation itself in a third way. The primitive, animal-like giants, from whom we all descend, were afraid of death. They lived in treacherous wilderness; they were exposed to the elements and to their most bewildering of expressions, that is to say, the lightning. As Vico explains, the first religious beliefs sprang out of a genuine "terror of Jove [or any other deification of the sky],[475] whom they feared as the wielder of the thunderbolt."[476] Modern languages contain the memory of such archaic beginnings in exclamations like "*moure bleu*! [or *morbleu*!]... *parbleu*!... [in which] *bleu* [is] the sky; and, as the gentile nations used 'sky' for Jove, the French must have used *bleu* for God".[477] Out of the same fear of death developed morality, in the form of conjugal love, which Vico believes to be inextricably linked to religion: "the virtue of the spirit began likewise to show itself among them, restraining their bestial lust from finding its satisfaction in the sight of heaven, of which they had a mortal terror."[478] Upon these first conjugal unions grew slowly civil society as well, in accordance with God's plan: "divine providence initiated the process by which the fierce and violent were brought from their outlaw state to humanity and by which nations were instituted... It did so by awaking in them a confused idea of divinity, which they in their ignorance attributed to that to which it did not belong."[479]

Interestingly, Vico adds that morality still relies upon this fear, at least as concerns the giant-equivalents of fully human societies, i.e. children: "Hence came the eternal property among all nations, that piety is instilled in children by the fear of some divinity".[480] Vico's interest in pedagogical matters is the result of his long professional experience *qua* university lecturer and mentor of youngsters from well-off families, as well as of profound epistemological concerns.[481] First of all, Vico was a humanist who tried to defend literary and historical studies from the rampant scientism of his age.[482] Different aspects of reality require different disciplines. Besides, he reminded his colleagues that the knowledge of the natural sciences was bound to be more superficial than the knowledge of the formal and human sciences. We can know better (i.e. both how and why) that which we make (e.g. geometry, law, poetry) than that which we have not made (e.g. planets, animals, ourselves; of which only how they are can be addressed). As he famously wrote: "*verum factum convertuntur*" [truth and made are mutually convertible]. Secondly, Vico did never forget that learning begins in childhood and that children must be approached in their own terms, just like the poets of ancient times.[483] Their most developed faculties are not rational, but sensorial and imaginative. More to the point, these faculties are still essential in reflective adulthood, e.g. imagination transcends the given categories of descriptive and explanatory thought in the natural sciences, which rely themselves upon imagination for their own coming into being and to which imagination cannot be reduced.[484] For Vico, the human mind is always and anyhow a "mind in a body".[485]

Burials, in their connection with the notion of the underworld, reveal another token of the triadic logic that pervades the development of human history. Initially, as Vico writes, "the first lower world must not have been any deeper than the source of the springs."[486] Then, "[w]ith the practice of burial the idea of the underworld was extended, and the poets called the grave the underworld... Thus the lower world was no deeper than a ditch, like that in which Ulysses, according to Homer, sees the underworld and the souls of the dead Heroes",[487] albeit "[l]ater... the underworld had the depth of a furrow. It is to this underworld that Ceres (the same as Proserpine, the seed of the grain) is carried off by the god Pluto".[488] "Finally", so as to emphasise the social divide of the heroic stage of civilisation, "the underworld was taken to be the plains and the valleys, as opposed to the lofty heaven set on the mountain tops."[489] The heroes' fatal severity discussed in the previous subsection

("Heroes") extends to this domain of human life too: the death of the hero's other, the enemy, the inferior. Vico notes that it was a widespread heroic custom "that of denying burial to enemies slain in battle, leaving their unburied bodies instead as a prey to dogs and vultures (on which account the unhappy Priam found so costly the ransom of his son's body, though the naked corpse of Hector had already been dragged by Achilles's chariot three times around the walls of Troy)."[490] Once more, Homer's heroic poetry discloses for Vico the true origins of humanity, which so much owes to the fearful awareness of mortality, the political usages of death, and death's sacralisation in religious funerary rites. In other words, Vico achieves historically the awareness of the importance of mortality in humanity's self-understanding, which Martin Heidegger also achieves, yet existentially, by focussing on the anxiety-ridden experience of the individual.[491]

Chapter 10
Contingency, Autonomy and Inanity: Cornelius Castoriadis on Human Mortality

Cornelius Castoriadis (1922–1997) was a Greek Trotskyite partisan, a student of law, philosophy and politics, a renowned Sovietologist of the Cold War era, a long-time OECD economic analyst, the leading member of the libertarian socialist group "Socialisme ou Barbarie", and in his maturity a practicing psychoanalyst. Above all, Castoriadis was a prolific writer and public speaker on the left of the political spectrum. During the 1960s, he became one of the most influential intellectuals in France, that is to say, the country to which he had fled because of the political persecution of left-wing activists in Greece and of which he became a citizen in 1970. A communist in his youth and a libertarian socialist his whole life, Cornelius Castoriadis abandoned officially Marxism already in the 1970s.[492] Nevertheless, as the Anglophone academe is concerned, the knowledge and circulation of Castoriadis' thought are still limited, especially in comparison with recent Continental 'stars' in the humanities such as Gilles Deleuze, Jürgen Habermas and Umberto Eco.[493] Therefore, the present chapter builds upon a substantial selection of passages from several texts by Castoriadis and offers an introduction to representative aspects of his work *via* the issue of mortality.[494]

At first glance, Castoriadis' conception of mortality falls into broad existentialist and psychoanalytic categories of thought. It refers repeatedly to the basic absurdity of the human condition, the anxiety caused by the awareness of one's own ineluctable demise, the believer's emotional investment underpinning religion as well as religion's unlikely reasonability, and the imposing authority of the Judeo-Christian god as a projection of the paternal figure. Within such a conception of finitude, analogies with Camus, Heidegger, Freud and Lacan are not greatly difficult to retrieve. Existentialist and psychoanalytic analogies notwithstanding, Castoriadis' approach to mortality possesses a truly original character, for it focuses upon the unique response to radical *contingency* developed in ancient Greece and the peculiar role played by this response in establishing the conditions for genuine human *autonomy*, which Castoriadis believes to be receding in the nominal democracies of the *inane* modernity.

Other scholars have mentioned or touched upon Castoriadis' conception of mortality when addressing his analysis of the birth of democracy in ancient Greece or juxtaposing his views with those of other thinkers.[495] As far as I know, none of these scholars has tackled Castoriadis' account of mortality *per se*, following the thread that weaves together the notions highlighted above i.e. contingency, autonomy and inanity.[496] By pursuing this thread, the present chapter offers a novel approach to Castoriadis' thought and fills at least one gap in the lacunose Anglophone literature devoted to him.[497]

Contingency

All is transient. All life on Earth, one day, will cease to be. According to Castoriadis, neither humanity and its most magnificent accomplishments, nor the fragile planet hosting us and every known life form in the universe are bound to last forever:

> *First of all, there is a fact that one day or another will have to be digested: we are mortal. Not only us, not only civilizations, but humanity as such and all its creations, its entire memory are mortal. Life expectancy for an animal species is, on average, two million years. Even if, mysteriously, we go indefinitely beyond that mark, the day the Sun attains its final phase and becomes a red giant, its edge will be somewhere between Earth and Mars; the Parthenon, Notre Dame, the paintings of Rembrandt and Picasso, and the books in which the Symposium and the Duino Elegies are recorded will be reduced to the state of protons that furnish this star with energy.*[498]

In the cosmos surrounding us, contingency is sovereign. Everything earthly perishes and so do celestial bodies. We, human beings, are bound to perish. This is not a novel realisation by any stretch of imagination. On the contrary, it is an insight that most individuals and all human societies have had to face at some point in their worldly journey. Indeed, according to Castoriadis, all cultures have developed strategies to cope with that event which contradicts life and yet defines it like no other event: death. Concerning these strategies, he acknowledges two key types:

Faced with that, two responses are possible. First, there's Pascal's, there's Søren Kierkegaard's response: I cannot accept that; I cannot or will not see it. Somewhere there has to be a meaning I am incapable of formulating, yet I believe in it. The "content" may be different—it being furnished by the Old Testament, the Gospels, the Koran, the Vedas, whichever. The other attitude is to refuse to close one's eyes and, at the same time, to understand that if one wants to live, one cannot live without meaning, without signification.[499]

Mortality, albeit certain, is not a condition that human beings have accepted lightly, easily, immediately, or gladly. As far as ordinary experience attests, not to mention the example of countless mystics and existentialist thinkers, the awareness of one's own bodily finitude and of the contingency colouring all beings around us is a source of great anxiety. Regularly, human societies have responded to this anxiety by means of forms of consciousness—Castoriadis' "figures of the thinkable"[500]—that provide consolatory meanings, such as reincarnation, otherworldly bliss, the resurrection of the flesh, divine election, or godly providence. This self-deceiving yet somewhat remedial response has been predominant in human history, and Sigmund Freud discussed it at length in his later works on neuroses and civilisation. Paying homage to the father of psychoanalysis, Castoriadis refers explicitly to Freud's insights on this issue:

Religion is an illusion, in the precise sense Freud defines on this occasion: not only erroneous belief, but belief sustained by a desire, a passionately cathected error. Socially speaking, it constitutes the keystone of the edifice of drive suppression... Psychically speaking, it works essentially through the "humanization of the world", so that... one feels at home (familiar) in strange surroundings... it anthropomorphizes the universe and relies on infantile projections, notably that of the all-powerful paternal imago... it furnishes a semblance of a solution to the most anxiety-ridden enigma of all, mortality. Freud does not, for all that, despair of the possibility of going beyond religion: "Men cannot remain children for ever; they must in the end go out into 'hostile life'."[501]

Along this Freudian line of analysis, the 'grown-up' alternative that Castoriadis endorses and pits against the 'immature' religious option is said to characterise uniquely the ancient Greek civilisation. In it, according to Castoriadis, the gods, though worshipped in countless numbers and forms, had no real salvation to offer to humankind. Even life after death, when acknowledged, was described as possessing little value: "For the Greeks (and, in my opinion, this is one of the reasons why they were able to create what they created), human beings are mortal beings in a very profound sense: there is nothing to expect from another life (if it exists, it is worse than this one)."[502] Castoriadis observes that our inescapable mortality was not underplayed by the ancient Greeks. Quite the opposite, mortality was taken to be humankind's essential feature:

Let us recall that Greek is the only tongue in which "mortal" (thnëtos) means "man." One will find in French or even in Latin some verses in which one says "mortals" in order to say "men": this is a borrowing from the Greek tongue. Elsewhere, men are men, they are the sons of God; in Greek, they are the mortals, and there are, moreover, no

185

other mortals: it will not be said of oxen that they are mortal.[503]

Despite being quintessentially contingent, the ancient Greek human being was shown a path to meaningfulness *within* and *of* life: to do something with it, to become one's own master, to create one's own meanings. Contingency was embraced for what it is and, rather than inducing paralysing fear and trembling, it was called upon so as to spur the human spirit to creative action. The example of the Homeric heroes is, in this sense, most revealing. Achilles preferred a short but glorious life to a long and anonymous one. Ulysses challenged the gods and fate itself by pitting his human wits against their higher decrees. And when the two Homeric heroes met in the abode of Hades, the former advised the latter to cherish his earthly existence, man's sole treasure. Evidently, the "afterlife" on offer was a worthless one.[504] According to Castoriadis, only the ancient Greeks were able to face our basically purposeless life and build an entire culture upon it, *contra* the illusive mystical consolations adopted by the other civilisations:

> *From the humbly human point of view, life would certainly be less absurd if we did not know that it is so. All religions are there to testify to this, to affirm that life is not absurd or, if it is, that there is also another life that, for mysterious (and, in fact, absurd) reasons, would not be, itself, absurd. The Greeks knew this absurdity quite well, and Aeschylus knew it when he has Prometheus say that he instilled in mortals "blind hopes".*[505]

> *Of course, these hopes are blind, since the future is unknown and the gods envious. But these are the two elements that make up man, at least Greek man: knowledge of death and the possibility of a prattein-poiein, a making/doing [faire]-creating this knowledge sharpens instead of stifles. Greece is the most brilliant demonstration of the possibility of transforming this antinomy into a source of creation.*[506]

There is an unequivocally brave, combative, heroic element in Castoriadis' account of the Greek acceptance of mortality "from Homer until the end of Athenian tragedy",[507] which is also the heroic time of the Hellenes in a Vichian sense, i.e. *qua* founding age of their civilisation:

> [T]he classical and preclassical Greek view that was current until the end of the fifth century... did not allow one to console oneself with stories of immortality and false hopes about life after death—[it] does not come here only as a reminder of the ultimate truth but also in order to underscore the deinotës of this being that, knowing all the while its mortality, does not for all that cease to "advance"... to "wear out [the earth for his profit]"... to "make [birds] prisoners"... to "make himself master [of savage beasts]"... and to "teach to himself".[508]

If there is anything worth worshipping, for Castoriadis as well as for many of his ancestors, that is humankind's autopoiesis, namely the specifically human ability to self-create on Earth in the face of radical contingency: "[M]an's self-creation... a mortal who is infinitely less strong than the gods, is more *deinos* than everything natural and more *deinos* than the gods—who are *natural*—because he is supernatural. Alone among all beings, both mortal and immortal, he himself alters himself."[509]

The main sources for Castoriadis' assessment of the ancient Greek interpretation of human mortality are not classical sophists and philosophers, of whom he could be regarded as a descendant. Such a choice of sources would not be possible because, according to Castoriadis, "any eventually positive connotations for the immortality of the soul appear only with the onset of the period of *decadence*, the fourth century B.C.E. and Plato."[510] Castoriadis' intellectual points of reference are located in earlier times and in alternative forms of cultural self-expression, such as the Homeric poems and the Athenian tragedies of Aeschylus and Sophocles:

People generally talk about "Greek tragedy": that's a being that does not exist: There is only Athenian tragedy, and that is no accident. It is only in Athens that there has been this powerful rise of democracy, and tragedy is a democratic institution in all its aspects and especially in its most deep-seated content. It is also and especially democratic on account of the central question it asks: What is human moira, what is human destiny? That question remains closed in all theological societies, where this moira, this destiny, is fixed once and for all by God or by other extrasocial forces. But tragedy interminably deepens this question. First of all, because it places at its center the conviction, central for all Greeks, of man's essential mortality.[511]

The quote above introduces a second fact that, according to Castoriadis, makes the ancient Greek approach to human finitude unique. It is the establishment of a causal relationship between human mortality and the first ever recorded experiments in democratic self-rule or, as Castoriadis dubs it, in genuine human "autonomy", which he defines as follows: "*the possibility of and the capacity for calling the established institutions and significations into question.*"[512]

Autonomy

Though doomed, fragile, and devoid of religious comforts, the ancient Greek human being was given an innovative instrument to lead a meaningful existence: autonomy. That meant that the Greek person, or at least those few male Greeks who were allowed to be educated and politically active in their polity, had the option of creating their own life-path, designing their own aims, and setting their own limits. This innovative instrument was not private and solipsistic, but eminently public. It is true that within the ancient *polis*, its potential beneficiary was each and every individual citizen, onto whom political freedom had been bestowed. However, as Castoriadis' work incessantly rejoinders, such a contingency-aware, self-directing anthropological type could exist exclusively within a collective entity that was capable of establishing the conditions for this type's subsistence in the first place. No contingency-aware and self-directing individual would have been possible amongst the Hellenes without autonomy-conducive social creations such as public assemblies, hoplite drills, or Athenian tragedies:

> *The work of genius is so important in our societies—and already in ancient Greece, with tragedy… because in its own way it calls social existence, and ultimately human existence itself, into question… beyond mere aesthetic pleasure… [it has] a political and educative importance. For, tragedy tells the Athenian demos: You are mortal, and you risk falling into hubris, which will lead to your ruin.*[513]

For Castoriadis, human self-creation is as much individual as it is collective. It is not just citizenship, but the very notion and experience of individuality that require forms of social organisation making them possible, both material and immaterial. Though capable of isolation, no man is an island.

First of all, at a fundamental level, there can be no thinking individual as such without prior socialisation of the human subject. Alone, separated from a community endowed with structures of signification, the subject would remain an infant-like, magmatic, desire-filled psyche. Not only it would be unable to act coherently beyond the level of basic instinctual behaviour, but it would also be devoid of any semiotic tool for inter-subjective communication as much as for self-understanding, which is the fabric of the intelligible world and includes the awareness of one's own mortality:

> *The socialization of the psyche—which implies a sort of forced rupture of the closure of the psychical monad—is not only what adapts the human being to this or that form of society; this is what renders it capable of living at all… That is the true sense of the term sublimation: sublimation is the subjective, psychical side of this process that, seen from the*

social side, is the fabrication of an individual for which there is diurnal logic, "reality", and even acceptance (more or less) of its mortality. Sublimation presupposes, obviously, the social institution, for it signifies that the subject succeeds in cathecting objects that no longer are private imaginary objects but, rather, social objects, the existence of which is conceivable only as social and instituted (language, tools, norms, etc.).[514]

Secondly, the process of socialisation does not entail *per se* the creation of autonomous individuals. The human being may well be a social and political animal since birth, but that does not translate automatically into free societies, democratic polities, or emancipated persons. Freethinking individuals are possible only under particular conditions of socialisation, which favour, say, openness to change, dialogical reason and a deep sense of human limitation over steadfast conservatism, dogmatism and the belief in manifest destinies or elections turning humans into demigods. Historically, most known societies instituted basic "figures of the thinkable" centred upon extra-social sources of authority (e.g. god, nature, objective facts) and related systems of government that were despotic and *de iure* unchallengeable (e.g. monarchies by divine right, aristocratic regimes, fascist dictatorships). Only a few historical societies proved capable of allowing public debates, critical inquiry and emancipatory projects to be conceivable and, to some extent, to be put to the test. The many former societies are tokens of heteronomy; the few latter societies are tokens of autonomy.

As autonomous societies are concerned, it is not possible to conceive of an autonomous individual outside, prior or above a social context that is responsible for the creation of the notion of autonomous individuality and the possibility for its concrete experience. Thinking for oneself, challenging prevailing opinions and institutions, doubting and criticising powerful authorities can be real activities of the individual if and only if they have been instituted socially. Society is primary, as exemplified by the emblematic inter-subjective medium of language, which the individual acquires and utilises creatively to attain self-awareness and express herself. In other words, autonomous individuals can be only the output of autonomous societies, which in turn require such individuals to look after the institutions that serve the cause of autonomy for this to have a chance to continue to be real in people's lives. As Norway's leading Castoriadis scholar Ingerid Straume states: "To Castoriadis, it is 'immediately obvious' that the project of an autonomous society becomes meaningless if it does not at the same time mean to bring forth autonomous individuals, and vice versa".[515]

On the one hand, if autonomous individuals lose sight of the social significations and political or cultural institutions that guarantee autonomy (e.g. political participation, workers' self-management, humanistic education), then they and their heirs are likely to lose their autonomy and become the subjects of something other than themselves (e.g. time-honoured procedures, unstoppable market forces, short-term and narrow-focussed business-directed training). On the other hand, if the existing significations and institutions (e.g. parliaments, enterprises, universities) hide from view the concrete opportunities for self-revision or the full awareness of their own socio-historical contingency (e.g. constitutional redrafting, cooperative ownership, critical thinking), then no genuinely autonomous individual will be fostered by them, but heteronomous ones (e.g. *de facto* subjects, alienated employees, parrot-like orthodox graduates). As Straume crystallises it, autonomy requires:

> *The collective realization that the political community has created, and is capable of changing, its own conditions; the laws to which it binds itself and their normative foundation (i.e. in the final instance, the social imaginary significations). When these insights are commonly accessible – not only in principle, but more importantly, psychologically thinkable as meaningful instituted cultural consciousness – we may say that this society is free or "autonomous".[516]*

There can be no freedom, no self-determination, no self-rule, no democracy or autonomy without actual, enduring awareness and participation of the individual in the creation, maintenance and revision of the social significations and politico-cultural institutions. As contingent as Castoriadis believes our fate and the universe itself to be, he admits of no necessary guarantee for autonomy's long-term persistence, especially if society's autonomous individuals do not fight for the preservation of the institutions that have fostered their anthropological type. After all, Greek democracies were lost to the imperial forces of Macedonia. Medieval communes were perverted into oligarchic regimes or conquered by foreign despots. Today, political parties, trade unions and national parliaments are being taken over by self-serving elites and corporate lobbies, whilst elected governments have been emasculated by the "planetary casino" unleashed by "the absolute freedom to transfer capital".[517]

If autonomy implies that we can act freely, that is to say, according to our own will, without prescribed adherence to sacred traditions or divine edicts, it is equally true that we can make a destructive use of our freedom, e.g. creating a scientific system of extermination camps or denying the preservation of the conditions for the social reproduction of autonomy. To be one's own rulers involves setting both one's aims and one's limits, and the risks and responsibilities that accompany them:

> [T]here is above all the question of human hubris, of the irresistible push of man toward excess and its limitations. Now, the central question of democracy, once extrasocial norms are set aside, is the question of self-limitation, which... is the main theme of Antigone... that is to say, the question of technique and of its necessary limits.[518]

Castoriadis' awareness of the issue of *hubris* (i.e. blinding pride) in human societies echoes the ancient Greeks' original notion of consubstantiality of utter contingency and self-creation, whereby the latter may turn into self-annihilation and reinforce *ipso facto* [by the fact itself] its profound tie to the former. Democracies can and must be able to change even that which is labelled "sacred" or "foundational", whether it is the alleged sanctity of private property or the supreme constitutional principles of a nation. If they can or must not do so, then they are not democracies. As Straume explains:

The opposite of autonomy (democracy) is of course heteronomy, which signifies that the collective does not possess this insight. Heteronomous societies maintain that society's laws are not a product of its own making, but rather spring from some extra-social source, like nature, reason, tradition, gods, a holy scripture or, more relevant today, the "laws" of the market. Here, the term "politics" refers merely to a "state of things"–an incarnated reason, given procedures, etc.–or law-like states which appears senseless or even blasphemous to question, let alone change. Under heteronomy, "politicians" can merely observe and follow the laws, implement, execute, etc.[519]

If genuine democracy requires doing away with the ultimate, allegedly non-human justificatory bedrocks of nature, gods, reason or the iron-laws of economics, which Ricardo claimed to be as unyielding as those of physics, then genuine democracy must be rare indeed. And rare it has been, according to Castoriadis' socio-historical analyses:

Societies in which the possibility of and the capacity for calling the established institutions and significations into question are a tiny exception in the history of humanity. In fact, we have only two examples of such societies: a first example in ancient Greece, with the birth of democracy... and a second example in Western Europe, after the long period of the Middle Ages.[520]

[I]n the interstices of the feudal world, [when] communities that wanted to be self-governed collectivities were reconstituted—new cities or bourgeois communes, in which a

protobourgeoisie (long before any idea or real existence of capitalism!) created the first seeds... of modern democratic and emancipatory movements.[521]

Embracing contingency has been, to many, a terrifying thought. Freedom can be as heavy as chains, if not heavier. That is why divine commands, historical materialism or natural selection by market competition are so alluring to many an intellect. Genuflecting before a superhuman, perhaps cruel, but certain power has been a desirable option for scores of human beings, who prefer believing that they have no alternative: TINA-like slogans are much older than Margaret Thatcher. Yet, the seeds for democracy—autonomy—are still with us. As Castoriadis states: "[T]hey are embodied in the individuals fabricated by these societies—you, me, and others—to the extent that these individuals are still capable—at least one hopes —of standing up and saying, *This law is unjust*, or, *The institution of society must be changed*."[522] According to Castoriadis, there is no large number of such individuals left around, especially in the so-called "affluent" societies of the self-proclaimed "democratic" West. Our political and business leaders may like repeating that we live in free, democratic nations devoted constitutionally to the protection and promotion of freedom, but Castoriadis detects very little genuine autonomy therein:

The test of freedom is becoming untenable to the extent that one happens to do nothing with this freedom. Why do we want freedom? We want it, in the first place, for itself certainly, but also to be able to make and do things. If one has nothing to do, if one can do nothing, if one does not want to do anything, this freedom is transformed into the pure figure of emptiness. Horrified by this void, contemporary man takes refuge in the laborious overfulfillment of "leisure" pursuits, in a more and more repetitive and ever accelerated performance of routine.[523]

Castoriadis claims apathetic, anomic, neurotic and, above all, heteronomous individuals to abound in post-industrial societies, which are characterised by the marketing expert's premeditated consumerist conformism rather than by each person's creative autonomous individuality.

Inanity

If death and mortality can help us to understand the birth of democracy in ancient Greece, so do death and mortality play a role in Castoriadis' denunciation of the absence of genuine autonomy in modern democracies and their astounding display of inanity:

> *People don't want to know that they are mortal, that they are going to die, that there is no afterlife nor any recompense or reward. After the subway and the workday, and so on, they forget while watching Bernard Tapie or Madonna on television. And that signifies that we are living not in a society of the spectacle but in a society of oblivion: forgetting of death, forgetting of the fact that life has no meaning other than the one one is capable of giving to it. The spectacle is there to facilitate and cover over this oblivion.*[524]

As afraid of death as human beings have been throughout history, nearly all societies have attempted to soothe the fears of their members by instituting imaginary sources of absolute stability. As seen in the opening pages of this chapter, Castoriadis connotes religion in a Freudian way, that is to say, *qua* highest example of cathected social signification aimed at letting the human being feel somewhat comfortable with her mortal nature:

> *For every society, the unbridgeable abyss that is the awareness of our own mortality has always been more or less covered over, in one way or another, without its ever being completely hidden from us. This is where religion comes into its own. Religion is a compromise formation in the grand*

sense of the term; it is the compromise formation from which all others derive. Religion has always said: You are going to die, but this death is not a true death.[525]

However, human societies need cast not these imaginary sources of absolute stability in the shape of gods or celestial intelligences. What does not change is the anxiety due to the contingent nature of being. Therefore, the 'immature' response to mortality can be reiterated in secular guises too, as the modern 'society of oblivion' exemplifies.

In the first place, Castoriadis claims that science and its technological manifestations have been employed to replace the gods of old. Contemporary human beings are still being told on countless occasions that a blissful future awaits us, thanks to the infinite wonders of technoscience, which embodies the masterly human ability to grasp rationally the laws of nature and subjugate her to our will. Death itself will be conquered, one day. That is the ideal terminus of humanity's prideful ascent to Mount Olympus. Human reason will triumph over our greatest source of anxiety. Meanwhile, as the white-gowned priests of reason climb the steep slopes of the gods' high quarters on our collective behalf, we can forget about mortality and try to lead as comfortably numb lives as possible, sheltered from death's ominous shadow and the uneasiness that it engenders in our souls. As Castoriadis sarcastically remarks: "If one lives to forget that one is mortal, one can always remain asleep while awaiting the series of medical miracles that will raise life expectancy from 72.1 to 72.3 years."[526] Relentlessly, technoscience has tried to remove mortality from view and convince humankind that we have become omnipotent, thanks to its 'miracles' and 'marvels', while in fact he believes that we are very far from it:

At the same time, the meaninglessness and emptiness of all this is masked by scientistic mystification, which is today more powerful than ever—and this, paradoxically, at a moment when genuine science has become more aporetic than ever as concerns its foundations and the implications of its results. Finally, we find again in this illusion of omnipotence the flight before death as well as its denial: I am perhaps mortal and weak, but there are strength and power somewhere, at the hospital, inside the particle accelerator, within the biotechnology laboratories, and so on.[527]

The myth of progress, which modern technoscience epitomises, is itself a variation on the theme of humanity's quest for immortality— our flight from contingency: "[T]he modern illusion of linearity, of 'progress', of history as cumulation of acquisitions or process of 'rationalization'… the phantasm of immortality (whose aim, as a matter of fact, is to abolish time)… or, in its vulgar form, from a guaranteed form of 'historical progress'."[528] Turned into an unquestionable providential destiny, Castoriadis claims technoscience to have grown incessantly, unfettered by any binding critical reflection upon its ultimate goals as well as upon its actual origins, social as much as psychological. It is believed that the white-gowned priests of reason are better left unhindered in their perilous journey to the top, upon which collective salvation depends. This is no cheap allegory, for the authority of technoscience is accepted like that of holy men and sorcerers:

What survives therefrom is the expansion of consumption of nearly anything and the autonomized expansion of technoscience, which takes the place of the religious beliefs of old. One can ask oneself to what extent, sociologically speaking, contemporary man's superstitious attitude toward technoscience differs essentially from primitive people's attitude toward magic: certainly, there is a difference as to the object, but what about the attitudes and modes of adherence? Does contemporary man know more about what technoscience is affirming, the reasons why technoscience affirms it and he believes in it? Does the mixture of hope and terror with which he regards technoscience have different effects?[529]

According to Castoriadis, technoscience ought to be questioned, for it is based upon mistaken factual assumptions and laden with unacknowledged emotional investments, of which religions used to be the recipient in previous ages. Moreover, the unquestioned growth of technoscience is causing havoc on a planetary scale, including the realistic threat of extinction for the human species as a whole:

> *The world, with its share of the chaotic and the forever unmasterable, will never be separable from the anthroposphere, and man will never master it. How could he master it, when he will forever be incapable of mastering the weft of his acts, from whose succession his own life is woven? This grandiose and empty phantasm of mastery serves as counterpart to the grotesque accumulation of ridiculous gadgets, the two operating in tandem as distraction and diverting entertainment in order to occult our basic mortality, to pervert our inherence in the cosmos, to make us forget that we are the improbable beneficiaries of an improbable and very narrow band of physical conditions that render life possible on an exceptional planet we are in the process of destroying.*[530]

Technoscience is claimed to be the pinnacle of human rationality, but in fact it displays superstitious belief at its highest level: its rationality is bogus. Technoscience promises control over nature and our own collective fate, but it delivers even bigger uncertainty: its mastery is bogus. The term "psuedorational pseudomastery" would describe it aptly.[531] However, Castoriadis reserves it for another imaginary source of absolute stability: capitalism. Capitalism, according to Castoriadis, has cultivated the same dream of ultimate mastery over nature and human destiny as technoscience. Hiding from consciousness and textbooks its long trail of theft, violence, extortion, fraud, cronyism and corrupt mercilessness, it has come to be described as "rational",[532] with strings of alleged experts in economic science glorifying it *qua* "natural", "fated"[533] and manifestly superior to all alternatives "through Darwinian selection".[534] Castoriadis is sceptical about such claims, which he argues to be:

(a) historically unjustified (e.g. capitalism took over the world because of free human agency, not fate); and

(b) scientifically untenable (e.g. there is no test planet to assess the necessity of the events that took place on our own planet).

Furthermore, he denies the alleged "rationality of capitalism" (the title of an essay of his on the subject), of which he detects instead the underlying irrationality:

This situation embodies and expresses all the traits of the contemporary age. The unlimited expansion of pseudomastery is pursued here for its own sake; it is detached from any rational or reasonably discussible end. Whatever can be invented will be invented; whatever can be produced (at a profit) is produced, the corresponding "needs" being stirred up afterward.[535]

[A]s long as people want this pile of junk, which is accumulating in a more and more haphazard way for a growing number of people, and with which they one day may or may not become saturated, the situation will not change.[536]

There is a push for indefinite expansion of an alleged mastery as well as a constellation of affects that curiously accompany it: irresponsibility and a carefree attitude. We have to denounce the hubris in ourselves and around us, to accede to an ethos of self-limitation and prudence, to accept this radical mortality in order to become finally, as much as we can be, free.[537]

On the one hand, Say's Law of endless supply and the scientific crafting of artificial demand uncoupled from any sensible overall goal indicate the profound irrationality of capitalism. Unquestioned growth is the other 'leg' of the fast-marching environmental breakdown that the world is experiencing (e.g. worldwide reduction of arable topsoil; disappearance of pluvial and boreal forests; depletion of the Ozone layer; reduction of oceanic plankton and marine biodiversity)—the first 'leg' being technoscience, as seen in the previous pages. On the other hand, the conspicuous indifference to the environmental losses suffered and the enormous risks taken in the name of profit-making (e.g. extraction, refining, transportation and consumption of fossil oil; construction and operation of nuclear power stations and atomic weapons; meltdown-inducing liberalised trade of capital and currency) are visible tokens of either shockingly short-sighted greed or superstitious overconfidence in our ability to steer planet-wide and ecosystem-specific LSS that we did not create and upon which we depend for our existence.

For Castoriadis, the supposedly rational overcoming of religion by technoscience and economic Darwinism is as irrational as it can be. A psychoanalytic assessment of mortality reveals the deeper absurdity of this overcoming, which is epitomised by the relentless pursuit of growth:

In The Future of an Illusion, *Freud links the roots of religion to the feeling of impotence in the face of a vast world... Now, the ultimate castration, if one wishes to use that term, is understanding that there is no answer to this question, which is the question of death... And that is what is very difficult for the individual patient in analysis, as well as for societies, to accept. A part of the disarray of contemporary society is this attempt, after the downfall of religion (I'm speaking now of the West), to replace this religious mythology with an immanent mythology, that of indefinite progress... The religion of history, whether it be in its Liberal form or its Marxist form. Instead, that is, of seeing that these are mythological constructs that don't rationally hold up. Why the devil must one increase the forces of production indefinitely?*[538]

What is more, Castoriadis believes the replacement of the religious significations of old with technoscience and capitalism to have enjoyed limited success, *pace* the analogies noted above: "Modern societies, which demolish the edifice of religious significations, have in most recent times proved incapable of setting up anything else in their stead."[539] Although he acknowledges the Freudian aetiology that lies behind the secularisation of Western religious creeds into scientism and the capitalist dogma, Castoriadis observes vast hopelessness, if not utter existential despair, in the societies of the late 20th century. Inanity pervades the lives of millions, who cannot find meaningfulness in either traditional religious hope or autonomous self-creation. This is particularly acute in Western societies, where at least the two widespread forms of "religion of history" indicated in the previous quote have caused considerable suffering by delivering no earthly paradise:

> *For the moderns, it's more complicated. For, among them, there has always been some more or less hidden leftovers from belief in a religious type of transcendence. That hasn't kept them from going quite far. But it has also occurred in terms of another shift: an earthly paradise has been posited at the "end of history" (Marxism) or as history's asymptotic direction (Liberalism). We have paid the price today to know that it was a matter of two forms of the same illusion, that there is, as a matter of fact, no "immanent meaning" in history and that there will be only the meaning* [le sens] *(or the non-sense) we will be capable of creating... And today's gloom no doubt also represents, in part, mourning over the death of this illusion of a paradisiacal future.*[540]

Failing in delivering their own streak of mundane heaven, technoscientific and capitalist self-delusions have failed also in removing the fear of mortality to the same extent as crucified sons of god, winged angels from above, or fire-tongued prophets used to do. Neurotically, modern secular self-delusions have merely been able to transpose the fear of mortality onto the objects that are used to distract the human mind from it, whether these objects are the bars of plutonium utilised for energy production or the new brand of perfume that, despite the televised promises, does not make us quite as happy as we had come to expect. Castoriadis claims the well-known psychoanalytic phenomenon of neurotic transposition to be observable already in the life of children, who symbolise egregiously the existential inanity of modern humankind:

> *The child enters an inane world. He is immediately inundated with an incredible flood of toys and gadgets (I am not talking about the projects and gang members, or about the children of millionaires; I am talking about 70 percent of the population); and he is bored shitless, drowned like a dead rat beneath all this junk, as witness the fact that he drops these toys and gadgets at every opportunity to go watch television, abandoning one inanity for another. The entire contemporary world is, in a nutshell, already placed in that situation. What does it all mean, if we go beyond the level of mere description? It is once again, of course, a desperate flight from death and mortality—which, moreover, as one knows, have been banished from contemporary life. Death is not really known; mourning exists neither in public nor as a ritual. It is also this that the present-day accumulation of gadgets and the state of universal distraction aim to mask. Here again, moreover, as we already knew from neurotics, we see that these gadgets and this distraction do nothing more than represent death itself, distilled into tiny droplets and transformed into the small change of daily life. This is death by distraction, death by staring at a screen on which things one does not live and could never live pass by.*[541]

For Castoriadis, as long as we keep refusing to face boldly our fundamentally contingent nature, then the genuine ability to experience freedom in its fullest sense is diminished, if not altogether lost, and therefore our ability to give meaning autonomously to our lives, individual as much as collective. Inane individuals, who keep the grim reaper as far from sight as possible, are unlikely heralds of democracy:

> [T]he test of freedom is indissociable from the test of mortality. ("Guarantees of meaning" are obviously the equivalent of a denial of mortality: here again the example of religions speaks volumes.) A being—an individual or a society—cannot be autonomous if it has not accepted its mortality. A genuine democracy—not a simply procedural "democracy"—a self-reflective and self-instituting society, one that can always put its institutions and its significations back into question, lives precisely in the test of the virtual mortality of all instituted signification... that... demonstrate, for all persons to come, the possibility of creating signification while living on the edge of the Abyss. Now, the ultimate truth of contemporary Western society is evidently to be found in the desperate and bewildered flight before death, the attempt to cover over our mortality. It is coined in a thousand ways: by the suppression of mourning, by "morticians", by the interminable tubes and hoses of the relentless health-care profession, by the training of psychologists specialized in "assisting" the dying, by the relegation of the aged to nursing homes, and so on and so forth.[542]

> [L]earning to live with this deep awareness of our mortality, of the very mortality of our works and of the meaning we have been able to create, is the prerequisite for all genuine democracy, and it is for this reason that democracy is the most difficult and tragic regime of all.[543]

To facilitate a return to Greek heroism and counter the neurotic trends identified in modern societies, Castoriadis suggests a rediscovery of philosophy as a critical tool for self-analysis. Echoing Montaigne and Nietzsche, he argues that a deep reflection upon our finite condition can open pathways for autonomy that we could not see before, as well as remind us of a healthy sense of self-limitation, of which technoscience and capitalism are dangerously devoid:

A rediscovery of philosophy as a whole would be beneficial, for we are going through one of the least philosophical periods, not to say antiphilosophical periods, in the history of humanity. The ancient Greek attitude, however, was not an attitude based on balance and harmony. It starts from the recognition of the invisible limits on our action, of our essential mortality, and of the need for self-limitation.[544]

Castoriadis claims philosophy to be able to help us face the truth of our condition and, at the same time, realise that we can establish meanings that give meaning to our lives, as circular as such a process may sound and is bound to be. The ancient Greeks' example is paramount: "Death is worse than life; there is no hope. That didn't keep the Greeks from creating things, in particular a democracy where it is clear that the law is posited by the people."[545] Philosophy, like ancient Athenian tragedy, can help us to stare contingency in the face and break free from monotonous, unfulfilling divertissements that stifle our autonomy:

We must summon Pascal to our aid here: the modern individual lives in a headlong flight from the knowledge both that he is going to die and that nothing he does, strictly speaking, has the slightest meaning. So he runs, he jogs, he shops in supermarkets, he goes channel surfing, and so on—he distracts himself. Once again, we are not talking about people on the fringes of society but about the typical, the average individual. Is this the sole possible "solution" after the dissolution of religion? I think not. I believe that there are other ends whose emergence society can bring about while recognizing our mortality. I believe that there is another way of seeing the world and human mortality, another way of recognizing our obligation to future generations—who represent the flip side of our debt to past generations, since none among us is what she is except as a function of hundreds of thousands of years of labor and human effort. Such an emergence is possible, but it requires that historical evolution turn in another direction and that society cease its slumber upon a huge pile of gadgets of all sorts.[546]

Horror Vacui

According to Castoriadis, restoring meaning in human life in the face of contingency requires rediscovering creativity, which is expressed in non-alienating work and collective self-direction. As born makers of things, both tangible and intangible, human beings can find fulfilment in forms of authentic agency conveying people's limited yet significant ability to steer their earthly journey:

The task of a free man is to know that he is mortal and to stand up at the edge of this abyss, in this chaos that is devoid of meaning and in which we make signification emerge... I am not even talking about great artists, thinkers, scientists, and so forth. Even the craftsperson worthy of the name who fashions not statues of gods but tables, vases, and so on was absolutely invested in her work; the fact that the vase was beautiful, that the house stood up, was an accomplishment. Such investment in form-giving, therefore meaning-giving, activity has existed in all civilizations, without exception. It exists less and less so today, because the way capitalism has evolved has led to the destruction of all meaning in work. Not everyone can be Ludwig van Beethoven... But everyone has to have a job he might invest in or be involved in.[547]

This philosophical reclaiming of meaningfulness in human life is, for Castoriadis, necessarily anticonsumerist and, to a significant extent, anticapitalist, at least if we understand "capitalism" as the supreme socio-political imperative of ever-increasing money-measured profit:

That [reclaiming] presupposes a radical modification of the notions of labor, contemporary technology, the organization of such labor, and so on—a modification that is incompatible with the maintenance of the contemporary institution of society and of the imaginary it embodies. This huge side of the question—the ecologists themselves don't see it; they see only the consumption and pollution side. But human life also takes place within work. Therefore, we have to give meaning back to the acts of working, producing, creating, and also participating in collective projects with others, engaging in individual and collective self-directing activities, and deciding on social orientations.[548]

Blinded by the quest for ever-growing profit and its mythical reification into a totemic fetish, capitalist societies have been reducing human work to a factor of production and forgotten about its potential as a means of personal and collective self-realisation. Whether in the alienating factories of the Industrial Revolution or in the equally alienating cubicles of the so-called "knowledge economy", most people's working life is characterised by drone-like repetitiveness, non-stimulating hyper-simplification of tasks, global yet minute subdivision of labour, pathological interaction with technologies, as well as performance intensification and unending job insecurity. All this avoidable unpleasantness serves the paramount end of generating money returns to money investors and/or managers, who themselves may be caged within the iron-bars of aptly named "fiduciary duty" to the same totemic fetish. Personal gratification, individual spontaneity, acquiring new skills or perfecting old ones, humane schedules and long-term job security do not inform the occupational settings of most individuals—not to mention the plight of the unemployed. Like trade unions or State regulation, they are deemed to be 'bad for business'; that is, they are believed to make firms less 'competitive', workers 'lazy', production lines 'inefficient', etc. Unprofitable yet humanising significations and institutions are accused of reducing the profit margin and contradicting the inherent, superior (pseudo)rationality of capitalism, which delivers crisis upon crisis in the name of growth, in spite of its alleged (pseudo)mastery over 'optimal allocation' of goods and services, the 'efficient' use of resources, the 'rational' computation of costs and benefits, etc.

Superstitiously incapable of acknowledging the wisdom of alternative conceptions (e.g. socialism, Catholic distributism) and the growing counterevidence to its alleged superior grasp of natural and human laws, capitalism marches on, surrounded by the hagiographer-economist and other sycophants, as well as by a world that gets poorer and poorer in both environmental resources and spiritual ones. As the inane modernity described by Castoriadis exemplifies, it is not only the planet's environment that is being depleted. According to him, the profit-dominated consumerist society promoted by capitalism has been erasing:

> [T]he pre-capitalist series of anthropological types it did not create and could not itself have created: incorruptible judges, honest Weberian-style civil servants, teachers devoted to their vocation, workers with at least a minimum of conscientiousness about their work, and so on. These types did not arise and could not have arisen by themselves; they were created during previous historical periods in relation to values that were considered at the time both sacrosanct and incontestable: honesty, service to the State, the handing down of knowledge, craftsmanship, and so forth. Now, we live in societies where these values have notoriously become a laughing stock; where the amount of money you have pocketed, it matters little how, or the number of times you have appeared on television alone count. The sole anthropological type created by capitalism, the one that was indispensable for its establishment at the outset, was the Schumpeter-style entrepreneur: someone who cares passionately about the creation of this new historical institution that is the business enterprise and who strives constantly to enlarge it through the introduction of new technical complexes and of new methods of market

penetration. Even this type is being destroyed by what is now occurring... [i.e.] managerial bureaucracy... [and] stock-market speculation.[549]

Given its dogmatic characterisation as manifestly better than all the alternatives and its powerful technoscientific armoury, capitalism has been destroying not only the ecological LSS that allow for its own being (e.g. the Earth's hydrologic cycles and its eco-systemic carbon-dioxide-absorption basins), but also the unprofitable cultural and socio-political significations and institutions inherited from pre-capitalist times that have made the anthropological emergence and continuation of capitalist society possible (e.g. humane and decent behaviour, devotion to truth and beauty, genuine entrepreneurship). If only "the amount of money you have pocketed, it matters little how, or the number of times you have appeared on television alone count",[550] then Viking raiders, criminal types, egomaniacs and sociopaths are likely to emerge victorious as leaders and role-models —and they have repeatedly, whether in bankrupt Iceland, Murdoch's and Berlusconi's TV empires, or in the City of London.[551]

What survives of any honest, 'irrationally' non-greedy and conscientious humanity is bound to feel at a loss. Whether envious, disgusted or desperate, such a share of humanity is going to be marginalised, at least until coordinated expressions of autonomy will succeed in "calling the established institutions and significations into question."[552] Also, as long as the dominant social imaginary remains capitalist, Castoriadis' original account can explain why and how contemporary children, men and women may spend their earthly existence training for and/or employed in jobs that may pay enough to purchase the consumer gadgets required not solely:

(a) to hide from view the *horror vacui* awaiting them *post mortem*; but also

(b) to cope with the *horror vacui* of lives that are managed by others for the supreme and manifestly 'rational' goal of increased shareholder value in the face of short-lived 'market miracles' and ecological collapse.

Life's absurdity would appear to have found a new grim face as modern technoscientific capitalism.

Concluding Remarks

A first critical remark to be made in connection with Castoriadis' understanding of human mortality is that it regularly underplays slavery and slave-like conditions in ancient Greece. It is probably true that "the two elements that make up man, at least Greek man" are "*knowledge* of death and the possibility of a *prattein-poiein*".[553] It is equally plausible that "Greece is the most brilliant demonstration of the possibility of transforming this antinomy into a source of creation", as explained in my previous contribution on Castoriadis.[554]   But it is also historically ascertained that this possibility was restricted to a tiny elite of wealthy males. Even if most inhabitants could be exposed to highly educative tragedies,[555] the vast majority of Greece's democracies were and remained slaves, or their legal like as women and young. Public assemblies, military drills and self-mastery were alien to them. Autonomy was alien to them.

This fact is not denied by Castoriadis, who mentions occasionally slavery in the context of ancient Greece,[556] yet mostly *en passant*, e.g. whilst discussing aesthetic judgments,[557] Marx's alienation of the means of production,[558] Freud's psychoanalysis,[559] capitalist ideology,[560] the idea of "absolute freedom",[561] or early Christianity.[562] Almost as frequent are his remarks on slavery in the contexts of the Arab world[563] and of modern forms of subjugation, both liberal-capitalist[564] and communist.[565] Even when addressing it openly in a 1993 work of his ("The Athenian Democracy: False and True Questions"),[566] Castoriadis seems uninterested in, if not even annoyed by, the "said and resaid" issue of slavery and the inferior condition of Hellenic women—no mention is made of the youth—in ancient Greek democracies.[567]   Rather, Castoriadis wishes to highlight the uniqueness of those early democracies, for they were, unlike slavery, a genuinely novel Greek invention. Moreover, the Greek ancient experiments in autonomous self-government proved to be the germinal elements of all ensuing emancipatory projects, whether successful in positing "direct democracy" or tamed into milder "representation".[568] In brief, whereas slaves and subjugated individuals were the norm in antiquity, democratic experiments were not.

Although one may sympathise with Castoriadis and his choice of emphasis, the abject condition of the largest part of ancient populations, even inside notable early tokens of autonomous self-direction, is hardly a small matter. Underplaying it has proven resilient in the received tradition of historical representation, which Castoriadis' own work reinforces overall. By doing so, he fails in "the possibility of and the capacity for calling the established institutions and significations into question",[569] since he follows the well-established glorification of ancient Greece as the cradle of democracy, whilst side-lining the life-reducing ordinariness of slavery and heteronomy inside it.

A second critical remark that I wish to make regards Castoriadis' insistence on the impossibility of "extrasocial" sources of authority and norms. This is a theme addressed especially *in Figures of the Thinkable* and in the third part of *The Rising Tide of Insignificancy*.[570] What Castoriadis had in mind when dealing with this notion are historical examples of justification of the *status quo*, or even of revolutionary programmes, by means of reference or appeal to superhuman forces, such as God, Reason, destiny, metaphysical or scientific Truth, and honoured tradition. Castoriadis rejected such a type of justification as untenable, for he claimed that there can be no other ultimate justificatory ground but society. For him, although this kind of references or appeals to non-human grounds could be psychologically understandable, for they soothe deep-seated fears of the human soul, they were logically flawed, since they posited as first causes of society society's effects. Also, Castoriadis opposed this sort of justification to true democracy, which originates as well within society and yet is fully aware of its contingent social origin, hence remaining capable of self-revision through time. Indeed, Castoriadis "hope[d]" that nobody "in the democratic tradition today seek extrasocial causes for their collective predicaments".[571]

His hope notwithstanding, is not the ecological system, as Hildegard of Bingen (the 'Sybil of the Rhine') comprehended long ago, precisely an extra-social normative system?[572] A life-value onto-axiology recognises this possibility by definition, for it locates human societies within the context of those natural LSS, the persistent abuse and destruction of which endanger the very existence of human societies and, *a fortiori*, the possibility of human autonomy as such. Castoriadis was by no means insensitive to the life-threatening destruction of the Earth's environment, as visible especially in the 1993 interview "The Revolutionary Force of Ecology".[573] He believed that humankind should treat the planet's ecosphere like "a gardener with an English garden".[574] He was even critical of Marx's oversight of this issue, which many 19th-century authors, not least Victor Hugo, had already been able to perceive in the face of modern industrialisation and urbanisation.[575] Besides, Castoriadis did state that "[a]utonomy—true freedom—is the self-limitation necessary not only in the rules of intrasocial conduct but also in the rules we adopt in our conduct toward the environment".[576] Nevertheless, Castoriadis did not conjoin together the predicate "extrasocial" and the notion of ecology, whose demands have been long recognised by human societies, as demonstrated by their civil commons for the sake of short-, medium- and long-term survival.[577]

Being symbolic and social animals does not make us less animal.[578] That ecological demands may have to be conceptualised and responded to *via* social institutions such as language and laws does not diminish their being extra-social. We humans may have been interpreting and understanding these demands through our socially created "figures of the thinkable", but we did not posit them ontologically. Contrary to what Castoriadis asserted, there are such things as "natural needs",[579] even if their precise determination may be difficult.[580] For example, their precise determination can be obfuscated by artificial needs, i.e. wants, created by interested social parties, e.g. the corporate concerns of consumerist societies. Still, discriminating between real needs and actual wants remains possible; in truth, it is necessary. Whether we like it or not, we must keep responding to the former in order to be able to live. If we fail in doing so, eventually, we die. Castoriadis was probably correct in arguing that technoscientific capitalist modernity is more and more likely to attain our demise as a species, despite its claims of superior knowledge and power over nature. What it offers regularly to contemporary humankind is, in fact, an illusory "psuedorational pseudomastery".[581] However, radical social contingency is equally illusory, for all societies stand upon the life ground.

A third critical remark concerns Castoriadis' treatment of religion. According to him, "religion has always said: *You* are going to die, but this death is not a true death", thereby postulating an otherworldly or equivalent dimension of being in which each mortal has a chance to continue to live: "the return of the ancestor in the child of the next generation, ancestor worship, the immortality of the soul, and so on".[582] In his recollections and analyses of the world's many religious traditions, Castoriadis seemed either unaware of, or unable to distinguish between, alternative forms of proposed overcoming of individual mortality. In particular, he did not seem capable of acknowledging the full spectrum of implications arising from the person's identification with the larger community of living beings that precedes, accompanies and follows each person's existence. This type of identification does not involve necessarily any otherworldliness, but rather relies upon the person's consciousness of her being part of the larger whole of earthly life, whether biological, emotional or conceptual.

Steeped as he was in classical and pre-classical Greek culture, and despite his profound insight into the social character of human existence, Castoriadis presupposed throughout his work the pre-eminence of each person's self-perception as a separate individual and the existential drama that this self-perception implies. Both presuppositions are exemplified and expressed in Castoriadis' recurrent reference to Homer's account of Achilles' profound sadness in continuing to be after his death, yet in the perpetual darkness of Hades: "I would prefer to be the slave of a poor peasant on earth than be king of all the shades".[583] Possibly, Castoriadis could not conceive of anything meaningful that surpasses the atomic notion of individual and society. This limitation of his own imaginary is manifested also in the following passage, which I have already quoted in my previous contribution: "*A being*—an individual or a society—cannot be autonomous if it has not accepted its mortality. A genuine democracy—not a simply procedural 'democracy'—a self-reflective and self-instituting society, one that can always put its institutions and its significations back into question, lives precisely in the test of the virtual mortality of all instituted signification… that… demonstrate, for all persons to come, the possibility of creating signification while living on the edge of the Abyss".[584] Autonomy is perhaps the only bliss that can be gained from the awareness of the utter contingency of each. Yet to say, as Castoriadis did, that "nothing [the person] does, strictly speaking, has the slightest meaning" is in this light the old snivelling of the existentialist ego, which cannot find adequate significance in one's ability to enmesh with and assist in the countless lives that we encounter on our mortal path.[585] However, each mortal being may be much more than itself alone, if it is one with the greater field of living being which it instantiates temporarily and partly.

Such an alternative outlook is likely to sound hopelessly mystical to many positivist ears—and mysticism was never Castoriadis' *forte*, for he dismissed it in his works as fundamentally irrational and quite simply irrelevant to his concerns.[586] Nevertheless, this kind of mysticism is one of the options that, for instance, the Taoist tradition, *War and Peace* author Lev Tolstoy and his follower 'Mahatma' Gandhi,[587] and today's life-value onto-axiology have considered in order to make sense of life *and* death as an ongoing, intertwined network of vital hence valuable experiences. Castoriadis was correct in suggesting that restoring meaning in human life in the face of contingency requires rediscovering creativity, which is expressed *inter alia* in non-alienating work and collective self-direction. However, Castoriadis neglected the possibility that a meaningful universal life good could transcend the atomic individual and society, whose contribution to the continuation of this good may render one with all life across generational time. This

213

comprehension, which eludes Castoriadis, is what the life-value onto-axiology stands for.

Chapter 11
Religion's *Gestalt*. Reflections on Michael Polanyi, Tacit Knowing and Mortality

When learning how to tie our shoelaces, we are not given a book to read or even told precisely what to do. At some point, someone shows us how to do it and utters onto us: "*do like this*". And what do we know of our own conscious bodily actions when swimming or cycling? As we perform these activities, we are striving. We are acting intentionally. We may be mimicking our old teacher, for instance, whether she was a sibling or a parent. But which muscles are we moving? In what order? And exercising how much pressure? How much air are we keeping in our lungs to stay afloat? How much are we concentrating mentally during the efforts that we consciously and intentionally perform? What do we pay most attention to? In which order? And to what degree? We simply cannot tell. Yet it is not ignorance. We do know how to swim, how to ride a bicycle— and we know that we know it. We *can* swim, cycle and tie our shoelaces, to the point of being able to teach it to our own children. Very few, however, can explain clearly how we can, i.e. explicitly, exactly, objectively. A gap endures between what our embodied thought can produce, i.e. a skilful performance, and the abstract language in which we wish to cast such a thought. This gap is what justifies the distinction between tacit and explicit knowledge, for which Michael Polanyi (1891–1976) has gained fame in the humanities and the social sciences. In what follows, Polanyi's distinction is elucidated and relevant implications *vis-à-vis* religion and mortality explored. Thus, in the present chapter, I offer some reflections on Polanyi's philosophy, not a critical appraisal of it or of the ample secondary literature it has been generating since the 1940s and 50s.

When reading as commonplace a written text such as a letter, we perform a "whole series of consecutive integrations simultaneously".[588] To begin with, we combine together sounds into words (tacit phonetics), words into sentences (tacit syntax) and sentences into prose (tacit stylistics). Moreover, and at the same time, we understand the sights and events therein described, we structure a verbal composition of what is understood, and we interpret the overall meaning of the composition. All these integrations are "tacit efforts" that allow us to make sense of the letter, the meaning of which we attend *to* by attending *from* the plethora of details that we integrate tacitly (more on this point in the pages to follow).[589] It is not the case that we are not aware of them. If we were genuinely unaware of them, then we could not operate upon them and grasp the meaning of the letter. Rather, we are aware of them in a secondary, instrumental manner, whilst we focus primarily upon their meaning (again, more on this point in the pages to follow).

Typically, especially if we are good at anything, we just do what we do, without much articulate thinking. We think fast, heuristically; not slowly, logically.[590] As a result, we may not even know how to explain clearly that which we can do very well. We can say we learned it. We may be able to show it, repeatedly and often flawlessly. Yet we may be at a loss for adequate words that can make it *explicit* to any satisfactory degree. It is a matter of know-how or *können*, rather than know-that or *wissen*—or *að kunna* rather than *að vita*, as the distinction goes in Icelandic. It is a knowledge that harkens back to pre-linguistic animal faculties of ours, which also explains why it is so difficult to elucidate it in articulate, objective, explicit terms. At best, we may produce convenient abstract formulations to refer to them, such as those of Piaget's genetic psychology, which Polanyi studied in his lifetime and referred to in his works.[591] Still, abstract lexical distinctions, though invariably popular among scholars and scientists, do not solve the problem. They exemplify it further. For my knowing that "know-how" means know-how means that I know how to make sense of the graphic signs that we call "graphemes", "letters", "words", etc., as well as of their mutual relations on the written page. *Mutatis mutandis*, the same holds for the spoken word, its "phonemes", "tones", etc.: "[T]he use of language is [itself] a *performance*".[592] Again, a gap endures between what our embodied thought can produce and the abstract language in which we may try to cast it. This thought and the language trying to express it are not one and the same thing, nor are they entirely equivalent. The former contains and constitutes implicit or tacit knowledge, the latter explicit knowledge; and only part of our implicit or tacit knowledge can be made explicit.

Consider, as a thought experiment, the ice-cream cake or *semifreddo* made by the present author's mother, which she prepares without consulting any cookbook or using any scale, but rather out of feelings of *quel che ci vuole* ["what is right"] and *quanto basta* ["what is enough"; *q.b.* in older cookbooks]. *Prima facie*, its preparation can be translated into a set of explicit instructions. Any contemporary cookbook is but a long series of such explicit instructions concerning types and quantities of ingredients, preparation methods and serving options. Tacit knowledge, in this case, has been made explicit—or at least some of it. Part of my mother's tacit knowledge, in fact, *cannot* be made explicit.

Firstly, let us say, thus continuing the experiment, that my mother makes the best *semifreddo* on Earth. Why is that? How is it that she makes a better cake than any other chef, cook, or experienced Italian housewife? The instructions are exactly the same for all of them. The equipment in her kitchen might be even deficient or out-of-date, in comparison. Why is she such a star, then? Why is her *semifreddo* so good? Is there no instruction on how to be the best that all could follow? No, there is not. Genius cannot be prescribed. There is no recipe that can turn any chosen person into the next Newton or a novel Mozart. Or ask Messi or Maradona how exactly they kick the ball to make the most astounding passes, so that any other player can do it too. They will not tell you. Not because it is a secret, but because they cannot tell you. They possess that knowledge, and we certainly know that they have it, for we can see it—not to mention the spectators paying good money precisely in order to see it. Nevertheless, they cannot articulate it in an explicit fashion. They can show it; but even then no other player can do the same as they do. Such a knowledge is beyond everyone else's grasp: it is "ineffable".[593]

Secondly, over her long life, my mother has been able to communicate quite aptly with a number of fellow Italian housewives, who are generally proficient in making cakes, if not in cooking in general. Discussing together culinary matters, they have been able to understand each other, as shown by the improvements that they have regularly introduced to a number of desserts and other dishes, even when nobody else around seemed to grasp quite fully what exactly they said. Over countless years, they have used a jargon, a slang, and seemingly odd terms or, from another angle, an *expert* language, exemplified by vague maxims such as "getting it just right", "soft but not too soft", "frothy but not too much", etc. As odd as these phrases may sound to most, these Italian housewives know well what they mean—the proof being truly in the puddings that get eaten. Also, they know which options to take seriously, i.e. which are plausible—and plausibility, like genius, cannot be prescribed either. These Italian housewives know what their odd terms mean, because they share similar experiences and a sense of what is to be done. They share an epistemic tradition, part of which is tacit, inasmuch as it cannot be rendered into clear and explicit terms for the non-initiated, whilst even the initiated make use of it while being aware of its inherent vagueness. Nonetheless, over countless years, these Italian housewives have spoken *like*, if not *as*, experts within an expert community, which exists precisely because there is non-transparent knowledge to be exchanged effectively only by people who have been trained inside and by it and who can therefore understand effectively what external observers would deem vague, too complex, perhaps equivocal, if not even mistaken.[594]

Thirdly, even if we translate my mother's *semifreddo* into the above-mentioned sets of instructions, one must still prove capable of understanding and carrying out the instructions. Comprehension of the rules and skilful execution may be facilitated, trained and evaluated, but they cannot be prescribed. Some persons succeed, while others fail. Again, tacit knowing of how to make effective sense of explicit knowledge is required throughout: "language [itself] is nothing unless it has conscious meaning".[595] That is why Polanyi claims that "*all knowledge… is either tacit or rooted in tacit knowledge*".[596] Even when expressing and/or grasping the most explicit forms of knowledge (e.g. formal logic, mathematics), we engage in a variety of familiar skilful performances which, however, we cannot entirely fathom (e.g. focusing our thought). As a matter of fact, most such tacit abilities have been trained and developed tacitly too, as when an infant acquires the mental, emotional and physical habits required to be interested in, look at, see and entertain mentally the objects around her as objects, or to speak her own mother tongue. If there were no capable persons around, who kept performing these actions and *ipso facto* teaching them to other persons (e.g. children, students, apprentices), whether by sheer proximity or by intended display, no knowledge would be possible, whether explicit or tacit, and entire cultures would collapse. No person, no knowledge; no knowledge, no culture. Hence is all knowledge *personal knowledge* —Polanyi's key-point, and the title of his most famous book.

To reiterate succinctly the three considerations at issue, there exists first of all the "ineffable domain", where "articulation is virtually impossible".[597] The reader can think of the sad, commonplace circumstance in which she may try to convey in writing her truly heartfelt condolences to a dear person, who knows very well that the written words she receives do not actually express all the grief engulfing both hearts—a grief that could actually be communicated more effectively by a silent hug. Then, Polanyi discusses the "domain of sophistication", i.e. the "area" where "the tacit and the formal fall apart", because: (A) "articulation encumbers the tacit work of thought" (e.g. children learning to speak, as studied by Piaget); or (B) symbolic systems produce peculiar results, upon which we must then exercise our tacit judgment (e.g. "new kinds of numbers" to be accepted or rejected).[598] Finally, even when dealing with the most explicit forms of knowledge available to us, the tacit component cannot be annihilated *in toto*, for one or more thinking bodily creatures will be called upon to exercise their faculties in order to engage with such forms of knowledge, hence succeeding or failing to a great variety of degree in their exercise, which can be trained, coached, guided, honed and supervised, but which remains a specific *person*'s skilful performance, i.e. one that cannot be prescribed and taken for granted in its entirety.

Polanyi's key-point is true of mathematics as much as of baking and confectionery. As far as we know, humans alone have minds capable of reading and understanding a cookbook, and bodies that can be used purposively to read and understand it (e.g. moving our eyes, turning the pages with our hand) in order to make a *semifreddo* out of it. There would be no *semifreddo* without a specific person that: (I) performs an integration of the instructions and the countless additional relevant pieces of information required in any given, historically unique context, most of which are not specified or specifiable (e.g. recognising the ingredients, assessing whether they are still good, determining whether they have been blended adequately); and (II) acts upon them with the specific purpose of producing a *semifreddo* (were we even to build a machine for making it, (I) and (II) would still apply to its engineers). It does not matter that the cookbook may be so detailed and so comprehensive as to tell the reader how to mix the ingredients down to the molecular level, *via* the most precise physico-chemical formulations. Someone would still have to commit herself, read and make sense of such a cumbersome cookbook in order to prepare the cake: "*numbers do not of themselves point to events*".[599]

Before turning to physical chemistry, Polanyi had studied medicine and served as a physician in the Austro-Hungarian Army during world War I. From these experiences, he developed a keen appreciation for the personal, inexact and indefinable aspects of knowledge, and "the *art* of knowing" that is incumbent upon us in order to pursue any rigorous scientific or intellectual investigation.[600] Medical diagnoses are particularly revealing, according to him, since: (A) "We cannot identify, let alone describe, a great number of the particulars which we are in fact noticing when we diagnose a case of the disease".[601] Also, (B) "[t]hough we can identify a case of the disease by its typical appearance, we cannot describe it adequately" because: (B1) "[w]e are ignorant of the unspecifiable particulars which would enter into the description" (cf. (A)); and (B2) "[t]he relation between the particulars—even if they could all be identified—could be described only in vague terms which the expert alone would understand".[602] Finally, (C1) "[o]ur identification of a disease in any one instance comprehends unspecifiably as its particulars the whole range of cases which, in spite of their differences, we have identified in the past"; and (C2) "[i]t relies on this comprehension for the future identification of an unlimited number of further cases which might differ from those known before in an infinite variety of unexpected ways".[603]

The same considerations apply to universals, concepts, classes and species. Connotation is always and inevitably partial; therefore, denotation is an art, whereby that which is inherently unique and different, such as an identifiable individual entity, is treated nonetheless as a token of another type of being, such as an idea, a kind of rocks or an animal species. No two lions are identical in any and every aspect, yet we acknowledge their being tokens of *Panthera leo* (and were a software for pattern-recognition devised, then living programmers would still have to judge its efficiency). A machine may emulate the activities of human beings, or "imitate" a human being, as Turing would say. Polanyi often refers to the work of his friend Alan Turing, whom he admired but "dissent[ed]" from.[604] Turing equated a computing machine's ability to "deceive us" into thinking of it as a thinking mind, and an actual thinking mind.[605] Thinking and understanding are no mere "experimental question", however, for successful deceit is not the genuine artefact.[606] It is still and only an imitation; not the real process. Machines know no meaning; they do not possess and do not exhibit understanding, though they may look like they do to the point of deceiving us. Machines are made, operated upon, and made to operate. In their case, Polanyi believes that meaning is situated in the persons that build, program and use the machines. There lie the actual imaginative, creative and responsible acts; those of the living *persons* involved.

In *Personal Knowledge*, Polanyi tackles crystallography and taxonomies in biology, precisely to exemplify and explain the apparent yet ordinary mystery of denotation. Still, in his view, medicine provides the most vivid and immediate examples. Inarticulable imprecision abounds in clinical practice, where "understanding" is also a matter of "mastering" ways of "grasping" physically bodily parts and sensing what may be at hand.[607] It is manifest that the identification of all relevant particulars in actual diagnoses is a factual impossibility, as shown by later discoveries, which cast light on particulars that had not been listed explicitly before in any medical record, textbook or memoir. Many such particulars had been noticed by physicians when realising that the patient suffered from a certain disease rather than another, but only some could be recalled later and fully accounted for. Furthermore, even when dealing with particulars that can be stated explicitly, there are components that cannot be made explicit, or that can only be addressed in vague terms, such as the muscular shifts required in using diagnostic tools, e.g. probes, sticks, microscopes, etc. (similar considerations apply to muscular shifts of the inquirer's ocular bulbs for the sake of seeing, or of her arms, hands and fingers for the sake of touching, palpating, pressing, manipulating, probing, etc.). In addition, the particulars change quality when isolated from the clinical context in which they were retrieved and focused upon. Skin colour depends on the surrounding environment (from the bodily parts in the background to the lights in a room). The dynamic character of complex movements in, say, pulmonary percussion or renal palpation is lost when single components thereof are concentrated upon. Words that were transparent when attended *from* become mysterious when attended *to*, as attested by the equally apparent yet ordinary mystery of language studied in semiotics, linguistics, etc. The subsidiary cannot be grasped focally *qua* subsidiary: "We cannot look *at* them [our glasses] since we are looking *with* them".[608] Finally, little can be said explicitly of the interrelations between particulars, e.g. whilst we can describe fairly accurately the main bodily organs, it is far more difficult to offer as accurate a description of the tissues between them.

In the sciences, and most notably in medicine, there abounds practical teaching, so that young students may acquire the practical abilities required to diagnose, such as pulmonary percussions or auscultations, and develop a 'feel' or 'sense' for the matter at hand. It is called "elbow knowledge" in contemporary common parlance. It is the sort of ability that scientists themselves acquire by interacting with their mentors in laboratories and that they keep cultivating later on through interpersonal exchanges, typically in a tacit fashion. Ask a senior diagnostician why she thinks that a certain medical sample points to a certain type of cancer, even if the symptoms could justify a dozen alternative possible conclusions, and she will not be able to tell you, but merely fall back on her professional experience and an 'instinct' or 'insight' or 'gut feeling'. They know it, but they cannot tell you how or why they produced their snap judgments, which in general are statistically less fallible than articulate reasoning.[609] Easy cases rely too upon a plethora of tacit integrations that any specialist would have trouble describing, such as the ability to ascertain the likely mood of a patient by attending from facial and vocal expressions to their psychological meaning, or all the concomitant bodily activities performed to grasp the words of the patient.[610] Any act of recognition, from the daily task of "recognising faces" to "identify[ing] cases of diseases and specimens" in the sciences as well as offering "ostensive definitions", is a personal performance.[611] As such, any act of recognition can fail or succeed, for it relies on the person's tacit bodily competences, as well as on her tacit mental abilities, beliefs, commitments and passions, which the person herself would have difficulty articulating. Thus, in the sciences too, the celebrated realm of rationality i.e. of explicit *ergo* objective knowledge, we actually rely daily on many a case of *je ne sais quoi* —this being one of the many French expressions describing awareness of the non-articulable features of human knowledge (others being, e.g., Blaise Pascal's *esprit de finesse* and *coeur*).[612]

If we do not preserve the awareness of this "art of knowing", many unmeasurable and possibly vague yet important dimensions of experience are at risk of being left out of the picture in the accounts and interpretations of science. For example, Henry laments that, in today's medicine, "patients' values, preferences, and beliefs" and "the significant tacit influence that industry funding exerts on research" are left out of medical studies.[613] Specialists prefer taking an "epidemiologic turn" instead, i.e. they concentrate upon "quantitative data", which are easier to gather and less controversial to debate.[614] Rather than admitting and dealing with possibly thorny and largely unquantifiable phenomena, reality is described as though such phenomena did not exist at all. It may not be blatant intellectual dishonesty, but it is certainly complacent, wilful blindness. And yet, some doctors are still better than others—morally too. Just like in theatre, ballet or sport, there are better and worse performers. Some persons are better than others in grasping tacitly what is tacitly transmitted and tacitly required for performance. Despite long lists of symptoms, vast databases and massive textbooks, which all medical students can read, the best diagnosticians may be at a loss when trying to tell you why they think that they have encountered a certain disease, when the available symptoms that can be made explicit and compared with accumulated explicit knowledge point in several different directions, or even in one that the expert, however, feels not to be correct. According to Polanyi, this happens because we grasp tacitly so many subsidiary elements and interrelations thereof that we ourselves may not be able to cast them into focal objects. With luck we, if not someone else, will do it, but even then only partially, on a future occasion: "We must accredit... our competence for comprehending unspecifiable entities, which will yet reveal themselves in the future in an unlimited number of unexpected ways... if all knowledge is fundamentally tacit".[615]

As some degree of abstract explicitness can be achieved *vis-à-vis* all human knowledge, for even the ineffable can be labelled "ineffable", so does a "personal coefficient" enter into all of it too.[616] Rejecting the positivist ideal of total objectivity, whilst trying to avoid relativist subjectivism, Polanyi writes: "*Nomothetic* and *idiographic*... [are] parts of *all* knowledge".[617] Knowledge is Janus-faced. On the one hand, it gazes upon abstract formulae encapsulating the laws of the universe itself. On the other hand, it requires a person's bodily and mental faculties, her willingness, her intellectual passions, and her responsible commitment. Un-understood, un-pursued and un-engaged, even the most profound, comprehensive and astounding abstract formula of the hardest science is no knowledge. On the one hand, we have reality, which Polanyi ardently believed we could come to know, *pace* critical doubt erected to modern methodological dogma. As the subtitle of Polanyi's *Personal Knowledge* reveals, he aspired to a "post-critical philosophy". On the other hand, there is the knower, whose belief in the existence of an external world, understanding of it, and curiosity for its biological, ethical or other aspects, are an essential part of the knowing process. We may pursue and obtain the highest peaks of explicitness, exactitude and objectivity, we may standardise hermeneutical criteria, but persons can never be scored off the picture in the name of abstract rationality: "deprived of their tacit [personal] coefficients, all spoken words, all formulae, all maps and graphs, are strictly meaningless... The ideal of a strictly explicit knowledge is... self-contradictory".[618]

When dealing with tacit knowledge, we are not talking only or even primarily of "unconscious" or "subconscious" information, though this may well exist and be part of our tacit knowledge.[619] Polanyi admitted that there could be subliminal information, which lies beneath our consciousness of it. Referring to the psychological studies conducted by Lazarus and McCleary, he writes of "subception" as well as of "learning" and "discovering without awareness" ("discovery [being] but learning from nature").[620] Yet Polanyi did not want tacit knowledge to be reduced to this particular sphere alone, which attracted much attention during most of the 20th century, especially but by no means solely in connection with psychoanalysis (though no typical behaviourists, both Lazarus and McCleary were experimental psychologists, unaffiliated with psychoanalysis). Rather, Polanyi emphasised that we are typically conscious or aware of information in two ways:

- as the *focus* of our attention; or
- as the *subsidiary* details that allow us to focus.

Consider a painting, for example.[621] Here you find a representation of the dramatic rendition of Jesus of Nazareth to the Sanhedrin in Jerusalem. It is entitled *Christ before Caiaphas* (ca. 1570).

It is one of the many masterpieces painted by the Genoese artist Luca Cambiaso, who painted at least two known copies of it (the one shown here is kept at the University of Glasgow's Hunterian Art Gallery, Scotland). What we are likely to perceive in it is a nocturnal scene from the *New Testament*, if we are familiar with Christian literature. If we are not familiar with it, depending on our eyesight and acculturation, we are very likely to see at least a group of people in a candle-lit room. If we look more closely, we may actually see the candles, as well as the people's faces, hats, a desk, weapons, armours, and a sandal. We see meaningful wholes. We see molar entities that make sense to us. They are the focus of our attention. What makes it possible for us to see those molar entities, though? Indeed, how is it that we can see a painting at all?

According to Polanyi, we can see a painting by way of multiple tacit integrations. On a first level, we integrate (i) the subsidiary details within the painting: brushstrokes; patches of light and dark pigment; lines of demarcation; etc. There are then (ii) the subsidiary details around the painting: the surface onto which it is projected; the light in a room; the wall behind the painting; etc. They too are integrated tacitly by the person observing the painting. Also, there are (iii) subsidiary details within each of us: our eyesight; our knowledge, or lack thereof, of Christian literature; our knowledge, or lack thereof, of mannerist and early baroque art; etc. They too are integrated tacitly in order to let us perceive what we perceive. All these details, i.e. (i)–(iii), are present to us, that is, we are aware of them, as we focus on the painting and see it *as* the painting before us. If we were not aware of them, we would not see that particular painting. Yet, the kind or degree of awareness differs. We pay attention *from* the subsidiary details *to* the painting, its meaning, and, if we shift our attention to a lower intermediate level, its meaningful molar elements. We can shift our focal attention further down, onto the subsidiary details too. We can focus on the brushstrokes, for instance, or on the threshold between dark and light areas, or on the contours of the characters, or on individual shades of colour. It is not that we were not aware of them before. Again, had we been not, then we would have not seen the painting. Rather, we are no longer aware of them in a subsidiary fashion. Thus, as we focus upon such details, the picture of Christ before the High Priest fades into the background and becomes one of the many subsidiary details allowing us to perceive the new focal objects. As *Gestalt* psychologists describe it, there has been a switch between *figure* (our focal object) and *ground* (our subsidiary details). Yet, as *Gestalt* psychologists would also warn us, "the whole is more than the sum of its parts"; or, as Polanyi writes: "While the features of a face have their meaning in a mood, the mood itself is even fuller of meaning than the features are... And again, while the meaning of a string of words lies in the sentence they form, the sentence is even more meaningful than the words which form it."[622]

Details form a greater whole, which, albeit necessitating them, cannot be reduced to them either. Specifically, subsidiary details have four main roles to play in tacit integrations: (1) *functional*–they provide "directedness" from one level of consciousness to another; (2) *phenomenal*–"we have a real coherent entity before us" thanks to the details;[623] (3) *semantic*–"details" or "clues" point to a higher whole, which is their meaning; and (4) *ontological*–"its result is an aspect of reality which, as   such may yet reveal its truth in an inexhaustible range of unknown and perhaps still unthinkable ways".[624] Once in focus, i.e. once made explicit, the subsidiary details are also no longer what they were before. They have lost some qualities and gained others. In the painting, for example, focusing upon the individual brushstrokes makes the viewer lose sight of their coherent meaning, i.e. they are no longer, say, a face or a body, but a patch of colour with a certain texture, direction and distribution. They become the prime object of study of the restoration specialist, not of the art critic or, for that matter, of the art lover or the curious tourist at the art gallery or national museum. In explicit terms, subsidiary details are no longer subsidiary details, but focal objects. They are no longer functional to identifying a coherent whole; they are no longer the elements of which we grasp the combined meaning. Once in focus, they become something else; hence does the gap between embodied thought and its explicit linguistic rendition endure.

Think again of swimming, cycling, or tying our shoelaces. We may provide a comprehensive list of the laws of physics required for them all. Still, were we to provide this list to a person that is trying to learn how to perform such activities, all this explicit information would be utterly pointless. Similarly, were we to produce all the possible physical and chemical analyses of a watch, we would still be unable to tell the time. We would have plenty of information, but all quite pointless. It is not pointless information *per se*. It is pointless *per* the aim that is being pursued.

Different aims produce, indeed require, different descriptions, different modes of experience, different lexicons, different disciplines or cultural frameworks—different forms or *Gestalten*. Dancers and sportspersons may focus upon and exercise specific muscles during training sessions, but they would not do it while dancing or playing a football match, for doing it would disrupt their performance. As the aforementioned examples of swimming, cycling and tying shoelaces are concerned, what the person needs is not a book or a list with explicit knowledge, but coaching, training, a form of "apprenticeship", as Polanyi would dub it, which can occur only inter-personally and, most importantly, tacitly, i.e. by mimicking and copying a mentor, partly without realising that we are doing it, for we are not focussing on the subsidiary details, such as each movement that we perform, but the end-results of the movements.[625] Think of language itself. Were we to teach a young child, or try to teach a child, all the phonetics, phonology, morphology, syntax, semantics, pragmatics, stylistics and semiotics involved in speaking her own mother tongue, would the child make any sense of them? No, she would not. All this information, all these rules, which are contained tacitly in any spoken language as tacit subsidiary elements, are transmitted tacitly in ordinary guardian- or parent-child interaction in the early years of a person's life. It is only after much schooling that some speakers will be able to describe accurately part of the information and of the rules contained within her own mother tongue.

As to the chemical or physical properties of specific muscles, they may be relevant if and only if a functional, medical problem occurs. Until then, dancers, footballers and speaking persons would happily make use of their muscular services without any concern for an explicit, objective, scientific account of them. Lower ontological levels are a precondition for the existence of higher ones that, *pace* reductionism, possess qualities that cannot be reduced to, and explained away with, the categories pertaining to the lower ones. Ontologically, chemistry requires physics, biology both, medicine all three. Though emerging thence, none can be reduced *in toto* to the lower ones: isomerism cannot be reduced to nuclei and electrons, and even less to quanta; growth and reproduction cannot be grasped in mere physical or chemical terms; caring and curing are beyond biological descriptors and require social-scientific categories of thought.[626] The example of a watch is what Polanyi used himself to show that not even "machines" can be reduced to, and explained away with, the categories of the hard sciences.[627] Neither physics nor chemistry could ever tell you what a watch is for, or that a watch is a watch. Engineering, with its value-filled human-centred operational principles and patented inventions, is already one step removed from the hard sciences and their non-patented discoveries. *A fortiori*, history, art, ethics, politics and spirituality are even less likely to be similarly reduced and explained away.

What is more, not even "mechanics… the show-piece of strict objectivity" in "mathematical formulae" that "predict strictly the observed positions and velocities of the planets" is entirely explicit or "objective": (A) "the observed readings will never coincide with theoretically predicted values"; (B) hence they must "ultimately be interpreted only by unformalizable mental activities"; (C) even statistical analyses have an intuitive beginning (i.e. selecting a plausible issue) and an interpretive end (i.e. accepting/rejecting results); (D) and more broadly, no rule exists to separate "order" from "noise": a *person* picks it.[628] Equally, (E) a *person*'s embodied skill to perform endless "hidden evaluations of not identifiable clues" is required in order to perceive meaningful wholes or patterns that are of relevance to any given discipline, namely an individual's ability that is acquired in infancy and later expanded through arduous training (e.g. academic studies).[629] Finally, (F) whether for the sake of collegial "orthodoxy" or risky "originality", individual scientists make "choices" about what they believe to be genuine knowledge, i.e. claims of universal validity for which they are personally responsible.[630] Galileo, for example, faced great peril in promoting his new conception of astronomical reality, which he nevertheless intuited and then pursued before he could provide any compelling demonstration for it. Why did he risk so much for something that he thought he could know but did not, in fact, know yet?

Polanyi's Personalist Religiousness

Polanyi's answer to the question above is, once again, centred upon the person: *faith*.

Galileo was driven by the passionate and logically ungrounded yet firm personal belief in the possibility of a novel rational theory of the universe that he had not yet produced, but merely intuited. Like a police investigator or a detective, Galileo acted wilfully on an initial hunch, which he decided to take most seriously. A committed scientist himself, aware of the hard toil and many pitfalls of both pure and applied research, Polanyi compares the scientist to a steadfast sculptor, who senses the final shape in the yet untouched block of marble and, after endless practice in her master's laboratory, strives arduously to achieve it, without certainty of success.[631] Polanyi recalls Camillo Golgi's account of his own scientific discoveries and research, which similarly proceeded from vaguely intuited novel phenomena and explanations to final explicit accounts of them.[632] Without belief in what might be, i.e. without a fiduciary ground in one's own intuitions, there would be no progress in science.

Discovery is not the only scientific context in which persons are central, for science relies on personal knowledge throughout. In this respect, Polanyi wrote of "knowing" far more often than "knowledge". For it to be, knowledge requires agency, which can succeed as well as fail. Knowledge requires knowing; and knowing requires performing, which only persons can do, whether well or badly. Performances are required at all levels of cognitive activity. How do we distinguish between relevant and irrelevant research aims? How do we know when to start and when to stop? How do we know that we are interpreting the available information correctly? How do we know that our interpretations of the received feedback are plausible? Which reasons should count as reasons? How and why do we bother? At all levels, a person, driven by her intellectual passions, must make an appraisal and a choice, possibly informed ones, and take *ipso facto* a risk. And taking risks means that a person is going to be responsible for modifying, or attempting to modify, the edifice of culture, which she therefore acknowledges, even if she did not erect it and within which she chooses to operate. It is a leap of faith, smaller or bigger that it may be, which each person must take. Normally, this leap and the attached responsibility are minimal. Occasionally, however, they can be a matter of life and death, as Galileo's case exemplifies, given the hardships that he faced at the papal court.

Polanyi enlists Gottlob Frege's modern logic in support of his own theses: "The significance of my writing down ' $\vdash$.p' is not that I make an assertion but that I commit myself to it... I *believe* what the sentence *p* says".[633] Unless a specific 'I', *someone*, commits to asserting the sentence *p* as an actual proposition about reality, thus revealing an implicit personal belief in its truth for all humankind, all we have is merely a possible proposition among many. This is what Frege called a "content of a possible judgment" and distinguished from the propositional "recognition" [*anerkennen*] that a sentence is true, which is "manifest[ed]" in " $\vdash$.p",[634] i.e. Polanyi's own "belief with universal intent".[635]

Polanyi was not inimical to explicit knowledge. He was himself an accomplished scientist, for one (and his son John went on to win in 1986 the Nobel Prize in chemistry that his father had been often close to, but never succeeded in receiving). Rather, Polanyi's intellectual work outside chemistry was motivated by his perceived collapse of Western culture, as shown in his lifetime by the two world wars, the Great Depression, fascism, the Holocaust and Stalinism. Polanyi regarded these tokens of self-proclaiming modern "progress" as the results of the West's rejection of its older cultural traditions.[636] In particular, Polanyi singled out anti-traditionalist Cartesian methodological scepticism and the arrogant "scientific obscurantism" of ensuing positivists, i.e. the victorious modern trends that take detached, impersonal, abstract, formalised, analytical reason, as best exemplified by the hard sciences, *qua* sole true path to knowledge.[637] Wherever and whenever these trends are predominant, theology, ethics, the humanities, common morals, common sense and, above all, "religion", are neglected or even abandoned.[638] They are deemed unscientific, *ergo* ultimately subjective, if not even plainly irrational. Science itself is misconceived, misrepresented and misunderstood, its multitude of tacit and personal elements disappearing from view. The paradoxes of such modern trends are evident, according to Polanyi: the horrors of the modern, rational, objective and scientific 'progress' mentioned above. That the two world wars, the Great Depression, fascism, the Holocaust and Stalinism are bad should be fairly obvious to all, or so he thought.

The logical contradictions of the same modern obscurantist trends were not, though, and they are what Polanyi endeavoured to reveal in his work, by showing how even the hard scientists rely on: (A) intuition or faith, as in the case of Galileo's wilful acceptance of risky innovation; plus (B) "authority, custom and tradition", like the Aristotelian scholars ridiculed in Brecht's *Life of Galileo*.[639] As Polanyi wrote: "In an ideal free society each person would have perfect access to the truth: to the truth in science, art, religion and justice, both in public and private life. But this is not practicable; each person can know directly very little of truth and must trust others for the rest."[640] The Royal Society's motto may have been *nullius in verba* ["take nobody's word for it"], but none of its members could ever keep truly to it.

On a deeper, basic level, no scientist could function without all the unscientific culture underpinning her from the cradle to the grave, and the culture of her fathers, forefathers and of their communities' at large. Without a natural language, without the elementary social skills that are required for interpersonal interaction, without the far more complex ones needed to graduate at a university and participate in the activities of the scientific community as a special section of the larger human community, there would be no science whatsoever. Such language and skills are acquired *without* sceptical doubt and *without* scientific means. Quite the opposite, they are based upon the fiduciary assumption of their inherent validity and relied upon throughout so as to acquire further, more complicated, discipline-specific languages and skills. On this discipline-specific level, Polanyi argues that "scientific discovery" is not inherently opposed to, or categorically distinct from, other cultural forms of knowing, religion included, since science operates itself upon: "the Pauline scheme of [1] faith", i.e. ungrounded personal belief in an undemonstrated reality; [2] "deeds", i.e. hard "labour night and day"; and [3] "grace", i.e. opening the "mind for receiving a truth from sources over which [the scientist] has no control."[641] Stressing further the continuity between religion and science, Polanyi quotes Saint Augustine: "*nisi credideritis, non intelligitis*" ["if you don't believe, you won't understand"].[642] A passionate fiduciary ground, typically endorsed tacitly, is needed for every specialist intellectual pursuit to take place. No alleged objective, scientific knowledge is possible without personal, unscientific faith: (A) in science as a worthy pursuit; (B) in the reality of the observed phenomena; (C) in the plausibility of the initial vaguest insights; (D) in the veracity of the non-assessable knowledge necessary to one's own early instruction and later research; (E) and in a host of other unscientific assumptions, including the validity of the received tradition that the great discoverer, on one fateful day, is going to question.

For decades, Polanyi practiced and specialised in the exact sciences, obtaining in Manchester the university chair that had been of John Dalton himself. Yet he never worshipped exactitude. In point of fact, he did not despise vagueness. On the contrary, he claimed that the closer you are to describing reality, the vaguer your language becomes. You can be extremely clear, extremely exact, if you simplify your picture of reality to carefully select aspects of it, which can be measured, quantified, compared, operated upon and tested (e.g. mass and motion in physics). You will get a much more genuine picture of reality, however, if you grasp *all* of its aspects and thus reproduce—if not even deepen by adding layers of human understanding to it—reality itself, in its immense variety and inherent polysemy. Film-makers, painters, poets, mystics and, sometimes, philosophers, have been the persons who, in our cultural tradition, have attempted such vast synthetic integrations. Whilst hard scientists have become masters of largely articulable particulars, soft scientists and, above all, humanists, artists and religious minds have been pursuing the mastery of a far less articulable generality, which can be destroyed by excesses of "lucidity" or "detailing", analogously to how you can spoil a joke or a poem by explaining it in too fastidious a manner.[643]

As Buddhist Zen koans exemplify, explanations by the best ones in a craft or organised form of human agency can be rather generic, elusive, even puzzling. It is only by practice over long stretches of time that pupils, students and apprentices may start making sense of the maxims, more or less hermetic, or the principles, more or less abstruse, that their mentors and teachers employ. Zen masters relished in their own enigmatic sentences, e.g. "even the grass and trees will become enlightened." But the same performative logic of apprenticeship is true in the exact sciences too, as young students spend years trying to grasp the meaning of complex, unintuitive mathematical formulations. Imagination is then engaged to the fullest extent, trying to grasp what still eludes understanding. Finally, in a conclusive and, typically, sudden act of imagination, a new plateau of comprehension is attained: a new coherent structure has finally been grasped with the available information. Under this respect, Polanyi refers often to Poincaré's accounts of imagination and creativity in mathematics, and to *Gestalt* psychology with regard to opaque processes of latent incubation and subsequent *aha Erlebnis* phenomena, whereby scientists can "discern… gestalten that indicate a true coherence in nature".[644] Disparate dots are connected and a meaningful new shape—a new form, figure or *Gestalt*—emerges.[645] This is how human comprehension works, including the most explicit, the most objective and the hardest sciences.

Also, imprecision lies at the heart of the scientific and, for that matter, of any other intellectual pursuit in yet another manner. Judges "rule according to law", artists seek "Beauty" in accordance to the established "Canon", scientists pursue "Reason" and the discovery of the "Law of Nature"; yet, all such "traditional standards" that each judge, artist and scientist decides personally to take seriously *before* knowing them to an expert extent, learn over a prolonged and arduous period of time, and eventually respect and apply in her adult life, "cannot be expressed precisely".[646] They are "ideal[s]" that underlie these social practices, which specific persons may decide to devote themselves to, hence acknowledging and submitting themselves to authorities and traditions that they will not be able to assess in a competent and accurate way until much later in their formative path. All who qualify as physicists, for instance, must have reached a certain plateau, which is something that only those who have already got there—the masters, the experts, the leaders of each particular socially sustained discipline a person may choose to devote herself to—can determine. Yet, not even the masters' plateau is necessarily the final one, for great scientific minds may keep discovering novel aspects, ramifications and implications buried within the very same mathematical formulations, which seemed defined and definitive to the other specialists.

The greatest minds—i.e. physics' Messis and Maradonas—can even come up with novel, alternative overall interpretations, which defy established truths and challenge accepted views. Objectivity shifts; positivism falters. Initially, these new interpretations are resisted as mistaken, nonsensical, if not even offensive. It can take years for them to become the new accepted views, i.e. when enough other experts may have come to understand whatever innovation the genius had introduced, *via* the wilful engagement of their "imagination" and repeated acts of spirited "persuasion" spurring them, so that a "*conversion*" may take place in people's fundamental beliefs in the nature of reality.[647] Through a long and murky process, that which was resisted and rebuked as mistaken, nonsensical or offensive becomes the new explicitness, even if the original formulation did not change a bit. Its interpretation changed, that is, a new framework or paradigm emerged, which created the conditions for a widespread hermeneutic shift (Polanyi's epistemology played a major influence on Thomas Kuhn, as the latter admits in Crombie's 1963 book, *Scientific Change*).[648] Textbooks and standard accounts of progress are likely to depict a neat, cumulative ascent towards better and better knowledge, though much of what allows for and accompanies the whole process is actually "unaccountable" and "unspecifiable", i.e. tacit, and takes place within the "republic science" by way of persuasive conversations, committed proselytising and generational substitution. [649]

But if we do take seriously all the murky, opaque and tacit elements that Polanyi insisted upon, how can we draw a line, then, between the humanities and the sciences? How can we separate between hard and soft science? Not to mention between charlatans, witch-doctors and proper physicians! Polanyi had no desire to rehabilitate cranks and failed old disciplines like astrology, which he often criticises in *Personal Knowledge*. Yet he has no trenchant answer to offer; and he knew it. Given an adequately rich and flexible interpretative apparatus, even magic could persist and accommodate new data. Different civilisations have produced different disciplines, fields of expertise, hermeneutical constructs and, to use Michael Oakeshott's famous phrase, a plurality of "modes of experience".[650] Societies, in their evolution, shed some of them, modify others, create new ones, and rediscover lost ones. Culture is a polymorphous, ever-changing beast. Apart from trying our best in utilising our faculties, both physical and mental, and choosing to participate in certain socially available disciplines, there is little else that a person can do. It is her own responsibility to do so, and so is the determination of which standards she is willing to claim to be valid for all: "All thought is incarnate; it lives by the body and by the favour of society. But it is not *thought* unless it strives for truth, a striving which leaves it free to act on its own responsibility, with universal intent."[651]

An educated person may choose as she deems fit. She takes the risk. It is her privilege and her burden. However, according to Polanyi, a responsible choice requires respecting whatever legacy our past may have brought to our attention. No single person can be an expert in each and every discipline that there is. One must therefore have faith in the significance of the tradition that has made her own acculturation possible. Western culture produced modern science after developing much older arts, literature, philosophy, history, pagan myths and Christian faiths. Why should we cultivate ignorance of this lore in the name of the newest member? How can we be certain that we cannot learn anything meaningful through the older ones? Enrichment *via* new forms of knowledge is preferable to impoverishment *via* abandonment of old ones. It is prudential reasoning—no more, no less. As such, it requires the awareness and acceptance of our fallibility, i.e. humility—another old, religious value. And that is what the sceptical mind-set of modern science finds hardest of all. Despite Galileo's original claims about the limited aims of his new science, which was meant to deal with some *affezioni particolari* ["particular aspects"] of observable nature, modern scientists and their sycophants have often displayed a desire to apply their methods and their standards to all other disciplines and disciplinary areas of inquiry.

If this application is pursued, however, then much can be lost, according to Polanyi, including the ability to grasp mentally and emotionally why and how there could be other disciplines employing other methods. Postmodern authors write often of "cultural imperialism". *Ante litteram* [before the term was coined], that is precisely what Polanyi tried to stop by advocating instead the paramount value of human knowledge in its plurality of expressions. Whether in physics, biology, chemistry, history or theology, Polanyi, especially in *The Tacit Dimension* and *Meaning*, characterises all knowledge as personally satisfying, sense-making, fiduciary, passionate, evaluative, traditional, imaginative, revisable *Gestalten* derived from personal experiences (e.g. intuitions) and aiming at universal validity. The more *Gestalten* we cultivate, the richer and more varied are the meanings that we can retrieve within and around ourselves. The more we discard and render ungraspable, the poorer and more disenchanted our inner and outer worlds become.

Polanyi developed his epistemology by considering expert domains such as the common-law judiciary, laboratory research in the hard sciences, and business management in free-market economies. In all these domains, substantial autonomy is granted to the individual agents, who pursue their aims in line with standards set by others (e.g. precedents, methodological standards, hard laws), whilst submitting voluntarily to them. The feedback received from the other experts in each domain leads to a process of "mutual adjustment" or overall coordination, which is not the result of anyone's planning, as in flower arrangements in a garden or soldiers' movements at a military parade.[652] Observing these professional or expert domains is what led Polanyi to talk about "dynamic order", "spontaneously arising order" and "spontaneous ordering", such that a coherent whole (e.g. a common-law system, a scientific tradition, a market economy) emerges from largely autonomous individual pursuits.[653] Though a little known fact, his friend and admirer Friedrich Hayek derived from Polanyi the idea and the term "spontaneous order", which is a concept that Polanyi himself derived in turn from *Gestalt* psychology and, in particular, from the study of human perception, which grasps molar entities upon the basis and in *lieu* of distinct multiple details.[654]

Differences among disciplines are inevitable: the ontological levels studied—history studies "actions", physicists "events"— require different "framework[s]" and "standards".[655] As we acquire and dwell in those frameworks and standards, we may learn to grasp the phenomena that each discipline concentrates upon. Once the modes of experience proper to the investigation of each ontological level are acquired and practiced, Polanyi's own "conception of knowing opens the way to them" all, from subatomic physics to "*divinity*".[656] Polanyi was particularly concerned with losing the *Gestalt* of religion, which offers opportunities to make sense of the most baffling contradictions (e.g. a virgin birth, a crucified god) and painful experiences (e.g. old age, death). Without ever spending many pages on it, he nevertheless included a few paragraphs on religion in all of his main works, which were devoted to issues and fields of inquiry that many educated minds would take as conspicuously unrelated to religion, e.g. epistemology, the history of modern science and semantics. Yet, insofar as human comprehension is the result of internalising concepts, sustaining intellectual passions and acquiring skills—many of which tacitly—that allow a person to experience the universe in ways that characterise each discipline, religion is not unlike physics or linguistics. One has to study, train and eventually succeed, or fail, in making sense of and through the categories and abilities of each discipline, religion included. Then, if successful, one can grasp the meaningful entities that each particular discipline can reveal to us. By then an old and severely ill man, Polanyi remarked in 1975: "*It is only through participation in acts of worship... that we see God*".[657] It is only by embracing, studying and dwelling within the categories and emotions of religion that we can make *sense* out of the holy texts: "Only a Christian who stands in the service of his faith can understand Christian theology and only he can enter into the religious meaning of the Bible."[658] The meaning or the sense that one extracts from the holy texts is a meaning or a sense that belongs to religion and theology, not to the *Gestalten* of physics or anthropology, which make use of other categories of thought, work upon the basis of different emotional drives and mental dispositions, engage other tacit skills, and cannot therefore agree with religion and theology, for there is not something that they should disagree upon to begin with. Religion and the sciences are indeed *Gestalten*, i.e. forms or modes of experience, but as different *Gestalten*, they do not pursue the same enquiry, they do not seek the same aim, they do not lead to the same sort of experience:

A heuristic impulse can live only in the pursuit of its proper enquiry. The Christian enquiry is worship. The words of prayer and confession, the actions of the ritual, the lesson, the sermon, the church itself, are the clues of the worshipper's striving towards God. They guide his feelings of contrition and gratitude and the craving for the divine presence, while keeping him safe from distracting thoughts.[659]

In his lifetime, Polanyi witnessed what he believed to be the terrifying success of a sceptical and positivist mind-set characterising modernity. Its unintended dreadful consequences were visible on a planetary scale, as exemplified most virulently by the technologically intensive world wars of the 20th century, the Nazis' efficient industrial network for mass extermination of anthropologically determined inferior races, and the brutal oppression required in communist countries by the laws of historical materialism in order to bring about a global classless society. Thanks to the committed implementation of the officially celebrated scientific method, which advocated or implied the rejection of pre-existing and time-honoured categories of interpretation *a priori*, all great ideals and profound drives of the past were 'unmasked' and eventually cast away as *else* than themselves, e.g.: love as biochemistry; ethics as evolutionary survival strategy; religion as neurosis; art as sublimation of sexual instincts; associated life as class interest or predation.[660] Even persons were no longer such. They were reduced by sceptical, scientific rationality to, say, social relations, unconscious drives, factors of production, genetic predispositions, or means of evolutionary development.

To Polanyi, who understood ideals, drives and persons on their own terms *via* the traditional cultural forms available to him, this reduction was nothing but "barbarism of reason", as Vico had already called the mishandling of past knowledge by misleading new approaches in his own early and vain attack on Cartesian rationalism.[661] To cast away centuries of civilisation, and especially religion and its associated traditional moral codes, because they cannot be handled by one of its by-products, i.e. the relatively young sciences of Newton, Dalton and Darwin, or alleged applications thereof in socio-scientific form (e.g. scientific Marxism, social Darwinism, racial anthropology, rational-expectation micro-economics), means performing dangerous cultural self-mutilations, which Polanyi wished to avoid at all costs.

Polanyi's motto, "we can know more than we can tell", is the beginning of wisdom here; not the end of it.[662] It is certainly true that self-proclaimed objective science can provide certain types of information that cannot be grasped by other forms of comprehension of reality. Polanyi was himself a chemist, after all. However, he argued that self-proclaimed objective science cannot truly perceive a plethora of phenomena that, in Western culture, have been the province of other disciplines. Rather than spreading blindness about them, science should better cast light on its own limitations. Without theology, philosophy, history, drama and common sense, we confine ourselves into a world that is poorer in meanings. Above all, without religion, we confine ourselves into this world, this mortal life and its existential burdens, such as its inevitable loads of physical and psychological pain. It is true that each and every person is responsible for deciding whether to believe or not, but how can anyone be given a fair chance to endorse religious belief, if social institutions undermine access to it? How can anyone begin to experience God's presence in her soul, for instance, if atheism has been the official State policy for three generations and no training, no apprenticeship, no coaching, either explicit or tacit, can be had?

Concluding Remarks

Science is a manifestation of reason's great power, but within reason. A military doctor, a student of biology and an accomplished chemist, Polanyi welcomed modern science, but rejected modern scientism, for in his view it had led to mental, emotional and existential self-impoverishment, both individual and social. The past has handed down to us a wealth of possible sources of meaning, including those that religious worship has to offer. Polanyi was a committed liberal throughout his life. He was a participant in the activities of the Mont Pelerin Society founded, *inter alia*, by Hayek, von Mises, Popper and Friedman.[663] However, he had also worshipped in Catholic and later Presbyterian and Methodist churches, and he wanted to preserve the sources of meanings created by our ancestors, religion *in primis* [first of all], and make them available to the generations to come.[664] Pluralism has merits, which extend beyond the political sphere alone.

Bibliography

The entries in the final bibliography are in alphabetical order, also as regards works by the same author. Depending on established conventions, classic, Medieval, early Renaissance Italian, and Icelandic authors are listed by first name. Whenever internet sources were utilised, the hyperlinks were removed in the bibliography for the sake of graphic quality. However, they can be retrieved in the endnotes.

Adams, Henry P., *The Life and Writings of Giambattista Vico*, London: Allen and Unwin, 1935.

Alktenhead, Decca, "Christine Lagarde: can the head of the IMF save the euro?", *The Guardian*, 25 May 2012.

Allen, Richard T., "The Meaning of Life and Education", *Journal of Philosophy of Education*, 25(1), 1991, 47–57.

Allen, Richard T., and Baruchello, Giorgio, "Life Responsibility versus Mechanical Reductionism", in *Philosophy and World* Problems, edited by John McMurtry, *Encyclopedia of Life Support Systems*, Paris & London: Eolss, 2002–16.

Ames, Roger T., "Death and Transformation in Classical Daoism", in *Death and Philosophy*, edited by Jeff Malpas and Robert C. Solomon, London: Routledge, 1998, 57–70.

Amore, Roy C., "The Heterodox Philosophical Systems", in *Death and Eastern Thought*, edited by Frederick H. Holck, Nashville: Abingdon, 1975, 114–63.

Anderson, Barbara, "Russia Faces Depopulation? Dynamics of Population Decline", *Population and Environment,* 23(5), 2002, 437–64.

Anderson, Sarah, and Cavanagh, John, *Report on the top 200 corporations*, Institute for Policy Studies, December 2000.

Andrady, Anthony L., Aucamp, Pieter J., Austin, Amy T., Bais, A.F., Ballaré, C.L., Björn, L.O., *et al.* "Environmental Effects of Ozone Depletion and Its Interactions with Climate Change: 2010 Assessment. Executive Summary", *Photochemical & Photobiological Sciences*, 10(2), 2011, 178–81.

Anonymous, *Njál's Saga*, translated by Hermann Pálsson and Magnus Magnusson, London: Penguin, 1960[13th century].

Aquinas, Thomas, *Summa Theologica*, translated by Fathers of the English Dominican Province, 1920[*ca.* 1268].

Ariès, Philippe, *Storia della morte in Occidente*, translated by Simona Vigezzi, Milan: BUR, 1997[1975].

Ariew, Roger, "Descartes and Pascal", *Perspectives on Science*, 15(4), 2007, 397–409.

Ash, Lucy, "France versus the World", *BBC* News, 22 April 2007.

Avant, Deborah D., *The Market for Force: The Consequences for Privatizing Security*, Cambridge: Cambridge University Press, 2005.

Bacon, Francis, *The New Atlantis*, in *Three Early Modern Utopias*, Oxford: Oxford University Press, 2009[1627].

Badenhausen, Kurt, Ozanian, Michael K., and Roney, Maya, "The Business of Football", *Forbes,* 31 August 2006.

"Bankers call for third LTRO", *Reuters*, 13 September 2013.

Barber, Benjamin, *Consumed: How Markets Corrupt Children, Infantilize Adults, and Swallow Citizens Whole*, New York: Norton, 2007.

Baruchello, Giorgio, "Classifying the Classics. *Gestalt* Psychology and the Tropes of Rhetoric", *New Ideas in Psychology*, 36, 2015, 10–24.

Baruchello, Giorgio, "Eight Noble Opinions and the Economic Crisis: Four Literary-philosophical Sketches à la Eduardo Galeano", *Nordicum-Mediterraneum*, 5(1), 2010.

Baruchello, Giorgio, "No Pain, No Gain. The Understanding of Cruelty in Western Philosophy and Some Reflections on Personhood", *Filozofia*, 65(2), 2010, 170–83.

Baruchello, Giorgio, "The Unscientific Ground of Free-Market Liberalism", in *Ethics, Democracy, and Markets*, edited by Giorgio Baruchello, Jacob Dahl Rendtorff and Asger Sörensen, Malmö: Nordic Summer University Press, 2016, 233–59.

Bayer, Thora I., "History as Symbolic Form: Cassirer and Vico", *Idealistic Studies*, 34(1), 2004, 49–65.

Bayer, Thora I. and Verene, Donald P., *Giambattista Vico. Keys to the* New Science. *Translations, Commentaries, and Essays*, Ithaca: Cornell University Press, 2009, 199–204.

Benedict XVI (Pope), "Omelia di Sua Santità Benedetto XVI", Piazza San Pietro, 3 June 2006.

Bergson, Henri, *Time and Free Will. An Essay on the Immediate Data of Consciousness*, London: George Allen, 1910[1888].

Berlin, Isaiah, "The Philosophical Ideas of Giambattista Vico", in *Art and Ideas in Eighteenth-Century Italy*. Rome: Edizioni di Storia e Letteratura, 1960, 156–233.

Berlin, Isaiah, *Three Critics of the Enlightenment: Vico, Hamann, Herder*, edited by Henry Hardy, London: Pimlico, 2000.

Berlin, Isaiah, *Vico and Herder: Two Studies in the History of Ideas*, New York: Viking, 1976.

Bhagwati, Jagdish, "Coping with Antiglobalization", *Foreign Affairs*, January/February 2002, 2–3.

Blanchard, Olivier, and Leigh, Daniel, "Growth Forecast Errors and Fiscal Multipliers", IMF Working Paper ref. WP/13/1, January 2013.

Blankenburg, Stephanie, and Plesch, Dan, *Corporate rights and responsibilities: Restoring legal accountability*, Royal Society for the encouragement of Arts, Manufactures & Commerce, 2007.

Blokland, Hans T., "Unhappily Trapped in the Emancipation Dilemma", *The Good Society*, 12(2), 2003, 58–62.

Boethius, Ancius Manlius Severinus, *The Consolation of Philosophy*, translated by Victor Watts, London: Penguin, 1999[523 A.D.].

Bowles, Samuel, and Park, Yongjin, "Emulation, Inequality and Working Hours: Was Thorstein Veblen Right?", *The Economic Journal*, 115, November 2005, 397–412.

Brower, Frank, Lintner, Valerio, and Newman, Michael (eds.), *Economic Policy Making and the European Union*, London: Federal Trust, 1994.

Brubaker, Elizabeth, "Privatizing Water Supply and Sewage Treatment: How Far Should We Go?", *Journal des Economistes et des Etudes Humaines*, 8(4), December 1998, 441–54.

Bulankulama and Others v. The Secretary, Ministry of Industrial Development and Others (Eppawala case), S.C. Application No. 884/99 (F/R), The Supreme Court of the Democratic Socialist Republic of Sri Lanka, 2000.

Bunting, Madeleine, *Willing Slaves: How the Overwork Culture is Ruling Our Lives*, New York: Harper Collins, 2004.

Burke, Edmund, *Reflections on the French Revolution,* London: Everyman's library, 1953[1790].

Burns, J.H., "Happiness and Utility: Jeremy Bentham's Equation", *Utilitas*, 17(1), 2005, 46–61.

Capongiri, A. Robert, *Time and Idea: The Theory of History in Giambattista Vico*, Chicago: Henry Regnery, 1953.

Castoriadis, Cornelius, *A Society Adrift: More Interviews and Discussions on The Rising Tide of Insignificancy, Including Revolutionary Perspectives Today*, translated and edited anonymously as a public service, 2010[1973–93].

Castoriadis, Cornelius, *A Society Adrift. Interviews and Debates, 1974–1997*, translated by Helen Arnold, New York: Fordham University Press, 2010.

Castoriadis, Cornelius, "De l'écologie à l'autonomie", transcription of a paper presented at Louvain-la-neuve (Belgium) on 27 February 1980.

Castoriadis, Cornelius, *Figures of the Thinkable. Including Passion and Knowledge*, translated and edited anonymously as a public service, 2005[1986–97].

Castoriadis, Cornelius, *Figures of the Thinkable*, translated by Helen Arnold, Stanford: Stanford University Press, 2007.

Castoriadis, Cornelius, *Postscript on Insignificancy. Including More Interviews and Discussions on the Rising Tide of Insignificancy. Followed by Five Dialogues, Four Portraits and Two Book Reviews*, translated and edited anonymously as a public service, 2011[1961–97], 194.

Castoriadis, Cornelius, *The Rising Tide of Insignificancy (The Big Sleep)*, translated and edited anonymously as a public service, 2003[1979–96].

Catholic Encyclopedia, New York: Robert Appleton Company, edited by Charles G. Herbermann, Edward A. Pace, Conde B. Fallen, Thomas J. Shahan and John J. Wynne, 1907–12.

Cazzullo, Aldo, "Tremonti e il G8", *Corriere della Sera*, 10 March 2009.

Central Bank of Iceland, Release n. 17/2006, 15 May 2006.

Chesterton, Gilbert Keith, *What I Saw in America*, London: Hodder & Stoughton, 1922.

Christian Aid, *Human tide: the real migration crisis*, May 2007.

Cicero, Marcus Tullius, *Academica priora et posteriora*, Fairbanks: PGLA, 2005[1st century B.C.].

Clark, Eric, *The Real Toy Story: Inside the Ruthless Battle for America's Youngest Consumers*, New York: Free Press, 2007.

Clark, Hannah, "Who's Afraid of Second Life?", *Forbes*, 27 January 2007.

Cobb, Cathy, and Goldwhite, Harold, *Creations of Fire: Chemistry from Alchemy to the Atomic Age*, New York: Basic Books, 2002.

Collina, Tom Z., and Poff, Erica, "The Green New Deal: Energizing the U.S. Economy", *Friedrich Ebert Stiftung*, 4, 2009.

Collingwood, Robin G., *The Philosophy of Giambattista Vico*, London: Howard Latimer, 1913.

Comte, Auguste, "The Positivist calendar", 2015[1849].

Cotroneo, Rocco, "Bio (o necro) combustibili", *Il corriere della sera*, 4 April 2007.

Croce, Benedetto, *La filosofia di G.B. Vico*, Bari: Laterza, 1965 (6th ed.) [1911].

Csikszentmihalyi, Mihaly, *Beyond Boredom and Anxiety: Experiencing Flow in Work and Play*, Chicago: Jossey-Bass, 2000.

Dante Alighieri, *La divina commedia*, 1966–7[1307–21].

Dawkins, Richard, *The Selfish Gene*, Oxford: Oxford University Press, 1976.

Deleuze, Gilles, *Difference and Repetition*, translated by Paul Patton, New York: Columbia University Press, 1994[1968].

Deleuze, Gilles, and Guattari, Félix, *A Thousand Plateaus*, translated by Brian Massumi, Minneapolis: Minnesota University Press, 1988[1980].

Descartes, René, *Meditations on First Philosophy*, translated by Elizabeth S. Haldane, Cambridge: Cambridge University Press, 1911[1641].

Descartes, René, *Treatise on Man*, in *The World and Other Writings*, translated and edited by Stephen Gaukroger, Cambridge: Cambridge University Press, 2004[1644], 99–169.

Di Miele, Andrea, "La cifra nel tappeto. Note su Paci interprete di Vico", *Bollettino del Centro di Studi Vichiani*, 37, 2007, 87–103.

Dickens, Charles, *Hard Times*, London: Penguin, 2007[1854].

Diels, Hermann, and Kranz, Walther, *Die Fragmente der Vorsokratiker*, translated by Kathleen Freeman, *Ancilla to the Pre-Socratic Philosophers*, Cambridge: Harvard University Press, 1983[6th century B.C.].

Dostoyevsky, Fyodor M., *Crime & Punishment*, translated by David McDuff, London: Penguin, 2002[1866].

Dostoyevsky, Fyodor M., *Demons*, translated by Richard Pevear and Larissa Volkhonsky, London: Vintage, 2010[1869].

Dostoyevsky, Fyodor M., *The Adolescent*, translated by Richard Pevear and Larissa Volkhonsky, London: Vintage, 2004[1875].

Dostoyevsky, Fyodor M., *Winter Notes on Summer Impressions*, translated by Kyril Fitz Lyon, London: Alma Classics, 2008[1863].

Du Bois Marcus, Nancy, *Vico and Plato*, New York: Peter Lang, 2001.

Durand, Mark, and Barlow, David H., *Essentials of Abnormal Psychology*, Pacific Grove: Wadsworth, 2005.

Economou, Marina, Madianos, Michael, Theleritis, Christos, Peppou, Lily E., and Stefanis, Costas N., "Suicidality and the Economic Crisis in Greece", *Lancet*, 380, 2012, 337–8.

Fairfield, Paul, *Moral Selfhood in the Liberal Tradition. The Politics of Individuality*, Toronto: University of Toronto Press, 2000.

Faresjö, Åshild, Theodorsson, Elvar, Chatziarzenis, Marios, Sapouna, Vasiliki, Claesson, Hans-Peter, Koppner, Jenny, Faresjö, Tomas, "Higher Perceived Stress but Lower Cortisol Levels Found among Young Greek Adults Living in a Stressful Social Environment in Comparison with Swedish Young Adults", *PLoS ONE* 8(9), 2013, e73828, doi:10.1371/journal.pone.0073828.

Feldman, Burton, and Richardson, Robert D., *The Rise of Modern Mythology, 1680–1860*, Bloomington: Indiana University Press, 1972.

Fontana, Enrico, *Rapporto ecomafia 2007*, Legambiente.

Foscolo, Ugo, *Poesie,* edited by Giuseppe Chiarini, Livorno: Raffaello Giusti, 1904[1803].

Frege, Gottlob, "The Thought: A Logical Inquiry", *Mind*, 65(259), 1956[1919], 289–311.

Galbraith, John Kenneth, *Money: Whence It Came, Where It Went*, Boston: Houghton Mifflin, 1975.

Galbraith, John Kenneth, *The Age of Uncertainty*, London: BBC, 1977.

Galbraith, John Kenneth, *The New Industrial State, with a new foreword by James K. Galbraith*, Princeton: Princeton University Press, 2007[1967].

Galeano, Eduardo, *Upside Down: A Primer for the Looking-Glass World*, translated by Mark Fried, New York: Picador, 2008[1998].

Galilei, Galileo, *Il Saggiatore*, Milan: Feltrinelli, 1965[1623].

Galilei, Galileo, *Lettere*, Turin: Einaudi, 1978[1615].

Galilei, Galileo, *Opere*, Florence: Barbera, 1890–1909 (1929–1939 reprint)[1638].

Geir Sigurðsson, "In Praise of Illusions: Giacomo Leopardi's Ultraphilosophy", *Nordicum-Mediterraneum*, 5(1), 2010.

Giannantonio, Valeria, *Oltre Vico. L'identità del passato a Napoli e Milano tra '700 e '800*, Lanciano: Carabba, 2009.

Gigante, Marcello, *Il libro degli epigrammi di Filodemo*, Naples: Bibliopolis, 2002.

Gilson, Etienne, *La philosophie au moyen-âge*, vols. I–II, Paris: Payot, 1988[1922]

Glyn, Andrew, *Capitalism Unleashed: Finance, Globalization, and Welfare*, Oxford: Oxford University Press, 2006.

Grafton, Anthony, "Fear and Loathing in Naples", a review of *G.B. Vico: The Making of an Anti-Modern*, by Mark Lilla (Cambridge, Mass.: Harvard University Press, 1993), *The New Republic*, 209(12), 1993, 51–3.

Hallie, Philip. P., "Cruelty", *Encyclopaedia of Ethics*, edited by Lawrence C. Becker, New York: Garland, 1992, 229–31.

Hallie, Philip P., "From Cruelty to Goodness", in *Vice and Virtue in Everyday Life*, edited by Christina H. Sommers and Fred Sommers, San Diego: Harcourt College Publishers, 1989[1981], 9–24.

Hallie, Philip P., *Lest Innocent Blood Be Shed: The Story of the Village of Le Chambon, and How Goodness Happened There*, New York: Harper & Row, 1979 (1985 reprint).

Hallie, Philip P., *The Paradox of Cruelty*, Middletown: Wesleyan University Press, 1969.

Hanson, Robin, *The Policy Analysis Market (and FutureMAP) Archive*, George Mason University, n.d.a.

Hardin, Garrett, "The Tragedy of the Commons", *Science*, 162, 1968, 1243–8.

Hartwell, Ronald M., *History of the Mont Pelerin Society*, Indianapolis: Liberty Fund, 1995.

Harvey, David, *A Brief History of Neoliberalism*, Oxford: Oxford University Press, 2005.

Heidegger, Martin, *Being and Time*, translated by John Macquarrie and Edward Robinson, San Francisco: Harper, 1962[1927].

Heidegger, Martin, *The Question Concerning Technology*, translated by William Lovitt, New York: Harper & Row, 1977[1953].

Henry, Stephen G., "Polanyi's tacit knowing and the relevance of epistemology to clinical medicine", *Journal of Evaluation in Clinical Practice*, 16(2), 2010, 292–97.

Hildegard of Bingen, *Selected Writings*, translated and edited by Mark Atherton, London: Penguin, 2001[12th century A.D.].

Hobbes, Thomas, *Leviathan*, London: Penguin, 1985[1651].

Hobsbawm, Eric, *Politics for a Rational Left: Political Writing, 1977–1988*, London: Verso, 1990.

Hobsbawm, Eric, *The Age of Axtremes, 1914–1991. The Short Twentieth Century*, London: Abacus, 1995.

Hobsbawm, Eric, *The New Century. In Conversation with Antonio Polito*, London: Abacus, 2000[1999].

Hosokawa, Migiwa, Tajiri, Shunichiro, and Uheata, Tetsunojyo (eds.), *Karoshi-Nou*, Tokyo: Roudou Keizaisha, 1982.

Iannello, Serena, "Pubblicità e tutela dei minori: sulla pubblicità di alimenti", *Altalex*.

"Iceland Collapse: Riots, Suicide, and Church Kitchens", *Business Pundit*, 24 January 2009.

"Il peccato peggiore? Lo shopping selvaggio", *Il corriere della sera*, 6 May 2007.

IMF, "Greece: Ex Post Evaluation of Exceptional Access under the 2010 Stand-By Arrangement", IMF Country Report No. 13/156, June 2013.

Jacobs, Struan, "Michael Polanyi and Spontaneous Order, 1941–1951", *Tradition and Discovery*, 24(2), 1997–1998, 14–28.

Jespersen, Jesper, "When the Treasury and its Models Seize Power", *Nordicum-Mediterraneum*, 11(1), 2016.

Jonas, Hans, *The Phenomenon of Life: Toward a Philosophical Biology*, Evanston, Ill.: Northwestern University Press, 2001[1973 part.].

Joseph, Peter, *Zeitgeist: Moving Forward*, documentary movie produced by TZMOfficialChannel, 2011.

Kahneman, Daniel, *Thinking, Fast and Slow*, New York: Farrar, Straus & Giroux, 2011.

Kant, Immanuel, "An Answer to the Question: What is Enlightenment?", in *Philosophy E-Server*, translated by Mary J. Gregor, 2006[1784].

Kant, Immanuel, *The Cambridge Edition of the Works of Immanuel Kant*, edited by Paul Guyer and Allen W. Wood, Cambridge: Cambridge University Press, 1992–2007.

Kassimatis, Georgios, "The Loan Agreement between the Hellenic Republic, the European Union and the International Monetary Fund", translated by S.G. Virna, 2010, Research paper prepared for Athens Bar Association.

Kempf, Hervé, *Comment les riches détruisent la planète*, Paris: Seuil, 2007.

Kentikelenis, Alexander, Karanikolos, Marina, Papanicolas, Irene, Basu, Sanjay, McKee, Martin, and Stuckler, David, "Health Effects of Financial Crisis: Omens of a Greek Tragedy", *Lancet*, 378, 2011, 1457–8.

Kimball, Roger, "The Nasty Nineties", a review of *Decade of Denial: A Snapshot of America in the 1990s*, by Herbert I. London (Lanham: Lexington Books, 2000), 2001.

Klestenic, Cynthia, *Theaters of Anatomy: Students, Teachers and Traditions of Dissection in Renaissance Venice*, Boston: Johns Hopkins University Press, 2011.

Kronsell, Amica, and Svedberg, Erika, "The Swedish Military Manpower Policies and their Gender Implications", in *The Changing Face of European Conscription*, edited by Pertti Joenniemi, Aldershot: Ashgate, 2006, 137–57.

Krugman, Paul, "Reconsidering a miracle", *The Conscience of a Liberal*, 16 April 2009 Blog entry, krugman.blogs.nytimes.com.

Kuhn, Thomas S., "The Function of Dogma in Scientific Research", in *Scientific Change: Historical Studies in the Intellectual, Social and Technical Conditions for Scientific Discovery and Technical Invention, from Antiquity to the Present*, edited by Alistair Crombie, New York: Basic Books, 1963, 347–69.

La Mettrie, Julien Offray de, *L'homme machine*, Leyde: Elie Luzac, 1748[1714].

Lafargue, Paul, *The Right to Be Lazy*, Chicago: Charles Kerr & Co., 1883.

Lamberg, Lynne, "If I work hard(er), I will be loved. Roots of Physician Stress Explored", *The Journal of the American Medical Association*, 282,1999, 13–4.

Lane, Robert, *The Loss of Happiness in Market Democracies*, New Haven: Yale University Press, 2001.

Lang, Helen S., *Aristotle's Physics and Its Medieval Varieties*, New York: State University of New York Press, 1992.

Laplace, Pierre Simon (Marquis de), *A Philosophical Essay on Probabilities*, translated by Frederick Wilson Truscott and Frederick Lincoln Emory, London: Chapman & Hall, 1902[1814].

Lavrin, Janko, "Tolstoy and Gandhi", *The Russian Review*, 19(2), 1960, 132–9.

Legrenzi, Paolo, *Storia della psicologia*, Bologna: Il mulino, 2002.

Leibniz, Gottfried W., *Monadology*, translated by Jonathan Bennett, 2007[1714].

Leonardo da Vinci, *Aforismi, novelle e profezie*, Rome: Newton, 1993[15th–16th century].

Leopardi, Giacomo, *Canti*, 1835.

Leopardi, Giacomo, *Operette Morali*, 1836.

Levine, Robert, "The Pace of Life in 31 Countries", *American Demographics*, 19, November 1997, 20–9.

Lilla, Mark, *G.B. Vico: The Making of an Anti-Modern*. Cambridge, Mass.: Harvard University Press, 1993.

Lorenzo de Medici, *Opera omnia*, 2007–16[1465–91].

Lovelock, James, *Gaia: A New Look at Life on Earth*, Oxford: Oxford University Press, 1979.

Lucretius, Titus Carus, *De rerum natura*, translated by William Ellery Leonard, London: Everyman's Library, 1942[*ca.* 50 B.C.].

Lutterbeck, Derek, "Policing Migration in the Mediterranean", *Mediterranean Politics*, 11(1), March 2006, 59–82.

Madsen, Kristen B. (ed.), *A History of Psychology in Metascientific Perspective*, special issue of *Advances in Psychology*, 53, 1988.

Marini, Cesare, *Giambattista Vico al cospetto del XIX secolo*, Napoli: Stamperia Strada Salvatore, 1852.

Marx, Karl, *Capital. Vol. 1*, edited by Friedrich Engels, translated by Samuel Moore and Edward Aveling, London: Lawrence & Wishart, 1970[1867].

Mastrolilli, Paolo, "Gli eroi del football dementi a 40 anni", *La Stampa*, 15 March 2007.

Mazzotta, Giuseppe, *The New Map of the World: The Poetic Philosophy of Giambattista Vico*, Princeton: Princeton University Press, 1999.

McCloskey, Donald (now Deirdre), "The Rhetoric of Economics", *Journal of Economic Literature*, XXI, June 1983, 481–517.

McMurtry, John (ed.), *Philosophy and world Problems*, vols. I-III, Oxford & Paris: Eolss, 2011.

McMurtry, John, *The Cancer Stage of Capitaism*, London: Pluto Press, 1999 (1st ed.) & 2013 (2nd ed.).

McMurtry, John, *Unequal Freedoms. The Global Market as an Ethical System*, Toronto: Garamond Press, 1998.

McMurtry, John, *Value Wars. The Global Market versus the Life Economy*, London: Pluto Press, 2002.

Mészáros, Istvan, *Beyond Capital*, London: Merlin Press, 1995.

Mimmo, Francesco, "Prodi lancia il piano anti-siccità. Blocco dei consumi non essenziali", *La Repubblica*, 7 March 2003.

Molner, David, "The Influence of Montaigne on Nietzsche: A Raison d'Etre in the Sun", *Nietzsche Studien*, 21, 1993, 80–93.

Montaigne, Michel de, *The Complete Essays*, translated by Donald Frame, Stanford: Stanford University Press, 1998[1580].

Morrison, Alan D. and Wilhelm, Jr., William J., *Investment Banking*, Oxford: Oxford University Press, 2006.

Nehamas, Alexander, "The Art of Living", *Philosophy Today*, 44(2), 2000, 190–205.

Newton, Isaac, *Philosophiae Naturalis Principia Mathematica*, Glasgow: James MacLehose, 1871[1687].

Nicolini, Fausto, *Giambattista Vico nella vita domestica: la moglie, i figli, la casa*, Venosa: Ossana, 1991.

Nicolini, Fausto, *La giovinezza di Vico*, Bari: Laterza, 1932.

Nicolini, Fausto, *Saggi vichiani*, Napoli: Giannini, 1955.

Nietzsche, Friedrich, *Also Sprach Zarathustra: Ein Buch für Alle und Keinen*, Zürich: Manesse, 2001[1883–91].

Nietzsche, Friedrich, *Beyond Good and Evil*, translated by Judith Norman, Cambridge: Cambridge University Press, 2002[1886].

Nietzsche, Friedrich, *Ecce Homo & The Antichrist*, translated by Thomas Wayne, New York: Algora, 2004[1888 & 1895].

Nietzsche, Friedrich, *The Gay Science*, translated by Josephine Nauckhoff, Cambridge: Cambridge University Press, 2001[1882].

Nietzsche, Friedrich, *The Will to Power*, translated by Walter Kaufmann and M.J. Hollingdale, New York: Random House,1968[1901].

Nietzsche, Friedrich, *Thus Spake Zarathustra*, translated by Thomas Common, 1891[1883–91].

Nietzsche, Friedrich, *Twilight of the Idols: or How to Philosophize with a Hammer*, translated by Duncan Large, Oxford: Oxford University Press, 2009[1889].

Noonan, Jeff, *Democratic Society and Human Needs*, Montreal & Kingston: McGill-Queen's University Press, 2006.

Nordicum-Mediterraneum. Icelandic E-journal of Nordic and Mediterranean Studies, edited by Giorgio Baruchello and Maurizio Tani, 3(2), 2008.

Norman, Donald A., *The Psychology of Everyday Things*, New York: Basic Books, 1988.

Ó Gráda, Cormac, "Markets and Famines in Pre-Industrial Europe", *Journal of Interdisciplinary History*, 36(2), Autumn 2005, 143–66.

O'Connor, John J., and Robertson, Edmund F., "Pythagoras of Samos", *MacTutor History of Mathematics Archive*, 1999[6th century B.C.].

O'Grady, Patricia, "Thales of Miletus", *Internet Encyclopaedia of Philosophy. A Peer-Reviewed Academic Resource*, 1995[350 B.C.].

Oakeshott, Michael, *Experience and Its Modes*, Cambridge: The University Press, 1933.

Oakeshott, Michael, "On Arriving at a University", in *What is History? And Other Essays*, Exeter: Imprint Academic, 2004[1961], 333–40.

"Obesity epidemic 'bigger threat than terrorism'", *The Guardian*, 3 March 2006.

OECD, "Is happiness measurable and what do these measures mean for policy", *OECD*.

Ólafur R. Grímsson, "Sáttmáli um Fæðuöryggi Íslendinga", *Búnaðarþing* 2008.

Orwell, George, *Nineteen Eighty-Four*, London: Penguin, 2000[1949].

Orwin, Alexander, *The Privatization of Water and Wastewater Utilities: An International Survey*, Toronto: Environment Probe, 1999.

Ostrow, Matthew, "Barrick Gold's Pascua Lama Drama", Brown-Watson Case 15-03, item prepared for Prof. Peter Gourevitch.

Ostry, Jonathan D., Loungani, Prakash, and Furceri, Davide, "Neoliberalism: Oversold?", *Finance & Development*, June 2016.

Overmeyer, Douglas T., "China", in *Death and Eastern Thought*, edited by Frederick H. Holck, New York: Abingdon, 1974.

Parkes, Graham, "Death and Detachment: Montaigne, Zen, Heidegger and the Rest", in *Death and Philosophy*, edited by Jeff Malpas and Robert C. Solomon, London: Routledge, 1998, 83–97.

Parmenides, *Poem*, translated by John Burnet, 1892[6th century B.C],.

Pascal, Blaise, *Pensieri. Testo francese a fronte*, Milan: Rusconi, 1993 [Copy B, 1669].

Payne, Sarah, "Poverty, Social Exclusion and Mental Health: Findings from the 1999 PSE Survey", Working paper no. 15, 1999.

Perelman, Chaïm, and Olbrechts-Tyteca, Lucie, *The New Rhetoric. A Treatise on Argumentation*, translated by John Wilkinson, Notre Dame: University of Notre Dame Press, 1969[1958].

Pethó, Eszter, "Introduction to Rhetorical Economics", *European Integration Studies*, 4(1), 2005.

Pickering, Mary, *Auguste Comte. An Intellectual Biography. Volume II*, Cambridge: Cambridge University Press, 2009

Pius X (Pope), "The Oath Against Modernism", 1 September 1910; and *Pascendi Dominici Gregis*, 8 September 1907.

Plato, *Gorgias and Timaeus*, translated by Benjamin Jowett, New York: Dover, 2003[*ca.* 380 B.C.].

Plato, *Plato in Twelve Volumes*, vols. 5–6 & 9–11, translated by Paul Shorey, W.R.M. Lamb and R.G. Bury, London: William Heinemann, 1925–69[*ca.* 360 B.C.].

Plato, *The Last Days of Socrates*, translated by Hugh Tredennick and Harold Tarrant, London: Penguin, 1993[4th century B.C.].

Plato, *The Works of Plato*, translated by Benjamin Jowett, New York: Tudor, 1936[*ca.* 360 B.C.].

Plato, *Theaetetus*, translated by John McDowell, Oxford: Oxford University Press, 2014[*ca.* 369 B.C.].

Polanyi, Michael, *Knowing and Being. Essays by Michael Polanyi*, London: Routledge & Kegan Paul, 1969.

Polanyi, Michael, "Life's irreducible structure", *Science*, 160, 1968, 1308–13.

Polanyi, Michael, *Personal Knowledge. Towards a Post-Critical Philosophy*, London: Routledge & Kegan Paul, 1958 (1962 reprint).

Polanyi, Michael, *Society, Economics & Philosophy. Selected Papers*, New Brunswick: Transaction, 1997[1917–72].

Polanyi, Michael, "The Growth of Thought in Society," *Economica*, 8(32), 1941, 428–56.

Polanyi, Michael, *The Study of Man*, Chicago: University of Chicago Press, 1959 (1969 reprint).

Polanyi, Michael, *The Tacit Dimension*, London: Routledge, 1966 (2009 reprint).

Polanyi, Michael, "What is a Painting?", *The American Scholar*, 39(4), 1970, 655–69.

Polanyi, Michael, and Prosch, Harry, *Meaning*, Chicago: Chicago University Press, 1975.

Pompa, Leon, *Vico. A Study of the 'New Science'*, Cambridge: Cambridge University Press, 1990 (2nd ed.)[1977].

Porphyry, *On Abstinence from Animal Food*, translated by Thomas Taylor, London: Thomas Rodd, 1823[3rd century A.D.].

Postone, Moishe, *Time, Labour, and Social Domination*, Cambridge: Cambridge University Press, 1993.

Putin, Vladimir, "Prime Minister Vladimir Putin's speech at the opening ceremony of the World Economic Forum", Geneva, 28 January 2009.

Reale, Giovanni, *Storia della filosofia antica in cinque volumi*, Milan: Vita e pensiero, 1991.

Reinstaller, Andreas, and Becker, Joachim, "Economics past and present: An interview with Kurt W. Rothschild", *European Association for Evolutionary Political Economy Newsletter*, 36, July/August 2006.

Ricardo, David, *On Protection to Agriculture*, in *The Works of David Ricardo*, edited by John R. McCullock, 2004–16[1820].

Ricci, Maurizio, "L'ecobenzina infiamma i prezzi del grano", *La Repubblica*, 20 July 2007.

Robischaud, Paul, "Joyce, Vico, and National Narrative", *James Joyce Quarterly*, 41(1–2), 2003, 185–96.

Rowe, Stan, "From Shallow to Deep Ecological Philosophy", *The Trumpeter*, 13(1), 26–31.

Saltykov Shchedrin, Mikhail E., *The Glovlyov Family*, translated by Natalie Duddington, New York: New York Review of Books Classics, 2001[1880].

Salvi, Carola, Bricolo, Emanuela, Kounios, John, Bowden, Edward, and Beeman, Mark, "Insight solutions are correct more often than analytic solutions", *Thinking & Reasoning*, [no volume & issue number yet], 2016, DOI: 10.1080/13546783.2016.1141798.

Santino, Umberto, "L'acqua rubata. Dalla mafia alle multinazionali", Palermo: Centro Siciliano di Documentazione "Giuseppe Impastato", 22 September 2006.

Sartre, Jean-Paul, *Being and Nothingness*, translated by Bernard Frechtman, London: Methuen, 1958[1943].

Schopenhauer, Arthur, *Complete Essays*, translated by T. Bailey Saunders, New York: Willey, 1942[1851].

Schopenhauer, Arthur, *Metaphysics of the Love of the Sexes*, translated by T. Bailey Saunders, 2013[1819].

Schopenhauer, Arthur, *Studies in Pessimism*, selected and translated by T. Bailey Saunders, Adeilaide: University of Adelaide, 2014[1851].

Schopenhauer, Arthur, *The World as Will and Representation*, translated and edited by Judith Norman, Alistair Welchman and Christopher Janaway, Cambridge: Cambridge University Press, 2010[1859].

Schopenhauer, Arthur, *The Basis of Morality,* translated by Arthur Brodrick Bullock, London: Swan Sonnenschein, 1903[1840].

Schrödinger, Erwin, *What is Life?,* Cambridge: Cambridge University Press, 1944.

Schwartz, Barry, *Paradox of Choice: Why More Is Less,* New York: Harper Collins, 2004.

Sepper, Dennis L., *Goethe contra Newton: Polemics and the Project for a New Science of Color*, Cambridge: Cambridge University Press, 2003.

Sharpe, Matthew, "Autonomy, Reflexivity, Tragedy: Notions of Democracy in Camus and Castoriadis", *Critical Horizons*, 3(1), 2002, 103–29.

Sheptycki, James W.E., *In Search of Transnational Policing. Towards a Sociology of Global Policing*, Aldershot: Ashgate, 2002.

Simon, Lawrence H., "Vico and Marx: Perspectives on Historical Development", *Journal of the History of Ideas*, 42(2), 1981, 317–31.

Slomp, Gabriella, *Thomas Hobbes and the Political Philosophy of Glory*, Houndmills: Macmillan Press, 2000.

Smith, Adam, *An Inquiry into the Nature and Causes of the Wealth of Nations*, edited by Edwin Cannan, Indianapolis: The Online Library of Liberty, 1901[1776].

Smith, Helena, "Greek police face investigation after protest violence", *The Guardian*, 1 July 2011.

Smith, Karl E., "Meaning and Porous Being", *Thesis Eleven*, 99(1), 2009, 7–26.

Smith, Karl E., "The Constitution of Modernity. A Critique of Castoriadis", *European Journal of Social Theory*, 12(4), 2009, 505–21.

Smith, Kevin, "'Obscenity' of carbon trading", *BBC News*, 4 April 2007.

Snorri Sturluson, *Egil's Saga*, translated by Hermann Pálsson and Paul Edwards, London: Penguin, 1976[*ca.* 1240].

Solomon, Robert C., "Death Fetishism, Morbid Solipsism", in *Death and Philosophy*, edited by Jeff Malpas and Robert C. Solomon, London: Routledge, 1998.

Sophocles, *The Oedipus Tyrannus*, translated and edited by Richard Jebb, Cambridge: Cambridge University Press, 1887[5th century B.C.].

Sorgi, Marcello, "I super ricchi. L'eredità di Blair", *La Stampa*, 2 April 2007.

Sperber Gapp, Kenneth, "The Universal Famine under Claudius", *The Harvard Theological Review*, 28(4), October 1935, 258–65.

Spindler, Amy M., "Review/Fashion; In Milan, Bold Visions and a Softer Silhouette", *The New York Times*, 1 July 1993.

Starobinski, Jean, *Montaigne in Motion*, translated by Arthur Goldhammer, Chicago: University of Chicago Press, 1985.

Starr., Ross M., "Money: In Transactions and Finance", in *Fundamental Economics*, edited by Mukul Majumdar, *Encyclopedia of Life Support Systems*, Paris & London: Eolss, 2002–16.

Stiglitz, Joseph, *Globalization and Its Discontents*, New York: Norton, 2003.

Straume, Ingerid, "Freedom and the Collective", *Nordicum-Mediterraneum*, 3(2), 2008.

Straume, Ingerid, and Baruchello, Giorgio (eds.), *Creation, Rationality and Autonomy: Essays on Cornelius Castoriadis,* Malmö: Nordic Summer University Press, 2013.

Stuckler, David, and Basu, Sanjay, *The Body Economic: Why Austerity Kills*, London: Allen Lane, 2013.

Taureck, Bernhard H.F., "Decentering Humanity: Nietzsche's Debt to Montaigne and Others", *New Nietzsche Studies* 2(3–4), 1998, 93–107.

"The Economics of Happiness", a review of *Happiness: Lessons from a New Science*, by Richard Layard (London: Penguin, 2005), *The Economist*, 2005.

Theognis of Megara, "The Elegiac Poems of Theognis", in *Elegy and Iambus, Volume I*, translated and edited by J.M. Edmonds, Cambridge, Mass.: Loeb Classical Library, 1931[6th century B.C.].

Theophrastus of Eresus, *On First Principles (known as his* Metaphysics*)*, translated by Dimitri Gutas, Leiden: Brill, 2010[*ca.* 340 B.C.].

Torrance, Thomas F., "Michael Polanyi and the Christian Faith—A Personal Report", *Tradition and Discovery* 27(2), 2000–2001, 26–33.

Townsend, Mark, and Harris, Paul, "Now the Pentagon tells Bush: climate change will destroy us", *The Guardian*, 22 February 2004.

Turgenev, Ivan, *Sketches from a Hunter's Notebook*, translated by Richard Freeborn, London: Penguin, 1990[1852].

UN Conference on Trade and Development, *World Investment report 1999: "Foreign Investment and the Challenge of Development"*, 1999.

UN News, "World's Hungry Swell to 852 Million Despite Promises to Eradicate Hunger", 26 October 2006.

UN, *Report of the third United Nations conference on the least developed countries*, 2001.

UNDP, *Human development report 1999*, 1999.

UNESCO, *Encyclopedia of Life Support* Systems, Oxford & Paris: Eolss, 2002–2016

UNESCO, "UNESCO Fact Sheet: Death at the Border—Statistics on Migrant Fatalities to Unauthorized International Border Crossings", 2005.

Utz, Arthur Fridolin, *Wirtschaftsethik*, Bonn: Scientia Humana Institut, 1994.

Varsava, Jerry A., "The 'Saturated Self': Don DeLillo on the Problem of Rogue Capitalism", *Contemporary Literature*, 46(1), Spring 2005, 78–107.

Verene, Donald P. (ed.), *Vico and Joyce*, Albany: State University of New York Press, 1987.

Verga, Giovanni, *Mastro Don Gesualdo*, Milan: Mondadori, 1984[1889].

Vico, Giambattista, *La scienza nuova*, La Spezia: Fratelli Melita, 1987[1744].

Vico, Giambattista, *On the Most Ancient Wisdom of the Italians Unearthed from the Origins of the Latin Language*, translated by Lucia M. Palmer, Ithaca: Cornell University Press, 1988[1709].

Vico, Giambattista, *On the Study Methods of Our Time*, translated by Elio Gianturco, New York: Bobbs-Merrill, 1965[1708].

Vico, Giambattista, *The New Science of Giambattista Vico*, translated by Thomas G. Bergin and Max H. Fisch, Ithaca: Cornell University Press, 1988 (3rd printing) [1744].

Villemaire, Diane, "What Kuhn Really Said", *New Vico Studies*, 12, 1994, 75–80.

Vincenzo, Joseph E., "Nietzsche and Epicurus," *Man and World*, 27(4), 1994, 383–97.

Vivarelli, Vivetta, "Montaigne und der 'Freie Geist': Nietzsche *im Uebergang*", *Nietzsche Studien*, 23, 1994, 79–101.

Voltaire, "Epitre à l'auteur du livre des *Trois imposteurs*", in *Oeuvres complètes de Voltaire*, vol. 10, edited by Louis Moland, Paris: Garnier, 1877[1769], 402–5.

Wang, Sinclair T., "Return to a Pristine Ecosphere via Molecular Nanotechnology", in *Death and Anti-Death, Volume 3*, edited by Charles Tandy, Palo Alto: Ria University Press, 2005, 375–404.

Wheelwright, Philip, *The Presocratics*, London: MacMillan, 1966.

Williams, Roy, and Preisser, Vic, *Preparing Heirs: Five Steps to a Successful Transition of Family Wealth and Values*, Bandon, Oregon: Robert D. Reed, 2003.

Williams, William D., *Nietzsche and The French: A Study of the Influence of Nietzsche's French Reading on His Thought and Writing*, Oxford: Blackwell, 1952.

WMO, *WMO statement on the status of the global climate in 2007*, Geneva: WMO, 2008.

World Bank, *Global economic prospects 2000*.

World Health Organization Europe, *Health risks of heavy metals from long-range transboundary air pollution*, Copenhagen: WHO Regional Office for Europe, 2007.

"You don't have to be smart to be rich, study finds", *The Washington Times*, 27 April 2007

Young, Damon A., "Being Grateful for Being: Being, Reverence and Finitude", *Sophia*, 44(2), 2005, 31–53.

Endnotes

[1] For instance, some critical remarks may now seem too harsh: The International Monetary Fund [hereafter IMF] is singled out in chapter 4 as a major proponent of so-called "free-market reforms" or "neoliberalism", which have had disastrous effects in terms of protection and enhancement of life-support systems. As of the 2010s, perhaps because of the collapse of international finance in 2007–8 and the ensuing unsuccessful austerity measures advised onto many governments (e.g. the Greek one), the IMF can no longer be depicted as die-hard neoliberal. Far too stark and startling is the self-criticism contained in recent self-evaluations by their own research department, e.g. Jonathan D. Ostry, Prakash Loungani, and Davide Furceri, "Neoliberalism: Oversold?", *Finance & Development*, June 2016, <https://www.imf.org/external/pubs/ft/fandd/2016/06/pdf/ostry.pdf>. Thirty-five years later, after much avoidable damage worldwide, the critics of Reagonomics and the Washington Consensus have been vindicated by one of their main foes.

[2] Cf. McMurtry's extensive interviews in Peter Joseph's popular 2011 documentary movie *Zeitgeist: Moving Forward* (<https://www.youtube.com/watch?v=4Z9WVZddH9w>). On 11th August 2016, the film uploaded on this major website by TZMOfficialChannel alone had been viewed by more than 23 million internet users, to whose number one should add at least three more million netizens who viewed it in translated and/or subtitled versions, plus the other English-language versions posted by other users. Few living philosophers have reached as wide an audience as McMurtry has reached by this medium.

[3] John McMurtry, *The Cancer Stage of* Capitalism, London: Pluto Press, 1999 (1st ed.) & 2013 (2nd ed.); the revised second edition includes a revealing subtitle, absent in the former: *From Crisis to Cure.*

[4] *Philosophy and World Problems*, vols. I-III, edited by John McMurtry, Oxford & Paris: Eolss, 2011.

[5] UNESCO, *Encyclopedia of Life Support Systems*, Oxford & Paris: Eolss, 2002–16, <http://www.eolss.net> (free access available only in developing countries).

[6] Regarding the final bibliography and the footnotes accompanying this book, I made use of the Chicago Style Citation standard, which is the most common among Anglophone academic philosophers, though rejecting some of its more quixotic aspects, along the way of what I did in the past as a book editor for the Nordic Summer University Press. In any case, given the amount of information provided, the reader should find it easy to retrieve, and if willing to go back to, the scholarly and scientific sources utilised for this book.

[7] As Martin Heidegger stressed in his most famous philosophical work, *Sein und Zeit*, each person's—i.e. the *Dasein*'s—first encounter with death is always and obviously somebody else's death (cf. *Being and Time*, translated by John Macquarrie and Edward Robinson, San Francisco: Harper, 1962[1927]).

[8] Philodemus of Gadara, Herculaneum Papyrus no. 1005, column W, line 1014, 1st century B.C., as cited in Marcello Gigante, *Il libro degli epigrammi di Filodemo*, Naples: Bibliopolis, 2002 (translation mine).

[9] The Latin expression "*contemptus mundi*" [despise of the world] is still well-known among educated people. It carries an exquisite sense of aversion to the mundane, as characteristic of much of the original Christian asceticism and monasticism (whose initial goal in the early Middle Ages was the most thorough *fuga mundi*, i.e. escape from the world). For the sake of linguistic and aesthetic consistency, and in order to take advantage of the tacit dimension of historical significance accompanying it, I use Latin phrases to denominate the remaining three pigeonholes of the first tetralogy of death: "*immortalis eris*" [you will be immortal]; "*bona mors*" [happy death]; and "*intra vitam*" [during life].

[10] Plato, *The Apology*, 40c-e, in *The Last Days of Socrates*, translated by Hugh Tredennick and Harold Tarrant, London: Penguin, 1993[ca. 399 B.C.]. Given the great variety of editions of Plato's dialogues, I do not refer to page numbers and use the standard scholarly referencing system instead, i.e. the so-called "Stephanus" system (from Renaissance French scholar Henri Estienne, who published in Geneva in 1578 the collected works of Plato in both the original Greek and the Latin translation).

[11] Michel de Montaigne, *The Complete Essays*, I, 33, translated by Donald Frame, Stanford: Stanford University Press, 1998[1580]. Given the great variety of editions of Montaigne's essays, I do not refer to page numbers and use the standard scholarly system instead, i.e. book and essay number.

[12] Ibid., I, 20.

[13] Significantly, the motto of the University of Rome *La Sapienza* recites: *immortalis eris, si sapias, iuvenis* [you will be immortal, young fellow, if you have knowledge].

[14] Plato, *The Apology*, 40c–41b.

[15] The outcome of one's death can be eternal damnation in Dante's *Inferno* or re-birth as an insignificant bug, neither of which appears to be very desirable. However, the task of the Christian religion, as well as of the Hindu and of most religions in general, is to warn humankind about this risk and to teach us how to prevent its occurrence. In this sense, *immortalis eris, si sapias, iuvenis, bonam mortem obtenere* [you will be immortal, young fellow, if you have knowledge about achieving a happy death].

[16] Achieving a good or happy death can be a demanding task. This truth was recognised by Father Vincenzo Carrafa, seventh General of the Society of Jesus, who established in 1648 the *Bona Mors* Confraternity (its actual title being Confraternity of "Our Lord Jesus Christ dying on the Cross, and of the Most Blessed Virgin Mary, his sorrowful Mother"), aimed at preparing its members to die happily by means of prayer and good deeds; cf. *The Catholic Encyclopedia* (edited by Charles G. Herbermann, Edward A. Pace, Conde B. Fallen, Thomas J. Shahan and John J. Wynne, New York: Robert Appleton, 1907–12), s.v. "The Bona Mors Confraternity", <http://www.catholic.org/encyclopedia/view.php?id=2002>.

[17] Snorri Sturlusson, *Egil's Saga*, translated by Hermann Pálsson and Paul Edwards, London: Penguin, 1976[*ca.* 1240], chapter 85. Given the great variety of editions of the Icelandic sagas, I do not refer to page numbers and use the chapter numbers instead. The same is done in this book with regard to thinkers and other authors, whose works are typically organised in numbered books, paragraphs, sections, etc.

[18] Anonymous, *Njál's Saga*, translated by Hermann Pálsson and Magnus Magnusson, London: Penguin, 1960[13th century], chapter 77.

[19] Ugo Foscolo, "A Zacinto", in *Poesie,* edited by Giuseppe Chiarini, Livorno: Raffaello Giusti, 1904[1803], stanza I, verse 1 (hereafter abbreviated with "s." and "v."). The Italian Romantic poet was born in a now Greek island that, for centuries, belonged to the Republic of Venice.

[20] Ivan Turgenev describes acutely the stoicism of the peasant Maxim's death in "Death", in *Sketches from a Hunter's Notebook*, translated by Richard Freeborn, London: Penguin, 1990[1852]. Alexander Solzhenitsyn's and Leo Tolstoy's views on the exemplary acceptance of mortality among the Russian peasantry are discussed in Philippe Ariès, *Storia della morte in Occidente*, translated by Simona Vigezzi, Milan: BUR, 1997[1975], 20 & 25 (translation mine).

[21] Robert C. Solomon, "Death Fetishism, Morbid Solipsism", in *Death and Philosophy*, edited by Jeff Malpas and Robert C. Solomon, London: Routledge, 1998, 172 & 175.

[22] Carlo Felice's death implied his succession by Carlo Alberto, who was acclaimed as a liberator by his subjects, who, for the most part, seemed to dislike Carlo Felice's domestic policy. Carlo Alberto would later promulgate the first liberal constitution in the history of the Kingdom of Sardinia, which would then become the Kingdom of Italy in 1861.

[23] Wishing somebody else's death is a rather common desire amongst human beings. The reason for such an expression of hatred (or of extreme love, as it may be in the case of a loved one who is agonising in a hospital bed) does not need to be highly moral. There exists not solely the citizen's hope that the tyrant's death may bring about a better time for the country; there is also the siblings' longing for the old parents' demise, so that they may get their hands on the inheritance.

[24] Martin Heidegger, *Being and Time*, 293.

[25] Michel de Montaigne, as cited in Graham Parkes, "Death and Detachment: Montaigne, Zen, Heidegger and the Rest", in *Death and Philosophy*, edited by Jeff Malpas and Robert C. Solomon, 93–4. I analyse this essay in finer detail in chapter 8.

[26] *"This large burden, follows then / on the donkey comes Silen / aged but drunk and jubilant / he's of flesh and of years plump / he can't well and upright stand / yet he laughs and has great fun / He who wants it merry be / for tomorrow can't foresee"* (Lorenzo il Magnifico, "Canzona di Bacco", s. VII, vv. 29-36, in *Opera omnia*, 2007–16[1490], <http://ilmagnifico.letteraturaoperaomnia.org/index.html>; translation mine).

[27] Douglas T. Overmeyer, "China", in *Death and Eastern Thought*, edited by Frederick H. Holck, New York: Abingdon, 1974, 206.

[28] Ibid.

[29] Roger T. Ames, "Death and Transformation in Classical Daoism", in *Death and Philosophy*, edited by Jeff Malpas and Robert C. Solomon, 61–2. I disregard hereby the distinction between *si* and *sheng*, namely between 'natural' and 'violent' death, as certain Taoists saw the latter as a dramatic interference with the harmony of the *wuhua*.

[30] Cf. Friedrich Nietzsche, *The Will to Power*, translated by Walter Kaufmann and M.J. Hollingdale, New York: Random House,1968[1901], §§580 & 1067; and Gilles Deleuze, *Difference and Repetition*, translated by Paul Patton, New York: Columbia University Press, 1994[1968], 259. With particular regard to the latter, it is interesting to notice that he interprets Freud's *eros* and *thanatos* as the two faces of the same energy-flow permeating the whole universe. This line of thought is remarkably close to the Taoist and Zen teaching of life and death as the two faces of the same *qi*.

[31] I use "West", "East", "Western", etc. to give a sense of the geographical origins of a certain school of thought or doctrine. As such, these categories serve my purpose and possess no deeper cultural or philosophical meaning. For a detailed exposition of the diverse Buddhist positions on *samsara* and death, cf. Roy C. Amore, "The Heterodox Philosophical Systems", in *Death and Eastern Thought*, edited by Frederick H. Holck, Nashville: Abingdon, 1975, 114–63. There are several, diverse interpretations of *nirvana*; still, all Buddhist schools, with no exception at all, teach that death has not to be feared and that, if it is capable of bringing forth *nirvana*, then it ought to be praised.

[32] I expect that the reader to keep in mind the types of conception of death corresponding to [I]–[IV] while reading the following pages of this chapter.

[33] Michel de Montaigne, *The Complete Essays*, I, 20.

[34] I do not discuss this issue further, which is nowadays widely debated in bioethics. Euthanasia, palliative care, medical experimentation on humans, live organ transplants, clinical and juridical definitions of death are all cases related to this topic. It is quite evident, in fact, that the line distinguishing between the human person (or the self) and the mere human being (or the individual body) is also the line determining the recognition or the withdrawal of specific legal rights.

[35] Quite rarely is the full, 'philosophical' awareness of mortality held responsible for a degeneration of the individual's morality, that is to say, to be responsible for 'darkness' rather than for 'enlightenment'. It may be of interest to recall Dostoyevsky's case, though. In some of his novels, he analyses in fine detail (although disapprovingly) the psychology of such cases of anti-wisdom, or of 'black' hedonism. Some individuals deduce from the consciousness of human frailty the deepest contempt for themselves and for their fellows, e.g. anti-heroes such as Svidrigailov in 1866 *Crime and Punishment*, the young Verkhovensky in 1871-2 *Demons*, and Andrei Versilov in 1875 *The Adolescent* (cf. final bibliography for full bibliographic references).

[36] Graham Parkes, "Death and Detachment: Montaigne, Zen, Heidegger and the Rest", 88.

[37] *"Forever will you rest from now, / my weary heart. The great pretence did die, / which I believed immortal. It died. I do feel, / in us for dear deceits / or hope, that the desire is gone. / Rest forever. Much / you did beat. No value have / your motions, nor it's worth lamenting for / the earth. Bitterness and boredom / nothing else life ever gave; and grime's the universe. / Calm yourself now. Despair / for the last time. To our species fate / granted nothing but death. Now loathe / yourself, nature, the evil / power that, hidden, rules for the ruin of all / and the infinite futility of all"* (Giacomo Leopardi, "A se stesso", in *Canti*, 1835, <http://digilander.libero.it/bepi/biblio3a/indice8.html>; translation mine).

[38] Michel de Montaigne, *The Complete Essays*, I, 20.

[39] It could be objected that, in the West at least, several voices have expressed such a dry, dramatic form of materialism (e.g. Leucippus, Lucretius, Hobbes, Condorcet). I do not have strong objections to adding further names to those of Nietzsche and Deleuze. Also, Greek and Roman atomism did not exclude completely the idea of a *logos* regulating the flux of atoms in space, and some materialists and sensists of the French Enlightenment did not deny the presence of a Mind behind the cosmos.

[40] Interestingly, many anthropologists have claimed that religions arose in order to provide answers to the mystery of death.

[41] Martin Heidegger, *Being and Time*, 310.

[42] The act of teaching presupposes an attribution of value to life, even when a comprehensive meaning of life is denied (e.g. Sartre's existentialism): at least, being aware of life's ultimate meaninglessness makes living worthier (or less worthless) than persevering in the ignorance of this truth (more on the tacit axiological dimension of life-approbation can be read in Richard T. Allen's 1991 article "The Meaning of Life and Education", *Journal of Philosophy of Education*, 25(1), 47–57).

[43] Michel de Montaigne, *The Complete Essays*, I, 20. More on both Nietzsche and Montaigne follows in chapter 8.

[44] *Pace* Heidegger, death is not the only fixed *datum* in human existence: there are birth, biological functions, inter-subjectivity, and, as Benjamin Franklin would add, taxes. Perhaps all of them, in their own special way, can assist us in reaching authenticity.

[45] Michel de Montaigne, *The Complete Essays*, I, 20.

[46] Friedrich Nietzsche's *Also Sprach Zarathustra: Ein Buch für Alle und Keinen*, Zürich: Manesse, 2001[1883–91] (translation mine). Further remarks will be presented in chapter 8.

[47] According to Leibniz's 1714 *Monadology* (translated by Jonathan Bennett, 2007, <http://www.earlymoderntexts.com/assets/pdfs/leibniz1714b.pdf>), monads are the "the true *atoms* of Nature", i.e. any existing substance, which can be legitimately considered as the centre of the universe, for all entities relate, no matter how indirectly, to all others, past, present and future (§3).

[48] John McMurtry, *Philosophy and World Problems*, s.v. "The Primary Axiom and the Life-Value Compass", §6.1.

[49] Further references to and explanations of life-value onto-axiology are found in chapters 2–4.

[50] Cf. Arthur Schopenhauer, "On Suicide", in *Studies in Pessimism*, translated by T. Bailey Saunders, Adelaide: University of Adelaide Press, 2014[1851], <https://ebooks.adelaide.edu.au/s/schopenhauer/arthur/pessimism/ contents.html>.

[51] Theognis of Megara, "The Elegiac Poems of Theognis", in *Elegy and Iambus, Vol. I*, translated and edited by J.M. Edmonds, Cambridge, Mass.: Loeb Classical Library, 1931[6th century B.C.], vv. 425-8.

[52] Sophocles. *The Oedipus Tyrannus*, translated and edited by Richard Jebb, Cambridge: Cambridge University Press, 1887[5th century B.C.], vv. 1529-30.

[53] Giacomo Leopardi, "Il sabato del villaggio", in *Canti*, 1835, <www.liberliber.it/biblio/L/Leopardi/canti.htm> (translation mine).

[54] Giacomo Leopardi, "Dialogo di Malambruno e Farfarello", in *Operette Morali*, 1836, <http://www.leopardi.it/operette_morali.php> (translation mine).

[55] Ibid., "Dialogo di Federico Ruysch e delle sue mummie", (translation mine).

[56] Ibid., "Dialogo della natura e di un islandese", (translation mine).

[57] Ibid.

[58] Ibid., "Dialogo di Tristano e di un amico", (translation mine).

[59] Increase of life-ranges applies also to the "ultraphilosophy" of consciously self-selected illusions that Leopardi also considered as a way to cope with life's meaninglessness, as discussed in Geir Sigurðsson's 2010 article "In Praise of Illusions: Giacomo Leopardi's Ultraphilosophy", *Nordicum-Mediterraneum*, 5(1), <http://nome.unak.is/wordpress/05-1/articles51/in-praise-of-illusions-giacomo-leopardis-ultraphilosophy/>.

[60] Cf. Giacomo Leopardi, "Dialogo della natura e di un islandese" and "Dialogo di Federico Ruisch e delle mummie", in *Operette morali*.

[61] Arthur Schopenhauer, *Metaphysics of the Love of the Sexes*, translated by T. Bailey Sounders, 2013[1819], <http://uncharted.org/frownland/books/Schopenhauer/Schopenhauer_Love_of_the_sexes.html>.

[62] Arthur Schopenhauer, "Sufferings of the World", in *Complete Essays*, translated by T. Bailey Saunders, New York: Willey, 1942[1851], 4–5.

[63] Friedrich Nietzsche, *Twilight of the Idols: or How to Philosophize with a Hammer*, translated by Duncan Large, Oxford: Oxford University Press, 2009[1889]; Nietzsche's work opens with this critique of Socrates, after the preface and forty-four Pythic "Maxims and Arrows" setting the tone of the book.

[64] The origins of negative nihilism may be found in religious myths pre-existing Western philosophy. However, I limit the present cultural exploration to philosophical sources.

65 Much has been written on pre-Socratic philosophy, typically with reference to the development of epistemic and metaphysical categories (e.g. 'truth', 'knowledge', 'principle', 'nature'). However, I do not know of any previous study that has attempted to evaluate pre-Socratic philosophy distinctively from the life standpoint and particularly the life-value standpoint. What I offer hereby is a novel interpretation of widely accepted readings of pre-Socratic philosophies and philosophers, whose surviving fragments and known accounts by other commentators can be found in encyclopaedias and standard reference books. Therefore, this chapter, unlike the previous one, does not include a large array of references.

66 UNESCO, *Encyclopedia of Life Support Systems*, s.v. "Definition of Life Support System in the context of the EOLSS".

67 Gilles Deleuze and Félix Guattari, "Postulates of Linguistics", in *A Thousand Plateaus*, translated by Brian Massumi, Minneapolis: Minnesota University Press, 1988[1980], 78.

68 Aristotle, *Metaphysics*, 983b23–25, as cited in *Internet Encyclopaedia of Philosophy. A Peer-Reviewed Academic Resource*, 1995[350 B.C.], s.v. "Thales of Miletus", by Patricia O'Grady, <http://www.iep.utm.edu/thales/>. As done for Plato, so do I utilise the standard scholarly referencing system for Aristotle, i.e. the so-called "Bekker numbers" (from August Immanuel Bekker, philologist and critic at the Prussian Academy of Sciences, who published between 1831 and 1836 the standard edition of the complete works of Aristotle).

69 Ibid., 983b26–7.

70 Aëtius, *Placita*, I.3, as cited in *Internet Encyclopaedia of Philosophy. A Peer-Reviewed Academic Resource* [2nd century B.C.], s.v. "Thales of Miletus".

71 Returning to a synthetic notion of living reality is the undertaking of current deep ecology, e.g. Stan Rowe, "From Shallow to Deep Ecological Philosophy", *The Trumpeter*, 13(1), 26–31.

72 Aristotle, *Metaphysics*, 411a7–8, as cited in *Internet Encyclopaedia of Philosophy. A Peer-Reviewed Academic Resource*, s.v. "Thales of Miletus".

73 I describe a life-permeated ("hylozoism") and divine universe ("pantheism" or 'pan-polytheism') in order to distinguish Thales' understanding of reality from animism, panpsychism and panentheism. These last three notions imply either the presence of soul or of one Supreme Being, namely notions that do not belong to Thales' lexicon but to that of successive philosophers.

74 As cited in Giovanni Reale, *Storia della filosofia antica in cinque volumi*, Milan: Vita e pensiero, 1991[6th century B.C.], vol. 1 (translation mine). Unless new and substantive original textual evidence is discovered, I suspect that the correct translation of "*apeiron*" is bound to remain contentious.

75 Ibid.

76 As cited in *MacTutor History of Mathematics Archive*, 1999[6th century B.C.], s.v. "Pythagoras of Samos", by John J. O'Connor and Edmund F. Robertson, <http://www-groups.dcs.st-and.ac.uk/history/Biographies/Pythagoras.html>.

[77] Heraclitus, DK 22 B 50 (i.e. according to the 20th-century scholarly standard classification by Hermann Diels and Walther Kranz, *Die Fragmente der Vorsokratiker*, as translated by, Kathleen Freeman, *Ancilla to the Pre-Socratic Philosophers*, Cambridge: Harvard University Press, 1983[6th century B.C.]).

[78] Heraclitus, DK 22 B 1.

[79] Parmenides, *Poem*, translated by John Burnet, 1892[6th century B.C], s.III, v.1, <http://philoctetes.free.fr/parmenidesunicode.htm>.

[80] Plato, *Apology* 33c.

[81] Ibid. 38a.

[82] Ibid.

[83] Ibid.

[84] Plato, *Crito* 54d–e, in *The Last Days of Socrates*.

[85] Ibid.

[86] Plato, *Apology* 40c (I am taking Plato's early dialogues as reliable written accounts of Socrates' teachings).

[87] Ibid. 40c–d.

[88] Ibid. 40e.

[89] Ibid. 41b.

[90] Plato, *Phaedo* 66e, in *The Last Days of Socrates*.

[91] Plato, *Theaetetus* 176b, translated by John McDowell, Oxford: Oxford University Press, 2014[ca. 369 B.C.].

[92] Plato, *Phaedo* 106e, in *The Last Days of Socrates*.

[93] Plato, *Gorgias* 527a, in *Gorgias and Timaeus*, translated by Benjamin Jowett, New York: Dover, 2003[ca. 380 B.C.].

[94] Plato, *Phaedo* 107d, in *The Last Days of Socrates*.

[95] Ibid. 79d.

[96] Ibid. 80e.

[97] Ibid. 81a.

[98] Plato, *Timaeus* 30c, in *Gorgias and Timaeus*, translated by Benjamin Jowett, New York: Dover, 2003[ca. 380 B.C.].

[99] Plato, *Laws* 899b, in *The Works of Plato*, translated by Benjamin Jowett, New York: Tudor, 1936[ca. 360 B.C.].

[100] Ibid. 898d, in *Plato in Twelve Volumes*, vols. 10 & 11, translated by R.G. Bury, London: William Heinemann, 1967–8[ca. 360 B.C.].

[101] Plato, *Timaeus* 40b, in *Plato in Twelve Volumes*, vol. 9, translated by W.R.M. Lamb, London: William Heinemann, 1925[ca. 360 B.C.].

[102] *Plato, Republic* 473d, in *Plato in Twelve Volumes*, vols. 5 & 6, translated by Paul Shorey, London: William Heinemann, 1969[ca. 360 B.C.].

[103] Ibid. 414d–415d.

[104] Ibid. 370d–371e.

[105] Ibid. 558d.

[106] Ibid. 559a–b.

[107] Giovanni Reale, *Storia della filosofia antica in cinque volumi*.

[108] Ibid.

[109] Democritus, DK 68 A 1.

[110] Giovanni Reale, *Storia della filosofia antica in cinque volumi*.

[111] Although being a disciple of Plato's and sharing much of his mentor's elitist intellectualism, including the notion of a rationally ordered universe, Aristotle was far less otherworldly and life-renouncing than Plato. He did inherit and maintain Plato's life- and order-giving forms underlying material reality, but he stressed their immanent character rather than their transcendent one. Additionally, as hinted in the main text, he had a genuine interest in biology and medicine, which Plato did not have. Nevertheless, as concerns the point that I am making in this paragraph, the differences between Plato and Aristotle can be underplayed.

[112] By "modern" I mean the period that, roughly, goes from the late 16th century (i.e. when the Italian Renaissance crossed the Alps) to the present day. In other words, I do not distinguish, as some other scholars would do, between a Modern Age and a Contemporary Age.

[113] Porphyry, *On Abstinence from Animal Food*, translated by Thomas Taylor, London: Thomas Rodd, 1823[3rd century A.D.], book III, §125. Possibly because of his mechanistic views, Theophrastus was tried for impiety.

[114] Theophrastus, *On First Principles (known as his* Metaphysics*)*, translated by Dimitri Gutas, Leiden: Brill, 2010[*ca.* 340 B.C.], 11a1.

[115] Ibid., 10a9-18.

[116] Marcus T. Cicero, *Academica priora et posteriora*, Fairbanks: PGLA, 2005[1st century B.C.], book 2, §xxxviii, line 121, <http://www.gutenberg.org/files/14970/> (translation mine). Aristotle's cosmology may have comprised concepts leading to Strato's mechanism (e.g. 'prime motor' and 'natural *loci*'). Still, they were tempered by his studies of animal life and the more spiritual aspects of his cosmology (e.g. ensouled matter and the function of love in causing entities to attract one another).

[117] For comprehensive synoptic accounts of medieval physics and the thinkers mentioned in the following two paragraphs, cf. Etienne Gilson, *La philosophie au moyen-âge*, vols I–II, Paris: Payot, 1988[1922]; and Helen S. Lang, *Aristotle's Physics and Its Medieval Varieties*, New York: State University of New York Press, 1992.

[118] E.g. Aquinas, *Summa Theologica*, 1920[*ca.* 1268], part I of Part II, question 57, art. 1.

[119] Dante Alighieri, *La divina commedia*, 1966-7[1307-21], <http://divinacommedia.weebly.com/introduzione-al-poema.html>.

120 Pius X (Pope), "The Oath Against Modernism", 1 September 1910, <http://www.franciscan-archive.org/bullarium/oath.html>; and *Pascendi Dominici Gregis*, 8 September 1907, <http://w2.vatican.va/content/pius-x/en/encyclicals/documents/hf_p-x_enc_19070908_pascendi-dominici-gregis.html>.

121 The 'eminent learning' and 'great sanctity' required to become an official Doctor of the Church were declared to be possessed by Aquinas in a Papal proclamation of 1568.

122 Galileo Galilei, *Lettere*, Turin: Einaudi, 1978[1615], 128–35.

123 Galileo Galilei, *Opere*, Florence: Barbera, 1890–1909, 1929–1939 reprint[1638], vol. V, 187.

124 Ibid., 187–8.

125 Cf. Francis Bacon, *The New Atlantis*, in *Three Early Modern Utopias*, Oxford: Oxford University Press, 2009[1627].Francis Bacon, an ambitious lawyer and corrupt politician under Queen Elisabeth I of England, did pursue some empirical studies himself. Indeed, his death in 1626 is attributed to a chill that he contracted while investigating the properties for food preservation of snow. However, his actual research is far inferior in both quantity and quality to his advocacy of inductive inquiry of material nature. Polemically, Bacon attacked the Platonic-Augustinian emphasis on faith-inspired deductive knowledge and the Aristotelian-scholastic tradition of syllogistic competence, both of which coloured most curricula in medieval universities, the latter in particular.

126 "He who is not mathematically minded should not read me" (Leonardo da Vinci, *Aforismi, novelle e profezie*, Rome: Newton, 1993[15th–16th century], 22; translation mine).

127 Psychologist Donald A. Norman offers a good example in his book, *The Psychology of Everyday Things* (New York: Basic Books, 1988), which I recall shortly hereby: I take a pistol and hold it in a perfectly horizontal position. At the same time, I also hold a bullet in the other hand, so that it is at the same distance from the ground as the bullet inside the pistol. Then, simultaneously, I fire the pistol and let the bullet in my other hand fall. Any physicist would expect that, in the absence of friction, the two bullets will touch the ground at the same time, for the horizontal component of the former's motion has no effect upon the vertical one, which is the same for both bullets. Anybody else, even if high-school-level-trained in Newtonian physics, would at least be tempted to expect that the shot bullet would take much longer to touch the ground much later than the one falling from the hand.

128 The Aristotelian-Ptolemaic geocentric universe is no longer obvious to the modern person, despite the persisting use of geocentric expressions like "the Sun rises at 6.30am" and "Venus will be in Taurus". The term "nature" does not suggest any longer, at least immediately and primarily, either the idea of "essence" or the soul-pervaded "cosmos" of the Aristotelian tradition. Rather, it suggests just the kind of material reality studied by the modern scientist.

129 Galileo Galilei, *Opere*, vol. VI [1624], 350.

[130] Famously, Johann Wolfgang von Goethe attempted to return Galileo's 'animal' to mainstream science, without much success (cf. his 1810 *Theory of Colours*, as discussed in Dennis L. Sepper, *Goethe contra Newton: Polemics and the Project for a New Science of Color*, Cambridge: Cambridge University Press, 2003). Today's research niches of fuzzy logic and naïve physics, very important for AI programmers, have inherited some of Goethe's concerns (e.g. an 'animal' perspective is needed when programming software for a mobile robot transporting infectious substances inside a hospital; cf. Donald A. Norman, *The Psychology of Everyday Things*).

[131] Galileo Galilei, *Il Saggiatore*, Milan: Feltrinelli, 1965[1623], 264.

[132] Galileo Galilei, *Opere*, vol. XVII [1639], 90.

[133] Henri Bergson, *Time and Free Will. An Essay on the Immediate Data of Consciousness*, London: George Allen, 1910[1888].

[134] Gottfried W. Leibniz, "Meditations on Knowledge, Truth and Ideas", in *Philosophical* Essays, translated and edited by Roger Ariew and Dan Garber, Indianapolis: Hackett, 1989[1684], 217.

[135] Cf. René Descartes, *Meditations on First Philosophy*, translated by Elizabeth S. Haldane, Cambridge: Cambridge University Press, 1911[1641], <http://selfpace.uconn.edu/class/percep/DescartesMeditations.pdf>.

[136] Cf. Cynthia Klestenic, *Theaters of Anatomy: Students, Teachers and Traditions of Dissection in Renaissance Venice*, Boston: Johns Hopkins University Press, 2011.

[137] As stated previously, medieval thinkers had already discussed the notion of impetus. Yet, it was only during the Modern Age that emerged a consistent and comprehensive explanation of physical phenomena based upon it.

[138] Cf. Isaac Newton, *Philosophiae Naturalis Principia Mathematica*, Glasgow: James MacLehose, 1871[1687], <http://www.wilbourhall.org/pdfs/newton/NewtonPrincipia.pdf>.

[139] Cf. René Descartes, *Treatise on Man*, in *The World and Other Writings*, translated and edited by Stephen Gaukroger, Cambridge: Cambridge University Press, 2004[1644], 99–169.

[140] Cf. James Lovelock, *Gaia: A New Look at Life on Earth*, Oxford: Oxford University Press, 1979.

[141] Ironically, the mechanistic picture of the world presents a problem analogous to that of the Holy Spirit's relationship with historical reality. As soon as it emerged, modern mechanism raised the question of how the knowing mind is related to the material body within which it appears to operate—a question that has become central to modern philosophy. However, the very terms of that question meant that the whole sphere of life—i.e. organisms, their organs and their distinctive environments—was completely ignored or denied.

[142] Friedrich Nietzsche, *The Gay Science*, translated by Josephine Nauckhoff, Cambridge: Cambridge University Press, 2001[1882], §372.

[143] In addition to Laplace, other famous cases of reductionism are 18th-century French 'sensism' (e.g. Julien Offray de La Mettrie, *L'homme* machine, Leyde: Elie Luzac, 1748[1714]) and 20th-century 'geneticism' by Richard Dawkins (cf. *The Selfish Gene*, Oxford: Oxford University Press, 1976; interestingly, Dawkins' theses are vividly reminiscent of Schopenhauer's, especially his *World as Will and Representation*, of which Dawkins was, apparently, totally ignorant when writing his book).

[144] In variously extreme forms, the 20th-century schools of reflexology in Russia and behaviourism in the USA endorsed a mechanistic approach to human psychology (cf. chapter 6 in *A History of Psychology in Metascientific Perspective*, edited by Kristen B. Madsen, special issue of *Advances in Psychology*, 53, 1988, 193–257).

[145] Cf. Pierre Simon Laplace, *A Philosophical Essay on Probabilities*, translated by Frederick Wilson Truscott and Frederick Lincoln Emory, London: Chapman & Hall, 1902[1814].

[146] Cf. Cathy Cobb and Harold Goldwhite, *Creations of Fire: Chemistry from Alchemy to the Atomic Age*, New York: Basic Books, 2002.

[147] Cf. Immanuel Kant, *Critique of Pure Reason*, sections VIII–IX, in *The Cambridge Edition of the Works of Immanuel Kant*.

[148] Cf. Roger Ariew, "Descartes and Pascal", *Perspectives on Science*, 15(4), 2007, 397–409.

[149] Voltaire, "Epitre à l'auteur du livre des *Trois imposteurs*, in *Oeuvres complètes de Voltaire*, vol. 10, edited by Louis Moland, Paris: Garnier, 1877[1769], 403.

[150] Immanuel Kant, "An Answer to the Question: What is Enlightenment?", in *Philosophy E-Server*, translated by Mary J. Gregor, 2006[1784], <http://philosophy.eserver.org/kant/what-is-enlightenment.txt> (emphasis added).

[151] Jean-Paul Sartre's *Being and Nothingness*, translated by Bernard Frechtman, London: Methuen, 1958[1943].

[152] Kant's formulation, with slight modifications, can be found in his *Groundwork of the Metaphysic of Morals*, *Critique of Practical Reason* and *Metaphysic of Morals* (cf. *The Cambridge Edition of the Works of Immanuel Kant*, edited by P. Guyer and A. Wood, Cambridge: Cambridge University Press, 1992–2007).

[153] Thomas Hobbes, *Leviathan*, London: Penguin, 1985[1651], part I, chapter XI, §2.

[154] Though already discussed by Helvetius, Voltaire and Beccaria, this notion of happiness became canonical in Western ethics thanks to the Utilitarian school of Bentham and John Stuart Mill (cf. J.H. Burns, "Happiness and Utility: Jeremy Bentham's Equation", *Utilitas*, 17(1), 2005, 46–61).

[155] Martin Heidegger, *The Question Concerning Technology*, translated by William Lovitt, New York: Harper & Row, 1977[1953], 9.

[156] Cf. Charles Dickens, *Hard Times*, London: Penguin, 2007[1854].

[157] Cf. Erwin Schrödinger, *What is Life?*, Cambridge: Cambridge University Press, 1944.

[158] Cf. Michael Polanyi, "Life's Irreducible Structure", *Science*, 160, 1968, 1308–12.

[159] Cf. Hans Jonas, *The Phenomenon of Life: Toward a Philosophical Biology*, Evanston, Ill.: Northwestern University Press, 2001[1973 part.].

[160] David Ricardo, *On Protection to Agriculture*, in *The Works of David Ricardo*, edited by John R. McCullock, 2004–16[1820], <http://oll.libertyfund.org/titles/ricardo-the-works-of-david-ricardo-mcculloch-ed-1846-1888>.

[161] Cf. Paolo Legrenzi, *Storia della psicologia*, Bologna: Il mulino, 2002.

[162] Ibid.

[163] Cf. Titus Lucretius Carus, *De rerum natura*, translated by William Ellery Leonard, London: Everyman's Library, 1942[*ca.* 50 B.C.].

[164] Cf. Francesco Mimmo, "Prodi lancia il piano anti-siccità. Blocco dei consumi non essenziali", *La Repubblica*, 7 March 2003, <http://www.repubblica.it/2007/03/sezioni/cronaca/emergenza-idrica/piano-anti-siccita/piano-anti-siccita.html>. Mainstream media sources are to be privileged in this chapter, in order to highlight, on the one hand, the widespread urgency and relevance of the issues discussed and, on the other hand, the pervasive nature of the neoclassical paradigm, which is not studied hereby as a lofty academic theory, but as a set of politically significant notions forming an active paradigm or ideology in today's world affairs. In this respect, John McMurtry speaks aptly of "the global market as an "ethical system" (*Unequal Freedoms. The Global Market as an Ethical System*, Toronto: Garamond Press, 1998). Facts and figures are 'out there', indeed in the mainstream media, but they regularly lack a consistent frame of understanding that exposes them as symptoms of a subjacent, life-destructive logic of insatiable money-capital accumulation dictated by the neoclassical paradigm. This operation of disclosure becomes possible by the adoption of a different line of analysis, springing from the serious consideration of the fundamental nature- and human-made systemic conditions that endorse and enhance life in depth and breadth. And this is exactly what is done by UNESCO's LSS and McMurtry's life-ground philosophy in particular, which I have already introduced in the previous chapters.

[165] Cf. Paolo Mastrolilli, "Gli eroi del football dementi a 40 anni", *La Stampa*, 15 March 2007, <http://www.luigiboschi.it/node/1633>.

[166] Cf. Marcello Sorgi, "I super ricchi. L'eredità di Blair", *La Stampa*, 2 April 2007, <http://pensiericonvulsi.blogspot.it/2007/04/i-super-ricchi-leredit-di-blair.html>.

[167] The notions of 'money capital', 'life capital' and, later in the text, 'life ground' are borrowed from John McMurtry's life-capital economics, i.e. part of life-value onto-axiology.

[168] Cf. Kenneth Sperber Gapp, "The Universal Famine under Claudius", *The Harvard Theological Review*, 28(4), October 1935, 258–65; and Cormac Ó Gráda, "Markets and Famines in Pre-Industrial Europe", *Journal of Interdisciplinary History*, 36(2), Autumn 2005, 143–66.

[169] Cf. Elizabeth Brubaker, "Privatizing Water Supply and Sewage Treatment: How Far Should We Go?", *Journal des Economistes et des Etudes Humaines*, 8(4), December 1998, 441–54.

[170] Cf. Alexander Orwin, *The Privatization of Water and Wastewater Utilities: An International Survey*, Toronto: Environment Probe, 1999.

[171] Cf. Umberto Santino, *L'acqua rubata. Dalla mafia alle multinazionali*, Palermo: Centro Siciliano di Documentazione Giuseppe Impastato, September 2006, <http://www.centroimpastato.it:80/publ/online/Acqua.php3>.

[172] To have a better idea of the money surrounding professional football in the US, the 2004 net revenues of the NFL teams ranged from a minimum of $167,000,000 to a maximum of $303,000,000 (cf. Kurt Badenhausen, Michael K. Ozanian and Maya Roney, "The Business Of Football", *Forbes,* 31 August 2006, <www.forbes.com/2005/09/01/sports-football-gambling-cz_05nfland.html>).

[173] The World Metereological Organization's [hereafter WMO] and United Nations' [hereafter UN] Intergovernmental Panel on Climate Change [hereafter IPCC] issued a report concerning measures to be taken in order to prevent our planet's environmental collapse (cf. *WMO statement on the status of the global climate in 2007*, Geneva: WMO, 2008). Tackling the issue of fossil-fuel production and consumption is amongst the priorities highlighted. The recommended cuts to greenhouse-gas emissions are calculated against their likely costs *vis-à-vis* global Gross Domestic Product [hereafter GDP], i.e. the estimated total market value of all goods and services produced within the borders of UN member nations during given periods of time. Whether intentional or not, this opposition clearly exemplifies that between money-capital and life-capital concerns.

[174] On the powerful and negative social effects of the emulation of the rich in recent decades, cf. Samuel Bowles and Yongjin Park, "Emulation, Inequality and Working Hours: Was Thorstein Veblen Right?", *The Economic Journal*, 115, November 2005, 397–412; and Hervé Kempf, *Comment les riches détruisent la planète*, Paris: Seuil, 2007.

[175] Sometimes the term "neoclassical" is used also with reference to pre-Keynesian economists like Alfred Marshall, Knut Wicksell and Irving Fisher, assuming that the Golden Age of Keynesianism goes from 1945 to 1973, or orbiting around Keynes himself, e.g. Piero Sraffa, Joan Robinson and Richard Kahn, when he was breaking the sacred equation of Say's Law. I stress the last three decades of the 20th century in order to avoid misunderstandings. Also, "neo-liberal" and "libertarian" are sometimes used to refer to some or all the tenets outlined in the main text. I prefer the term "neoclassical" in order to emphasise their origin in economics and avoid confusion with the term "liberal", which describes very different views, including those of John Stuart Mill and John M. Keynes.

[176] Adam Smith, *An Inquiry into the Nature and Causes of the Wealth of Nations*, edited by Edwin Cannan, Indianapolis: The Online Library of Liberty, 1901[1776], <http://oll.libertyfund.org/titles/smith-an-inquiry-into-the-nature-and-causes-of-the-wealth-of-nations-cannan-ed-in-2-vols> (known also as *The Wealth of Nations* and referred here as Smith's *Inquiry*).

[177] Ibid., "Of Restraints upon the Importation from Foreign Countries of such Goods as can be Produced at Home".

[178] Ibid., "Of the Expences of the Sovereign or Commonwealth".

[179] Ibid., "On the Extraordinary Restraints on the Importation of Goods of almost all Kinds" and "Of the Accumulation of Capital, or of Productive and Unproductive Labour".

[180] Ibid., "Of the Expences of the Sovereign or Commonwealth".

[181] Alan D. Morrison and William J. Wilhelm, Jr., *Investment Banking*, Oxford: Oxford University Press, 2006, 42.

[182] The list above is far from original. Analogous observations can be found already in the works of other scholars, e.g. *A Brief History of Neoliberalism* (Oxford: Oxford University Press, 2005) by David Harvey and *The Cancer Stage of Capitalism* by John McMurtry.

[183] Cf. World Health Organization Europe, *Health risks of heavy metals from long-range transboundary air pollution*, Copenhagen: WHO Regional Office for Europe, 2007.

[184] UNESCO, *Encyclopedia of Life Support Systems*, s.v. "Money: In Transactions and Finance", by Ross M. Starr.

[185] Private companies must frighten their potential customers into buying their services; cf. James W.E. Sheptycki, *In Search of Transnational Policing. Towards a Sociology of Global Policing*, Aldershot: Ashgate, 2002.

[186] Fighting must take place for the armaments and security business to prosper; cf. Amica Kronsell and Erika Svedberg, "The Swedish Military Manpower Policies and their Gender Implications", in *The Changing Face of European Conscription*, edited by Pertti Joenniemi, Aldershot: Ashgate, 2006, 137–57; and Deborah D. Avant, *The Market for Force: The Consequences for Privatizing Security*, Cambridge: Cambridge University Press, 2005.

[187] The 2007 source no longer being available, cf. as a short introduction Matthew Ostrow, *Barrick Gold's Pascua Lama Drama*, Brown-Watson Case 15-03 (prepared for Prof. Peter Gourevitch), <https://gps.ucsd.edu/_files/faculty/gourevitch/gourevitch_cs_ostrow.pdf>.

[188] It must be noted that Newtonian physics and its practical expression as mechanical engineering were extremely popular in the 18th and 19th centuries, thus suggesting that classical economics reflected somehow the *Zeitgeist* within which it was born (cf. UNESCO, *Encyclopedia of Life Support Systems*, s.v. "Life Responsibility versus Mechanical Reductionism", by Richard T. Allen and Giorgio Baruchello).

[189] It should be observed that already in the year 2000, 51 of the 100 largest economies in the world were corporations, not States (cf. Sarah Anderson and John Cavanagh, *Report on the top 200 corporations*, Institute for Policy Studies, December 2000, <https://www.globalpolicy.org/component/content/article/221/47211.html>).

[190] Interestingly, classical economics influenced the lexicon of a very different field of scientific study: 19th-century biology. Contrary to common belief, the language of 'competition', 'necessary death' and 'cruelty' typically associated with modern evolutionary theory originates first in economics, i.e. in the works of Smith, Malthus and Ricardo (cf. for example "Of the Wages of Labour" in Adam Smith's already-cited *Inquiry*). From there, combined with the Buddhist pessimism of Arthur Schopenhauer, it reaches Charles Darwin, father of that theory, and finally returns to the social and economic sphere in the guise 'social Darwinism', the creation of Herbert Spencer, who also coined the famous expression 'survival of the fittest'. As regards what counts as 'fitness' for survival, it should come as no surprise to most readers that ruthlessness seems to play a bigger role than intelligence or virtue, as suggested by psychologist Jay Zagorsky (cf. "You don't have to be smart to be rich, study finds", *The Washington Times*, 27 April 2007, <http://www.eurekalert.org/pub_releases/2007-04/osu-ydh042307.php#>).

[191] Awareness is not absent *in toto* [completely} from the political and scientific scene. A conference was held in Rome's University of Tor Vergata in April 2007 on the topic of happiness, in which economists, political and social scientists took part, in the attempt to develop a better set of parameters for the assessment of human well-being to be used by policy-makers, since standard neoclassical categories seem inadequate. The conference was funded and organised, amongst others, by the Bank of Italy and the OECD (cf. OECD, "Is happiness measurable and what do these measures mean for policy", 2007,).

[192] As cited in Istvan Mészáros, *Beyond Capital*, London: Merlin Press, 1995, §3.2.1.

[193] Eszter Pethó, "Introduction to Rhetorical Economics", *European Integration Studies*, 4(1), 2005, 110 (emphasis added). The birth of rhetorical economics in the 1980s, with Deirdre McCloskey as its champion (e.g. "The Rhetoric of Economics", *Journal of Economic Literature*, XXI, June 1983, 481–517), reflects the influence of the great Belgian scholar Chaïm Perelman who, in the 1950s and 1960s, returned to the humanities and the social sciences the serious study and consideration of rhetoric (cf. Chaïm Perelman and Lucie Olbrechts-Tyteca, *The New Rhetoric. A Treatise on Argumentation*, translated by John Wilkinson, Notre Dame: University of Notre Dame Press, 1969[1958]).

[194] Andreas Reinstaller and Joachim Becker, "Economics past and present: An interview with Kurt W. Rothschild", *European Association for Evolutionary Political Economy Newsletter*, 36, July/August 2006, <http://www.uv.es/ftoboso/news6/rothschild-interview2006.pdf>.

[195] In a recent e-mail exchange of mine with Oxford economist Andrew Glyn, he suggested that the economists' widespread blindness to the life-ground may be due to the fact that "environmental constraints/issues have not yet had a strong effect on the growth & distributional pattern in the North (which does not imply that the pattern of growth should NOT have taken these issues into account)".

[196] I wish to highlight hereby that de-spiritedness and abstractedness are two key-features of the lifelessness of modern science, as extensively discussed in my previous chapter.

[197] The 2007 source no longer being available, cf. Jesper Jespersen, "When the Treasury and its Models Seize Power", *Nordicum-Mediterraneum*, 11(1), 2016, <http://nome.unak.is/wordpress/volume-11-no-1-2016/01_double-blind-peer-reviewed-article/treasury-models-seize-power/>, dealing with the case of Denmark.

[198] Other economic paradigms have been capable of life-destruction, but by betrayal of their life-aware principles (e.g. Stalin's *de facto* denial of Marx's principle "From each according to his abilities, to each according to his needs", the ecological disasters of several former Warsaw Pact countries), not by assumption of life-blind principles.

[199] Biological movement or motility is the first of the three planes of life identified by life-value onto-axiology, the other two being felt being and thought. Together, these three planes of life identify the life-ground as the ultimate ground of value, upon which all axiological assessments stand, whether tacitly or explicitly (e.g. well-being, desirability, utility, optimal flow, subjective and objective standards for happiness), as well as all controversies about what is to value most or more.

[200] In this chapter I am intentionally anthropocentric, in order to show even more starkly the fundamental inadequacy of the neoclassical paradigm.

[201] John McMurtry, *Value Wars. The Global Market versus the Life Economy*, London: Pluto Press, 2002, 155–7.

[202] Cf. Rocco Cotroneo, "Bio (o necro) combustibili", *Il corriere della sera*, 4 April 2007, <http://americas.corriere.it/2007/07/bio_o_necro_combustibili.html>.

[203] Cf. Maurizio Ricci, "L'ecobenzina infiamma i prezzi del grano", *La Repubblica*, 20 July 2007, <http://www.repubblica.it/2006/12/sezioni/ambiente/biocarburanti/ecobenzina/ecobenzina.html>.

[204] As cited in Kevin Smith, "'Obscenity' of carbon trading", *BBC News*, 4 April 2007, <http://news.bbc.co.uk/2/hi/science/nature/6132826.stm>.

[205] Believers in the neoclassical paradigm may argue that the depletion of the world's LSS caused by the pursuit of money-capital accumulation is to become unprofitable and, as a result, that the free market is going to take care of the problems it generates without the need of any external intervention (e.g. State regulation, green taxes). This, however, is a non-falsifiable hypothesis, indeed a wish, which stems from the more fundamental non-falsifiable hypothesis of the 'invisible hand', or self-correcting ability of free markets, as I have argued elsewhere (the 2007 original source no longer being available, cf. Giorgio Baruchello, "The Unscientific Ground of Free-Market Liberalism", in *Ethics, Democracy, and Markets*, edited by Giorgio Baruchello, Jacob Dahl Rendtorff and Asger Sörensen, Malmö: Nordic Summer University Press, 2016, 233–59). Apart from being a modern instance of superstitious thought, this belief does not address the issue of why one should still refer to the neoclassical paradigm *vis-à-vis* ecological concerns, given that this paradigm is unable to distinguish between, to name a few, life and death (e.g. commonly traded life-destructive commodities such as hand-grenades and landmines), life-needs and wants (e.g. affordable junk food *contra* nourishing food that the poor cannot purchase), biodiverse forests and monocultures (e.g. commercial pinewoods in Finland).

[206] Kevin Smith, "'Obscenity' of carbon trading"—Not to mention the attempted creation in the USA of an exchange market trading possible acts of terrorism and political violence, to be based on "the Policy Analysis Market, a DARPA-funded research project, within the FutureMAP program, which was suddenly cancelled amid a media storm on July 29, 2003" (Robin Hanson, *The Policy Analysis Market (and FutureMAP) Archive*, George Mason University, n.d.a., <http://mason.gmu.edu/~rhanson/policyanalysismarket.html>).

[207] Jagdish Bhagwati, "Coping with Antiglobalization", *Foreign Affairs*, January/February 2002, 2–3. Bhagwati dismisses rhetorically the widespread opposition to the neoclassical paradigm as "nostalgia for vanished dreams", whilst not considering that free-market competition was, according to Adam Smith's *Inquiry* itself, "a Utopia or an Oceana" ("Of the restraints upon the importation from foreign countries of such goods as can be produced at home"). Furthermore, he does not tackle the reasons of the many opponents that he lumps together under the "antiglobalization" label. Still, he strikes the right chord as concerns a line of continuity between traditional socialism and green thought, i.e. their shared awareness of human (at least) life-needs, which the neoclassical paradigm ignores, for it focuses on the self-maximising individual's property rights as its axiological and hermeneutical bedrock.

[208] In the USA, assessing the outcomes of for-profit mass-marketed junk-food and advertising-induced overeating habits, Dr Richard Carmona stated: "Unless we do something about [obesity], the magnitude of the dilemma will dwarf 9/11 or any other terrorist attempt" ("Obesity epidemic 'bigger threat than terrorism'", *The Guardian*, 3 March 2006, <https://www.theguardian.com/world/2006/mar/03/usa.mainsection>). In Italy, a recent research by the University of Rome Three has calculated that, between 16.00 and 19.00, minors are exposed to one TV advert every five minutes and 36% of them aim at selling junk food (the original 2007 source no longer being available, cf. Serena Iannello, "Pubblicità e tutela dei minori: sulla pubblicità di alimenti", *Altalex*, 2010, <http://www.altalex.com/documents/news/2010/04/02/pubblicita-e-tutela-dei-minori-sulla-pubblicita-di-alimenti>).

[209] Some 'Green' points are now commonplace in the political agenda of most world leaders. What matters, however, is whether they are actually pursued or not!

[210] Benedict XVI, "Omelia di Sua Santità Benedetto XVI", Piazza San Pietro, 3 June 2006, <http://w2.vatican.va/content/benedict-xvi/it/homilies/2006/documents/hf_ben-xvi_hom_20060603_veglia-pentecoste.html> (translation mine).

[211] Cf. Sinclair T. Wang, "Return to a Pristine Ecosphere via Molecular Nanotechnology", in *Death and Anti-Death, Volume 3*, edited by Charles Tandy, Palo Alto: Ria University Press, 2005, 375–404.

212 As cited in Mark Townsend and Paul Harris, "Now the Pentagon tells Bush: climate change will destroy us", *The Guardian*, 22 February 2004, <https://www.theguardian.com/environment/2004/feb/22/usnews.theobserver>. A recent report by UK-based Christian Aid tells instead of one billion climate refugees by the year 2050, i.e. one seventh of the world's population (Christian Aid, *Human tide: the real migration crisis*, May 2007, <https://www.christianaid.org.uk/Images/human-tide.pdf>).

213 The Cancer Council of Australia has issued repeatedly results of medical research conducted in both Australia and New Zealand showing astounding increases of skin cancer over the past decade (the 10 May 2007 original source no longer being available, cf. Anthony L. Andrady *et al.*, "Environmental Effects of Ozone Depletion and Its Interactions with Climate Change: 2010 Assessment. Executive Summary", *Photochemical & Photobiological Sciences*, 10(2), 2011, 178–81).

214 It is somehow easier to recognise the pattern of life-destruction on a global scale than on an individual scale, perhaps because the latter feels too close to home and reminds individuals of their responsibilities and of the effort that meeting such responsibilities involves. Tragically, in today's worldwide consumerist culture, where whims are reinforced artificially over reflection and the critical use of reason, notions like 'virtue', 'sacrifice' and 'duty' sound unintuitive and anachronistic, if they are understood at all. As Benjamin Barber discusses in his recent book *Consumed: How Markets Corrupt Children, Infantilize Adults, and Swallow Citizens Whole* (New York: Norton, 2007), basic impulses, not self-critical thinking, are fostered by market strategists since early childhood (it has been calculated that an average USA child is exposed to 40,000 TV commercial a year, not to mention billboards and vicarious advertising; cf. Eric Clark, *The Real Toy Story: Inside the Ruthless Battle for America's Youngest Consumers*, New York: Free Press, 2007). This means that feeling, rather than thought, informs individual life, thus leading to privileging short-term gratification over long-term gratification. Selfish concerns are the focal point in this cultural *milieu*, rather than collective ones, and the most palpable manifestation of the same lie in the triumph of individualism over community and private interest over public interest.

215 In 2006, illegal dumping, abusive development and animal trafficking, either committed or relied upon by private enterprises, constituted an estimated €26,000,000,000 business in Italy alone, i.e. the eighth largest economy on the planet (cf. Enrico Fontana *et al.*, *Rapporto ecomafia 2007*, <http://www.legambiente.it/contenuti/dossier/rapporto-ecomafia-2007-premessa>).

216 Edmund Burke, *Reflections on the French Revolution,* London: Everyman's library, 1953[1790], §134.

217 Burke's example shows how even an anti-radical, free-market prone thinker, indeed an icon of British conservatism, was able to acknowledge the priority of life-needs over money-capital concerns.

[218] Whereas UNESCO speaks in this respect of "human-engineered" systems furthering "life in the biosphere in a sustainable fashion" in order to "provide all of the sustainable needs required for continuance of life… far beyond biological requirements" alone (UNESCO, *Encyclopedia of Life Support Systems*, s.v. "Definition of Life Support System in the Context of EOLSS"), John McMurtry conceives of a "life-sequence economy" as the expression of the "civil commons", i.e. "the unseen substructure of history… bearer of the underlying life ground, and the regulating foundation of a life economy on the local or the global level" (*The Cancer Stage of Capitalism*, 1999, viii).

[219] Cf. World Bank, *Global economic prospects 2000*, <http://econ.worldbank.org/ WBSITE/EXTERNAL/EXTDEC/EXTDECPROSPECTS/0,,contentMDK: 23102090~pagePK:64165401~piPK:64165026~theSitePK:476883,00.html>.

[220] Cf. UN, *Report of the third United Nations conference on the least developed countries*, 2001, <http://www.un.org/en/conf/ldc/pdf/aconf191d13.en.pdf>.

[221] Cf. Andrew Glyn, *Capitalism Unleashed: Finance, Globalization, and Welfare*, Oxford: Oxford University Press, 2006; and UN Conference on Trade and Development, *World Investment report 1999: "Foreign Investment and the Challenge of Development"*, 1999, <http://unctad.org/en/Docs/wir1999_en.pdf>.

[222] Cf. UN Development Programme [hereafter UNDP], *Human development report 1999*, 1999, <http://hdr.undp.org/sites/default/files/reports/260/ hdr_1999_en_nostats.pdf>.

[223] Adam Smith, *An Inquiry into the Nature and Causes of the Wealth of Nations*, "Of Colonies".

[224] I write "marginal" because Smith, in his *Inquiry*, was more than willing to accept massive life-destruction in the name of economic logic, whereas as death by starvation of the labouring poor in times of recession "and a great part of the children which their fruitful marriages produce" ("Of the Wages of Labour"), or the successful "colonisation" of a "barbarous country" by means of "cruel destruction of the natives" and replacement by bodily fitter slaves ("Of the Expence of Defence" & "Causes of the Prosperity of new Colonies"). All this, while the "Civil government, so far as it is instituted for the security of property, is in reality instituted for the defence of the rich against the poor, or of those who have some property against those who have none at all" ("Of the Expence of Justice").

[225] Analogous considerations apply to other complex forms of animal life. As Arthur Schopenhauer had already observed almost two centuries ago in *The Basis of Morality* (translated by Arthur Brodrick Bullock, London: Swan Sonnenschein, 1903[1840]), there is a substantial difference between an animal in its own natural environment and the one caged at the zoo, where it is reduced to nodding or trotting monotonously, after its initial rebellion was crushed by its captors. The compassion such animals elicit in us reach into the common yet generally unrecognised dread of living that all individual creatures share. It is the root of the *pietas* that Schopenhauer addresses as *noluntas* in his major work, *The World as Will and Representation* (translated and edited by Judith Norman, Alistair Welchman and Christopher Janaway, Cambridge: Cambridge University Press, 2010[1859]).

[226] George Orwell, *Nineteen Eighty-Four*, London: Penguin, 2000[1949].

[227] If it were not for the *de facto* application of neoclassical categories of thought to the human search for happiness, this question would result unfair, for such categories are *de iure* unable to address it.

[228] "The Economics of Happiness", a review of Richard Layard's *Happiness: Lessons from a New Science* (London: Penguin, 2005), in *The Economist*, 2005, <http://www.economist.com/node/3555887>.

[229] It should be observed that the end of fulfilling these conditions does not imply capitalism as the exclusive means to achieve it.

[230] John McMurtry, *The Cancer Stage of Capitalism*, London: Pluto, 1999, 164.

[231] UNESCO, "UNESCO Fact Sheet: Death at the Border - Statistics on Migrant Fatalities to Unauthorized International Border Crossings", 2005, section 1.2, <http://portal.unesco.org/shs/en/file_download.php/8426e9451a9ce452eed861619 3911003fact+sheet+migrants+death.pdf >.

[232] Derek Lutterbeck, "Policing Migration in the Mediterranean", *Mediterranean Politics*, 11(1), March 2006, 59–82.

[233] Cf. UN News, "World's Hungry Swell to 852 Million Despite Promises to Eradicate Hunger", 26 October 2006, <https://www.globalpolicy.org/social-and-economic-policy/world-hunger/general-analysis-on-hunger/46191-worlds-hungry-swell-to-852-million-despite.html>.

[234] An interesting shift has occurred from the classical paradigm to the neoclassical one. Whereas the former regarded the majority of humankind as bound to serve as cheap labour for the benefit of their employers (Adam Smith's *Inquiry* speaks of the "race of labourers", in contrast with those of "proprietors of land" and "employers"; cf. "Of the Rent of Land"), the latter regards it also as potential consumers of mass-produced priced goods, thus running into the dilemma of guaranteeing adequate purchasing power while, at the same time, reducing costs of production, which involves paying low wages.

[235] Cf. Robert Lane, *The Loss of Happiness in Market Democracies*, New Haven: Yale University Press, 2001.

[236] Michel de Montaigne, *The Complete* Essays, I, 3.

[237] For a recent analysis of the existential insanity arising from the dogma of self-maximisation of preferences and the underlying contradiction with the moral presumptions that make capitalism viable (e.g. trust, good will, honesty), cf. Jerry A. Varsava, "The 'Saturated Self': Don DeLillo on the Problem of Rogue Capitalism", *Contemporary Literature*, 46(1), Spring 2005, 78–107.

[238] Jeff Noonan, *Democratic Society and Human Needs*, Montreal & Kingston: McGill-Queen's University Press, 2006, 57.

[239] Ibid.

[240] A recent inquiry by the British Broadcasting Corporation [hereafter BBC] News presenter Lucy Ash reveals that "only just over a third of French people think a free market economy is the best system to develop the country" and, in response to this finding, she advocates strategies to "educate French citizens" to appreciate "business acumen" and avoid "misgivings". The author is so steeped in the neoclassical paradigm that she cannot conceive of any sensible reason why the majority of the population in an advanced country like France could ever claim that "profit is somehow unclean", suggesting instead that this belief results from prejudice with "roots in French Catholicism", whilst at the same time reporting, in the same article, one of the most life-devastating failures of that very paradigm, i.e. post-communist Russia, where "many… have suffered in a painful transition to a market economy" (Lucy Ash, "France versus the world", *BBC* News, 22 April 2007, <http://news.bbc.co.uk/2/hi/programmes/documentary_archive/6511945.stm>). In point of fact, Russia depopulated from the year 1991 at a rate comparable to that of a country at war: even the most optimistic studies on this phenomenon acknowledge its dramatic proportions (cf. Barbara Anderson, "Russia Faces Depopulation? Dynamics of Population Decline", *Population and Environment*, 23(5), 2002, 437–64).

[241] Jeff Noonan, *Democratic Society and Human Needs*, 57. It may not be always easy to distinguish between wants and needs, especially when the 'revision' of one's 'self-interpretation' could result long and painful. Paedophilia and homosexuality, to mention two divisive issues in today's cultural and legal arena, would be condemned by several Christian and Islamic theologians as unacceptable wants, although the sexual proclivities of paedophiles and homosexuals may present themselves to the paedophile and to the homosexual as most powerful needs, for the fulfilment of which they may be willing to put their life at risk (paedophilia is universally condemned, whilst homosexuality is so in many countries). However, whatever the conclusion of an extensive study on either controversial phenomenon may be, the ground for their condemnation or approval could not but be the life-ground, i.e. what consequences these behaviours will ultimately have onto the lives affected.

[242] Traces of this wisdom persist also in the modern times, for example in the thought of Immanuel Kant, for whom moral duty precluded any want, and Arthur Schopenhauer, for whom even life-needs ought to be reduced.

[243] Paul Fairfield, *Moral Selfhood in the Liberal Tradition. The Politics of Individuality*, Toronto: University of Toronto Press, 2000.

[244] Cf. Gabriella Slomp, *Thomas Hobbes and the Political Philosophy of Glory*, Houndmills: Macmillan Press, 2000.

[245] Barry Schwartz, *Paradox of Choice: Why More Is Less,* New York: Harper Collins, 2004.

[246] Ancius Manlius Severinus Boethius, *The Consolation of Philosophy*, translated by Victor Watts, London: Penguin, 1999[523 A.D.], 26.

[247] Hans T. Blokland claims contemporary consumerism to be the most dramatic expression of modern Western culture, in which Weber's Reformation-inspired individualism and capitalist ethics dominate the scene ("Unhappily Trapped in the Emancipation Dilemma", *The Good Society*, 12(2), 2003, 58–62). As already denounced by Tönnies, Simmel, Fromm and Mumford, this culture trains people into working hard instead of spending time with their families, friends and communities, hoping that an opportunity for self-gratification may eventually come. Academics can themselves fall victim of this culture. The perplexing results of this culture are known: sleeplessness, reduced leisure time, noisiness, several avoidable endemic pathologies, and even the increased walking speed of people living in urban centres (cf. Robert Levine, "The pace of life in 31 countries", *American Demographics*, 19, November 1997, 20–9).

[248] Forty years ago, confronted with the British government's uncritical adoption of market growth as the Alpha-and-Omega of political action, Michael Oakeshott remarked: "Economics is trying to explain human conduct when human beings are in the position of having to make a choice between different courses of action. It does not tell you what to do... Oh I know that, in these days, economists spend half their time telling the Chancellor of the Exchequer what to do. But don't be misled... economics itself is not knowing what to do—it is giving an explanation of a situation, it is exploring a world of explanatory, not practical, ideas" ("On Arriving at a University", in *What is History? And Other Essays*, Exeter: Imprint Academic, 2004[1961], 333–40). Today, economists are often leading politicians themselves, eager to 'reassure the markets' as their paramount mission.

[249] Amy M. Spindler, "Review/Fashion; In Milan, Bold Visions and a Softer Silhouette", *The New York Times*, 1 July 1993, <http://www.nytimes.com/1993/07/01/garden/review-fashion-in-milan-bold-visions-and-a-softer-silhouette.html> (emphasis in the original).

[250] The essentially unreflective nature of the consumerist way of life is captured by the successful slogan of Nike's advertising campaign: "Just do it".

[251] Cf. Roy Williams and Vic Preisser, *Preparing Heirs: Five Steps to a Successful Transition of Family Wealth and Values*, Bandon, Oregon: Robert D. Reed, 2003.

[252] Paul Lafargue, *The Right to Be Lazy*, Chicago: Charles Kerr & Co., 1883.

[253] Madeleine Bunting, *Willing Slaves: How the Overwork Culture is Ruling Our Lives*, New York: Harper Collins, 2004.

[254] Cf. Giovanni Verga, *Mastro Don Gesualdo*, Milan: Mondadori, 1984[1889].

[255] Cf. Mikhail E. Saltykov Shchedrin, *The Glovlyov Family*, translated by Natalie Duddington, New York: New York Review of Books Classics, 2001[1880].

[256] Verga's Mastro Don Gesulado is obsessed with the accumulation of *roba* [stuff].

[257] Hans T. Blokland, "Unhappily Trapped in the Emancipation Dilemma".

[258] Cf. Migiwa Hosokawa, Shunichiro Tajiri and Tetsunojyo Uheata (eds.), *Karoshi-Nou*, Tokyo: Roudou Keizaisha, 1982.

[259] It should be noted how the demand for actual free time has been one of the oldest, loudest and most frequent in the history of industrial labour and trade unionism (cf. Moishe Postone, *Time, Labour, and Social Domination*, Cambridge: Cambridge University Press, 1993).

[260] Roger Kimball, "The Nasty Nineties", a review of Herbert I. London's *Decade of Denial: A Snapshot of America in the 1990s* (Lanham: Lexington Books, 2000), 2001, <http://sagamoreinstitute.org/ao/index/article/id/1508>.

[261] If one considers Schiller's Romantic notion of free, creative play as the most fulfilling dimension of human life, echoed in the recent psychological theory of flow by Mihaly Csikszentmihalyi, then the potential loss of life capital is enormous, as most time is spent under circumstances that do not allow the free and fullest expression of our higher faculties (cf. Mihaly Csikszentmihalyi, *Beyond Boredom and Anxiety: Experiencing Flow in Work and Play*, Chicago: Jossey-Bass, 2000).

[262] Fyodor M. Dostoyevsky, *Winter Notes on Summer Impressions*, translated by Kyril Fitz Lyon, London: Alma Classics, 2008[1863].

[263] Ibid., "Essay on the Bourgeois", "Continuation of the Preceding" and "'Bribri' and 'Mabiche'".

[264] As already observed, cheap labour has not disappeared from view, but the neoclassical paradigm focuses on the human being as consumer, rather than as producer.

[265] Cf. Lynne Lamberg, "If I work hard(er), I will be loved. Roots of Physician Stress Explored", *The Journal of the American Medical Association,* 282,1999, 13–4.

[266] A recent research by *Riza Psicosomatica* suggests that self-soothing "wild shopping" is as common as it is commonly recognised as negative. The majority of interviewed Italians claim it to be "the worst sin", more serious than "neglecting one's own children" ("Il peccato peggiore? Lo shopping selvaggio", *Il corriere della sera*, 6 May 2007, <http://www.corriere.it/Primo_Piano/Cronache/2007/05_Maggio/06/colpe_shopping_tradimento_figli.shtml>; translation mine).

[267] Emblematic is the worldwide success of the homonymous videogame, which *Forbes* commentator Hannah Clark commends as having "the potential to be a big business" ("Who's Afraid of Second Life?", *Forbes*, 27 January 2007, <http://www.forbes.com/corporatecitizenship/2007/01/27/second-life-marketing-lead-citizen-cx_hc_davos07_0127disrupt.html>).

[268] Cf. Mark Durand and David H. Barlow, *Essentials of Abnormal Psychology*, Pacific Grove: Wadsworth, 2005.

[269] Cf. Sarah Payne, *Poverty,* "Social Exclusion and Mental Health: Findings from the 1999 PSE Survey", Working paper no. 15, 1999, <http://www.bristol.ac.uk/poverty/pse/99PSE-WP15.doc>.

[270] As cited in *Bulankulama and Others v. The Secretary, Ministry of Industrial Development and Others* (Eppawala case), S.C. Application No. 884/99 (F/R), The Supreme Court of the Democratic Socialist Republic of Sri Lanka, 2000, <http://www.southasianrights.org/wp-content/uploads/2011/07/Bulankulama-and-Others-v.-Secretary-Ministry-of-Industrial-Development-And-Others-Eppawela-Case-2000SLR3V2431.htm>. Korten's thought moves along analogous lines as McMurtry's, although it is less inclined to fine theoretical analysis and more prone to outright advocacy.

[271] John McMurtry, *Unequal Freedoms*, 376.

[272] In his famous article, "The Tragedy of the Commons", Garrett Hardin argues that a system of private ownership is the only way to prevent mismanagement of commonly held resources and stresses the importance of strict legislation to avoid overpopulation and environmental pollution (*Science*, 162, 1968, 1243–8).

[273] Jeff Noonan's *Democratic Society and Human Needs* offers a good overview of the long history of pro-civil-commons struggles in the Western world.

[274] One of the most dramatic examples of subjection to money-capital is embodied by today's corporate business being granted 'limited liability', like pre-modern aristocrats throughout Europe. Equality before the law, one of the supposed great achievements of our civilisation, is in fact denied (cf. Stephanie Blankenburg and Dan Plesch, *Corporate rights and responsibilities: Restoring legal accountability*, Royal Society for the encouragement of Arts, Manufactures & Commerce, 2007, <http://www.cisd.soas.ac.uk/Files/docs/56182498-rsa-corporate-rights-plesch-and-blankenburg.pdf>).

[275] Cf. Frank Brower, Valerio Lintner and Michael Newman (eds.), *Economic Policy Making and the European Union*, London: Federal Trust, 1994 (in particular the chapter by Lintner).

[276] Tom Z. Collina and Erica Poff, "The Green New Deal: Energizing the U.S. Economy", *Friedrich Ebert Stiftung*, 4, 2009, <http://library.fes.de/pdf-files/bueros/usa/06873.pdf>.

[277] Ólafur R. Grímsson, "Sáttmáli um Fæðuöryggi Íslendinga", *Búnaðarþing 2008*, <http://www.bondi.is/lisalib/getfile.aspx?itemid=306> (translation mine). Contrary to the nations discussed in the paragraphs immediately above the one to which this note refers, the case of food security in Iceland has not been debated by the international media, hence a specific bibliographic reference is provided.

[278] The topic of crisis-related suicides in Iceland did reach the international news (e.g. "Iceland Collapse: Riots, Suicide, and Church Kitchens", *Business Pundit*, 24 January 2009, <http://www.businesspundit.com/iceland-collapse-riots-suicide-and-soup-kitchens-in-churches/>).

[279] "In civilized society it is only among the inferior ranks of people that the scantiness of subsistence can set limits to the further multiplication of the human species; and it can do so in no other way than by destroying a great part of the children which their fruitful marriages produce." (Adam Smith, *Inquiry*, "Of the Wages of Labour").

280   The works of Castoriadis and McMurtry are dealt with in this book (respectively, in chapters 10 and 1–4). As regards the Guelph alumnus John Kenneth 'Ken' Galbraith, he is only briefly referred to in the present chapter, hence I recommend the following three books: *Money: Whence It Came, Where It Went*, Boston: Houghton Mifflin, 1975; *The Age of Uncertainty*, London: BBC, 1977; and *The New Industrial State, with a new foreword by James K. Galbraith*, Princeton: Princeton University Press (2007)[1967]. Concerning British historian Eric Hobsbawm, cf. instead *Politics for a Rational Left: Political Writing, 1977–1988*, London: Verso, 1990; *The Age of Extremes, 1914–1991*, London: Abacus, 1995; and *The New Century*, London: Abacus, 2000[1999].

281 Larry Elliott has been for the past twenty years the main economics editor of the Manchester's *Guardian*, one of Britain's most distinguished newspapers.

282 The privatisation of this State-run fund was a long-time pet-project of the IMF, given its tragically mistaken appraisal of the local financial institutions as solid and prosperous (cf. Central Bank of Iceland, Release n. 17/2006, 15 May 2006, <http://www.sedlabanki.is/?PageID=13&NewsID=1208>). Eventually, it must be acknowledged, the IMF did not insist on this point ("Óska eftir 6 milljördum dala", *Mbl.is.*, 20 October 2008, <http://www.mbl.is/mm/vidskipti/frettir/2008/10/20/oska_eftir_6_milljordum_dala/>).

283 Cf. Joseph 'Joe' Stiglitz, Stiglitz, *Globalization and Its Discontents*, New York: Norton, 2003.

284   Eduardo Galeano, *Upside Down: A Primer for the Looking-Glass World*, translated by Mark Fried, New York: Picador, 2008[1998], 151–2.

285 Cf. Paul Krugman, "Reconsidering a miracle", *The Conscience of a Liberal*, 16 April 2009 Blog entry, <http://krugman.blogs.nytimes.com/2009/04/16/reconsidering-a-miracle/>; and Vladimir Putin, "Prime Minister Vladimir Putin's speech at the opening ceremony of the World Economic Forum", Geneva, 28 January 2009, <http://www.weforum.org/pdf/AM_2009/OpeningAddress_VladimirPutin.pdf>.

286 Cf. Aldo Cazzullo, "Tremonti e il G8", *Corriere della Sera*, 10 March 2009, <http://www.corriere.it/politica/09_marzo_10/aldo_cazzullo_tremonti_manifesto_g8_0023d768-0d46-11de-82af-00144f02aabc.shtml>.

287   Philip P. Hallie, *The Paradox of Cruelty*, Middletown: Wesleyan University Press, 1969, 14.

288   Philip P. Hallie, *Lest Innocent Blood Be Shed: The Story of the Village of Le Chambon, and How Goodness Happened There*, New York: Harper & Row, 1985[1979], 2.

289 *Encyclopaedia of Ethics* (edited by Lawrence C. Becker, New York: Garland, 1992), s.v. "Cruelty", by Philip P. Hallie, 229–31, 229.

290 Philip P. Hallie, *The Paradox of Cruelty*, 5–6.

291 Ibid., 22–4.

292 Ibid., 13–4 & 29–31.

293 Philip P. Hallie, "From Cruelty to Goodness" in *Vice and Virtue in Everyday Life*, edited by Christina H. and Fred Sommers, San Diego: Harcourt College Publishers, 1989[1981], 11.

294 Philip P. Hallie, *The Paradox of Cruelty*, 55.

295 Ibid., 41.

296 Ibid., 33.

297 Ibid., 15–20.

298 Giorgio Baruchello, "No Pain, No Gain. The Understanding of Cruelty in Western Philosophy and Some Reflections on Personhood", *Filozofia*, 65(2), 2010, 172–5 (emphases removed).

299 Cf. Michael Trice, *Encountering Cruelty: The Fracture of the Human Heart*, Leiden: Brill, 2011.

300 Giorgio Baruchello, "No Pain, No Gain", 171–2 (emphases removed).

301 Cf. Philip P. Hallie, *The Paradox of Cruelty*.

302 Georgios Kassimatis, "The Loan Agreement between the Hellenic Republic, the European Union and the International Monetary Fund" (Research paper prepared for Athens Bar Association, inclusive of all the initially confidential 2010 loan agreements, known also under the formal title *The Loan Agreements between the Hellenic Republic, the European Union and the International Monetary Fund*), translated by S.G. Virna, 2010, foreword, §2, <http://www.kassimatisdimokratia.gr/index.php/law-science/item/129-the-loan-agreements-between-the-hellenic-republic-the-european-union-and-the-international-monetary-fund>. Kassimatis' hefty paper was circulated among the participants at the conference entitled "Sovereign Debt and Fundamental Social Rights", organised by the International Association of Constitutional Law in Athens, Greece (28–9 June 2013), to which I was invited to deliver the paper "The Presupposed Oncological Model of Paul Krugman's Banking Metastases: An Introduction to John McMurtry's Philosophy".

303 Georgios Kassimatis, "The Loan Agreement between the Hellenic Republic, the European Union and the International Monetary Fund", 54.

304 Ibid., 3.

305 Ibid., 52 (emphasis added).

306 Ibid., 51–9.

307 Ibid., 69–79.

308 Ibid., 52 & 54.

309 Cf. Decca Alktenhead, "Christine Lagarde: can the head of the IMF save the euro?", *The Guardian*, 25 May 2012, <http://www.theguardian.com/world/2012/may/25/christine-lagarde-imf-euroAZ>.

310 Cf. Helena Smith, "Greek police face investigation after protest violence", *The Guardian*, 1 July 2011, <http://www.theguardian.com/world/2011/jul/01/greek-police-investigation-protest-violence>.

311 Cf. Olivier Blanchard and Daniel Leigh, "Growth Forecast Errors and Fiscal Multipliers", IMF Working Paper ref. WP/13/1, January 2013, <http://www.imf.org/external/pubs/ft/wp/2013/wp1301.pdf>.

312 Cf. IMF, "Greece: Ex Post Evaluation of Exceptional Access under the 2010 Stand-By Arrangement", IMF Country Report No. 13/156, June 2013, <http://www.imf.org/external/pubs/ft/scr/2013/cr13156.pdf>.

313 Cf. Alexander Kentikelenis et al., "Health Effects of Financial Crisis: Omens of a Greek Tragedy", Lancet, 378, 2011, 1457–8.

314 Cf. Marina Economou et al., "Suicidality and the Economic Crisis in Greece", Lancet, 380, 2012, 337; and Åshild Faresjö et al., "Higher Perceived Stress but Lower Cortisol Levels Found among Young Greek Adults Living in a Stressful Social Environment in Comparison with Swedish Young Adults", PLoS ONE 8(9), 2013, e73828, doi:10.1371/journal.pone.0073828.

315 Cf. David Stuckler and Sanjay Basu, The Body Economic: Why Austerity Kills, London: Allen Lane, 2013.

316 Cf. Joseph Stiglitz, Globalization and Its Discontents.

317 Cf. Olivier Blanchard and Daniel Leigh, "Growth Forecast Errors and Fiscal Multipliers".

318 Cf. "Bankers call for third LTRO", Reuters, 13 September 2013, <http://www.reuters.com/assets/print?aid=USL5N0H820C20130912>.

319 Cf. John McMurtry, The Cancer Stage of Capitalism. From Crisis to Cure.

320 Cf. David Stuckler and Sanjay Basu, The Body Economic.

321 On Nietzsche's debt to Montaigne, in particular with respect to scepticism, corporeity, and writing style, cf. Alexander Nehamas, "The Art of Living", Philosophy Today 44(2), 2000, 190–205; David Molner, "The Influence of Montaigne on Nietzsche: A Raison d'Etre in the Sun", Nietzsche Studien, 21, 1993, 80–93; and William D. Williams, Nietzsche and The French: A Study of the Influence of Nietzsche's French Reading on His Thought and Writing, Oxford: Blackwell, 1952. On the issue of the "decentering of humankind," cf. Bernhard H.F. Taureck, "Decentering Humanity: Nietzsche's Debt to Montaigne and Others", New Nietzsche Studies 2(3–4), 1998, 93–107. On solitude and the free spirit, cf. Vivetta Vivarelli, "Montaigne und der 'Freie Geist': Nietzsche im Uebergang", Nietzsche Studien, 23, 1994, 79–101.

322 Parkes is the first commentator to argue in favour of a similarity between Montaigne's conception of death and Nietzsche's (cf. "Death and Detachment: Montaigne, Zen, Heidegger and the Rest"). On Montaigne alone and the issue of death, cf. Jean Starobinski, Montaigne in Motion, translated by Arthur Goldhammer, Chicago: University of Chicago Press, 1985. On Nietzsche and death, cf. Joseph E. Vincenzo, "Nietzsche and Epicurus," Man and World 27(4), 1994, 383–97, where the author stresses the "tragic joy" that guides Nietzsche's acceptance of death, beyond the quietist "inverted Platonism" of the Epicureans.

323 Graham Parkes, "Death and Detachment: Montaigne, Zen, Heidegger and the Rest", 83–4.

324 Michel de Montaigne, The Complete Essays, I, 20.

[325] Friedrich Nietzsche, *The Gay Science*, §278.

[326] Michel de Montaigne, *The Complete Essays*, I, 20.

[327] Graham Parkes, "Death and Detachment: Montaigne, Zen, Heidegger and the Rest", 83.

[328] Ibid.

[329] Ibid.

[330] Ibid.

[331] Michel de Montaigne, *The Complete Essays*, I, 20.

[332] Ibid.

[333] Ibid.

[334] Ibid., I, 12.

[335] Ibid., II, 31.

[336] Ibid., I, 3.

[337] Ibid., I, 23.

[338] Friedrich Nietzsche, *The Will to Power*, §124.

[339] Ibid., §778.

[340] Ibid., §933.

[341] Friedrich Nietzsche, *Thus Spake Zarathustra*, translated by Thomas Common, Part I, "Zarathustra's Prologue", §4, 1891[1883-91], <http://www.eserver.org/philosophy/nietzsche-zarathustra.txt> (I opted for this translation because it conveys with rare effectiveness both the rhetorical power and the sense of word- and structure-construction that are so distinctive of Nietzsche's German *Zarathustra*).

[342] Friedrich Nietzsche, *Beyond Good and Evil*, translated by Judith Norman, Cambridge: Cambridge University Press, 2002[1886], §61.

[343] Friedrich Nietzsche, *The Will To Power*, §113.

[344] Ibid., §4.

[345] Friedrich Nietzsche, *Beyond Good and Evil*, §56.

[346] Michel de Montaigne, *The Complete Essays*, I, 20.

[347] Friedrich Nietzsche, *The Gay Science*, §11.

[348] Michel de Montaigne, *The Complete Essays*, II, 2.

[349] Friedrich Nietzsche, "Thus Spoke Zarathustra", in *Ecce Homo*, §1, in *Ecce Homo & The Antichrist*, translated by Thomas Wayne, New York: Algora, 2004[1888 & 1895].

[350] Friedrich Nietzsche, *The Will To Power*, §407.

[351] Michel de Montaigne, *The Complete Essays*, III, 10.

[352] Friedrich Nietzsche, *The Will to Power*, §55.

[353] Ibid., §701.

[354] Michel de Montaigne, *The Complete Essays*, II, 3.

[355] Ibid., III, 13.

[356] As cited in Graham Parkes, "Death and Detachment: Montaigne, Zen, Heidegger and the Rest", 86.

[357] Ibid.

[358] Michel de Montaigne, *The Complete Essays*, I, 20.

[359] Ibid., I, 33. This concept is bound to become milder in the later writings of Montaigne.

[360] Friedrich Nietzsche, *The Will To Power*, §§ 482–90.

[361] Ibid., §489.

[362] Ibid., §§ 523 & 529.

[363] Cf. Giovanni Battista Vico, *La scienza nuova*, La Spezia: Fratelli Melita, 1987[1744]; *The New Science of Giambattista Vico*, translated by Thomas G. Bergin and Max H. Fisch, Ithaca: Cornell University Press, 1988 (3rd printing) [1744].

[364] Cf. A. Robert Capongiri, *Time and Idea: The Theory of History in Giambattista Vico*, Chicago: Henry Regnery, 1953.

[365] Cf. Benedetto Croce, *La filosofia di G.B. Vico*, Bari: Laterza, 1965 (6th ed.) [1911].

[366] E.g. Fausto Nicolini, *La giovinezza di Vico,* Bari: Laterza, 1932; *Saggi vichiani*, Napoli: Giannini, 1955; and *Giambattista Vico nella vita domestica: la moglie, i figli, la casa*, Venosa: Ossana, 1991.

[367] Cf. Robin G. Collingwood, *The Philosophy of Giambattista Vico*, London: Howard Latimer, 1913.

[368] Cf. Henry P. Adams, *The Life and Writings of Giambattista Vico*, London: Allen and Unwin, 1935.

[369] Cf. Isaiah Berlin, "The Philosophical Ideas of Giambattista Vico", in *Art and Ideas in Eighteenth-Century Italy*. Rome: Edizioni di Storia e Letteratura, 1960, 156–233; *Vico and Herder: Two Studies in the History of Ideas*, New York: Viking, 1976; and *Three Critics of the Enlightenment: Vico, Hamann, Herder*, edited by Henry Hardy, London: Pimlico, 2000.

[370] Cf. *Vico and Joyce*, edited by Donald P. Verene, Albany: State University of New York Press, 1987; and Paul Robischaud, "Joyce, Vico, and National Narrative", *James Joyce Quarterly*, 41(1-2), 2003, 185–96.

[371] Cf. Thora I. Bayer and Donald P., Verene. *Giambattista Vico. Keys to the* New Science. *Translations, Commentaries, and Essays*, Ithaca: Cornell University Press, 2009, 199–204.

[372] Anthony Grafton, "Fear and Loathing in Naples", a review of Mark Lilla's *G.B. Vico: The Making of an Anti-Modern* (Cambridge, Mass.: Harvard University Press, 1993), *The New Republic*, 209(12), 1993, 52.

[373] Cf. Valeria Giannantonio, *Oltre Vico. L'identità del passato a Napoli e Milano tra '700 e '800*, Lanciano: Carabba, 2009.

[374] Cf. Cesare Marini, *Giambattista Vico al cospetto del XIX secolo*, Napoli: Stamperia Strada Salvatore, 1852.

[375] Ibid., 127 (translation mine).

[376] Mary Pickering, *Auguste Comte. An Intellectual Biography. Volume II*, Cambridge: Cambridge University Press, 2009, 297.

[377] Cf. Auguste Comte, "The Positivist calendar", 2015[1849] <http://positivists.org/calendar.html>.

[378] Karl Marx, *Capital. Vol. 1*, edited by Friedrich Engels, translated by Samuel Moore and Edward Aveling, London: Lawrence & Wishart, 1970[1867], 372n3.

[379] Anthony Grafton, "Fear and Loathing in Naples", 51.

[380] Cf. Mark Lilla, *G.B. Vico: The Making of an Anti-Modern*.

[381] Giambattista Vico, *The New Science of Giambattista Vico*, §129.

[382] Ibid., §130.

[383] Leon Pompa, *Vico. A Study of the 'New Science'*, Cambridge: Cambridge University Press, 1990 (2nd ed.)[1977], 203; this "death" too will be addressed here.

[384] Giambattista Vico, *The New Science of Giambattista Vico*, §7.

[385] Ibid., §§ 43–118.

[386] Cf. A. Robert Capongiri, *Time and Idea: The Theory of History in Giambattista Vico*.

[387] Giambattista Vico, *The New Science of Giambattista Vico*, §780.

[388] Ibid., §894.

[389] Ibid., §786.

[390] Ibid.

[391] Ibid.

[392] Ibid., §787.

[393] Ibid.

[394] Cf. ibid., §§ 404–8, 806–8.

[395] Ibid., §364.

[396] Ibid., §780.

[397] Ibid., §375.

[398] Cf. ibid., §81.

[399] Cf. Anthony Grafton, "Fear and Loathing in Naples".

[400] Giambattista Vico, *The New Science of Giambattista Vico*, §880.

[401] Ibid., §873.

[402] Ibid., §904.

[403] Burton Feldman and Robert D. Richardson, *The Rise of Modern Mythology, 1680–1860*, Bloomington: Indiana University Press, 1972.

[404] Giambattista Vico, *The New Science of Giambattista Vico*, §80.

[405] Ibid., §81.

[406] Ibid., §558.

[407] Ibid., §802.

[408] Ibid., §1021.

[409] Ibid., §619.

[410] Ibid., §664; cf. also § 26.

[411] Ibid., §668.

[412] Ibid.

[413] Ibid.; cf. also §115.

[414] Cf. ibid., §§ 115, 997 & 1021.

[415] Ibid., §317; Vico's references to these pagan nations and to the "Patagonian giants" (§338) in the same paragraph of the present chapter appear in the Italian text and in the first printing of the English translation of the *New Science* cited in my bibliography, but not in the third printing of the latter.

[416] Ibid., §521.

[417] Ibid., §338.

[418] Ibid., §296.

[419] Ibid., §16.

[420] Ibid., §449.

[421] E.g. ibid., §§ 25, 110, 549 & 627.

[422] E.g. ibid., §§ 513, 582–3 & 964.

[423] E.g. ibid., §§ 517, 582 & 670.

[424] Ibid., §§ 25, 1069 & 1079.

[425] Ibid., §558.

[426] Ibid., §§ 720–1.

[427] Ibid., §659.

[428] Cf. Thora I. Bayer, "History as Symbolic Form: Cassirer and Vico", *Idealistic Studies*, 34(1), 2004, 49–65.

[429] E.g. Giambattista Vico, *The New Science of Giambattista Vico*, §§ 5 & 29.

[430] Ibid., §592.

[431] Ibid., §112.

[432] Ibid.

[433] Cf. Ibid., §1022.

[434] Ibid., §2.

[435] Ibid., §31; cf. also §630.

[436] Ibid., §699.

[437] Ibid., §159.

[438] Cf. ibid., §564.

[439] Ibid., §159.

[440] Ibid., §40.

[441] Leon Pompa, *Vico. A Study of the 'New Science'*, 203.

[442] Giambattista Vico, *The New Science of Giambattista Vico*, §1106.

[443] Ibid., §§ 1106–11.

[444] Ibid., §1106.

[445] Lawrence H. Simon, "Vico and Marx: Perspectives on Historical Development", *Journal of the History of Ideas*, 42(2), 1981, 317.

[446] Giambattista Vico, *The New Science of Giambattista Vico*, §713.

[447] Ibid., §§ 919–21.

[448] Ibid., §§ 932-6.

[449] Ibid., §§ 942-6.

[450] Ibid., §§ 1021–2.

[451] Ibid., §§ 975-9.

[452] Ibid., §§ 402-8.

[453] Cf. Giuseppe Mazzotta, *The New Map of the World: The Poetic Philosophy of Giambattista Vico*, Princeton: Princeton University Press, 1999.

[454] Giambattista Vico, *The New Science of Giambattista Vico*, §404.

[455] Ibid., §402.

[456] Ibid., §230.

[457] Ibid., §403.

[458] Ibid., §929.

[459] Ibid., §407.

[460] Ibid., §406.

[461] Ibid., §407.

[462] Ibid., §408.

[463] Cf. Nancy Du Bois Marcus, *Vico and Plato*, New York: Peter Lang, 2001.

[464] E.g. Giambattista Vico, *The New Science of Giambattista Vico*, §§ 12–3, 40 & 333.

[465] Ibid., §721.

[466] Ibid., §8.

[467] Ibid., §11.

[468] Ibid., §12.

[469] Ibid.; cf. also §537; from religion and, in particular, from burials, originates also the belief in the immortality of the soul, e.g. §360.

[470] Ibid., §337.

[471] Ibid., §333.

[472] Ibid., §529.

[473] Ibid., §531.

[474] Cf. ibid., §§ 529, 531, 637 & 1051.

[475] E.g. ibid., §§ 62, 377, 383, 689 & 712.

[476] Ibid., §502; since fear of death expresses a desire to live, it is implied that life, rather than death *per se*, is the ultimate onto-axiological springboard of religion (cf. McMurtry, *Philosophy and World Problems*).

[477] Giambattista Vico, *The New Science of Giambattista Vico*, §482.

[478] Ibid., §504.

[479] Ibid., §178; cf. also §518.

[480] Ibid., §503.

[481] Cf. Giuseppe Mazzotta, *The New Map of the World: The Poetic Philosophy of Giambattista Vico*.

[482] Giambattista Vico, *On the Most Ancient Wisdom of the Italians Unearthed from the Origins of the Latin Language*, translated by Lucia M. Palmer, Ithaca: Cornell University Press, 1988[1709].

[483] Giambattista Vico, *On the Study Methods of Our Time*, translated by E. Gianturco, New York: Bobbs-Merrill, 1965[1708].

[484] Cf. Diane Villemaire, "What Kuhn Really Said", *New Vico Studies*, 12, 1994, 75–80.

[485] Andrea Di Miele, "La cifra nel tappeto. Note su Paci interprete di Vico", *Bollettino del Centro di Studi Vichiani*, 37, 2007, 98.

[486] Giambattista Vico, *The New Science of Giambattista Vico*, §714.

[487] Ibid., §715.

[488] Ibid., §716.

[489] Ibid., §717; there is not always an exact correspondence between the three ages of historical development and each and every area of human life that Vico subdivides in three parts. Thus, the three forms of underworld that he discusses in §§ 715–21 would seem to apply to the first two ages only.

[490] Ibid., §781.

[491] Cf. Martin Heidegger, *Being and Time*.

[492] Cf. Cornelius Castoriadis, "Why I am No Longer a Marxist", in *A Society Adrift. Interviews and Debates, 1974–1997*, translated by Helen Arnold, New York: Fordham University Press, 2010, 11–44.

[493] The multidisciplinary journal *Thesis Eleven* and its editor, Johann P. Arnason, must be commended for having tried to widen the knowledge and circulation of Castoriadis' work in the Anglophone countries over the past three decades.

[494] Concerning the sources utilised for the present chapter, I refer extensively to four 'bootleg' collections of essays that an anonymous translator published online in order to foster worldwide the knowledge and appreciation of Castoriadis' thought. Given the large number of references to the many essays collected in these books and the overall consistency of Castoriadis' work over the years, I list individual essay titles only when relevant; otherwise, I refer to the books alone. Also, when available and known to me, I include in the final bibliography the official and 'respectable' hardcover English translations corresponding to the anonymous collections of essays that I utilise. I am aware of the apparent oddity of my choice, which is only made worse by the deplorable invectives at relatives of Castoriadis and at Castoriadis scholars contained in the anonymous collections. Nevertheless, I refer to the anonymous collections because: (A) they constitute a very effective means of propagation of Castoriadis' thought, which is also an aim of the present chapter; and (B) they are excellent translations, which I deem better than the existing alternatives, and remarkably closer to the French originals in both thought and style.

[495] E.g. Matthew Sharpe, "Autonomy, Reflexivity, Tragedy: Notions of Democracy in Camus and Castoriadis", *Critical Horizons*, 3(1), 2002, 103–29.

[496] The most thorough scrutiny of Castoriadis' conception of mortality is probably contained in Damon Young's article "Being Grateful for Being: Being, Reverence and Finitude", *Sophia*, 44(2), 2005, 31–53, which deals however with notions of "gratitude" and "reverence" in religious experience and not with issues of autonomy and inanity in modern democracies.

[497] As also an introduction to Castoriadis' work based upon his understanding of mortality, this chapter makes little use of the sparse Anglophone secondary literature devoted to him, most of which has been published in Johann P. Arnason's *Thesis Eleven*. However, for the sake of completeness, cf. the 2008 special issue 3(2) of *Nordicum-Mediterraneum. Icelandic E-Journal in Nordic and Mediterranean Studies*, comprising several articles and a survey of the relevant online sources of literature by and on Castoriadis in many languages, as well as the book *Creation, Rationality and Autonomy: Essays on Cornelius Castoriadis,* edited by Ingerid Straume and Giorgio Baruchello, Malmö: Nordic Summer University Press, 2013.

[498] Cornelius Castoriadis, *A Society Adrift: More Interviews and Discussions on The Rising Tide of Insignificancy, Including Revolutionary Perspectives Today,* translated and edited anonymously as a public service, 2010[1973–93], 260, <http://www.notbored.org/ASA.pdf> [hereafter ASA].

[499] Ibid.

[500] Cornelius Castoriadis, *Figures of the Thinkable. Including Passion and Knowledge*, translated and edited anonymously as a public service, 2005[1986–97], i, <http://www.notbored.org/FTPK.html> [hereafter FT].

[501] Cornelius Castoriadis, *The Rising Tide of Insignificancy (The Big Sleep)*, translated and edited anonymously as a public service, 2003[1979–96], 242–3, <http://www.notbored.org/RTI.html> [hereafter RTI].

[502] Cornelius Castoriadis, ASA, 84.

503 Cornelius Castoriadis, FT, 5–6n1.

504 Ibid., 21.

505 Ibid., 63.

506 Ibid., 21–2.

507 Ibid., 21.

508 Ibid., 34.

509 Ibid., 49–50.

510 Cornelius Castoriadis, RTI, 267.

511 Cornelius Castoriadis, FT, 5–6n1.

512 Ibid., 129 (emphasis added).

513 Cornelius Castoriadis, ASA, 107.

514 Cornelius Castoriadis, RTI, 42.

515 Ingerid Straume, "Freedom and the Collective", *Nordicum-Mediterraneum* 3(2), 2008, §4, <http://nome.unak.is/nome2/issues/vol3_2/straume.html>.

516 Ibid.

517 Cornelius Castoriadis, FT, 82.

518 Ibid., 5–6n1.

519 Ingerid Straume, "Freedom and the Collective", §4.

520 Cornelius Castoriadis, FT, 129.

521 Ibid., 162.

522 Ibid., 162–3 (emphasis in the original).

523 Cornelius Castoriadis, RTI, 84.

524 Cornelius Castoriadis, ASA, 259.

525 Cornelius Castoriadis, RTI, 226.

526 Cornelius Castoriadis, ASA, 187–8.

527 Cornelius Castoriadis, RTI, 94–5.

528 Ibid., 96–7.

529 Cornelius Castoriadis, FT, 245.

530 Ibid., 245–6.

531 Ibid., 146.

532 Ibid., 89.

533 Cornelius Castoriadis, RTI, 47–8.

534 Cornelius Castoriadis, FT, 89–90.

535 Cornelius Castoriadis, RTI, 94.

536 Cornelius Castoriadis, FT, 115.

537 Ibid., 245–6.

538 Cornelius Castoriadis, *Postscript on Insignificancy. Including More Interviews and Discussions on the Rising Tide of Insignificancy. Followed by Five Dialogues, Four Portraits and Two Book Reviews*, translated and edited anonymously as a public service, 2011[1961–97], 194, <http://www.notbored.org/PSRTI.pdf> [hereafter PSRTI].

539 Cornelius Castoriadis, RTI, 226–7.

540 Cornelius Castoriadis, ASA, 262.

541 Cornelius Castoriadis, RTI, 221–2.

542 Ibid., 84–5.

543 Cornelius Castoriadis, PSRTI, 251–2.

544 Cornelius Castoriadis, RTI, 121.

545 Cornelius Castoriadis, PSRTI, 197.

546 Cornelius Castoriadis, RTI, 227–8.

547 Cornelius Castoriadis, ASA, 261.

548 Ibid.

549 Cornelius Castoriadis, RTI, 88–9.

550 Ibid., 88.

551 Cf. Giorgio Baruchello "Eight Noble Opinions and the Economic Crisis: Four Literary-philosophical Sketches à la Eduardo Galeano", *Nordicum-Mediterraneum*, 5(1), 2010, <http://nome.unak.is/nm/5-1/12-reflection-on-the-economic-crisis-/228-eight-noble-opinions-and-the-economic-crisis-four-literary-philosophical-sketches-a-la-eduardo-galeano>.

552 Cornelius Castoriadis, FT, 129.

553 Ibid., 21.

554 Ibid., 22.

555 Cornelius Castoriadis, RTI, 96.

556 Cf. ibid., 150, 204 & 289; cf. also Cornelius Castoriadis, PSRTI, 237.

557 Cf. Cornelius Castoriadis, FT, 66.

558 Cf. ibid., 92n9.

559 Cf. ibid., 375.

560 Cf. Cornelius Castoriadis, ASA, 152.

561 Cf. Ibid., 193.

562 Cf. Cornelius Castoriadis, RTI, 204.

563 Cf. Ibid., 51, 59 & 141–2; cf. also Cornelius Castoriadis, ASA, 235.

564 Cf. Cornelius Castoriadis, RTI, 270; FT, 199 & 212n4; ASA, 8, 19, 52n15 & 102; and PSRTI, 17 & 29–30.

565 Cf. Cornelius Castoriadis, RTI, 380; ASA, 139 & 242; and PSRTI, 56 & 113.

566 Cf. Cornelius Castoriadis, "The Athenian Democracy: False and True Questions", in RTI, 2003[1993], 311–28.

567 Ibid., 326.

568 Cornelius Castoriadis, RTI, 377–8.

569 Cornelius Castoriadis, FT, 129.

570 Cf. Cornelius Castoriadis, Part III—Polis of RTI, 259–359.

571 Cornelius Castoriadis, FT, 129.

572 Cf. Hildegard of Bingen, *Selected Writings*, translated and edited by Mark Atherton, London: Penguin, 2001[12th century A.D.].

573 Cf. Cornelius Castoriadis, "The Revolutionary Force of Ecology", in RTI, 2003[1993], 109–23.

574 Cornelius Castoriadis, PSRTI, 114.

575 Cf. Cornelius Castoriadis, RTI, 114

576 Ibid., 123.

577 Cf. John McMurtry, *Value Wars*.

578 Cf. Karl E. Smith, "The Constitution of Modernity. A Critique of Castoriadis", *European Journal of Social Theory*, 12(4), 2009, 505–21.

579 Cornelius Castoriadis, "De l'écologie à l'autonomie", transcription of a paper presented at Louvain-la-neuve (Belgium) on February, 27th 1980, n.d.a.[1980], <http://www.les-renseignements-genereux.org/var/fichiers/textes/Tex_Casto_ecologie.pdf> (translation mine).

580 Cf. Jeff Noonan, *Democratic Society and Human Needs*.

581 Cornelius Castoriadis, FT, 146.

582 Cornelius Castoriadis, RTI, 227.

583 Cornelius Castoriadis, PSRTI, 197; cf. also ASA, 261–2.

584 Cornelius Castoriadis, RTI, 84–5.

585 Ibid., 228.

586 Cf. Karl E. Smith, "Meaning and Porous Being", *Thesis Eleven*, 99(1), 2009, 7–26.

587 Cf. Janko Lavrin, "Tolstoy and Gandhi", *The Russian Review*, 19(2), 1960, 132–9.

588 Michael Polanyi, *Knowing and Being. Essays by Michael Polanyi*, London: Routledge & Kegan Paul, 1969, 186.

589 Ibid.

590 Cf. Daniel Kahneman, *Thinking, Fast and Slow*, New York: Farrar, Straus & Giroux, 2011.

591 E.g. Michael Polanyi, *Personal Knowledge. Towards a Post-Critical Philosophy*, London: Routledge & Kegan Paul, 1958 (1962 reprint).

592 Michael Polanyi, *Knowing and Being*, 193 (emphasis added).

593 Michael Polanyi, *Personal Knowledge*, 87.

594 Cf. Michael Polanyi, *Knowing and Being*, 132.

595 Ibid., 195.

596 Ibid. (emphasis added).

597 Michael Polanyi, *Personal Knowledge*, 87 & 94.

598 Ibid., 87–94.

599 Michael Polanyi and Harry Prosch, *Meaning*, Chicago: Chicago University Press, 1975, 30 (emphasis added).

600 Michael Polanyi, *Personal Knowledge*, 1 (emphasis added).

601 Michael Polanyi, *Knowing and Being*, 141.

602 Ibid.

603 Ibid.

604 Cf. Michael Polanyi, *Personal Knowledge*, 20n, 126n, 191n, 261 &, above all, 263n.

605 Ibid., 263n.

606 Ibid.

607 Michael Polanyi, *Knowing and Being*, 126.

608 Michael Polanyi and Harry Prosch, *Meaning*, 61 (emphasis in the original).

609 Cf. Carola Salvi, Emanuela Bricolo, John Kounios, Edward Bowden and Mark Beeman, "Insight solutions are correct more often than analytic solutions", *Thinking & Reasoning* (vol. & issue ns. n.a.), 2016, DOI: 10.1080 / 13546783.2016.1141798.

610 Cf. Stephen G. Henry, "Polanyi's tacit knowing and the relevance of epistemology to clinical medicine", *Journal of Evaluation in Clinical Practice* 16(2), 2010, 292–7.

611 Michael Polanyi, *The Tacit Dimension*, London: Routledge, 1966 (2009 reprint), 5–6.

612 Blaise Pascal, *Pensieri. Testo francese a fronte*, Milan: Rusconi, 1993[Copy B, 1669].

613 Stephen G. Henry, "Polanyi's tacit knowing and the relevance of epistemology to clinical medicine", 296.

614 Ibid.

615 Michael Polanyi, *Knowing and Being*, 133.

616 Ibid., 145.

617 Michael Polanyi, *The Study of Man*, Chicago: University of Chicago Press, 1959 (1969 reprint), 100 (emphasis added).

618 Michael Polanyi, *Knowing and Being*, 195.

619 Ibid., 194.

620 Ibid., 142–3.

[621] Cf. Michael Polanyi, "What is a Painting?", *The American Scholar*, 39(4), 1970, 655–69.

[622] Michael Polanyi, *Knowing and Being*, 185.

[623] Ibid., 141.

[624] Michael Polanyi, *The Tacit Dimension*, 11.

[625] Michael Polanyi, *Personal Knowledge*, 207.

[626] Cf. Michael Polanyi, "Life's Irreducible Structure".

[627] Michael Polanyi, *Personal Knowledge*, 328.

[628] Michael Polanyi, *Knowing and Being*, 106–15.

[629] Ibid.

[630] Michael Polanyi, *The Tacit Dimension*, 55, 94 & 76.

[631] Cf. Michael Polanyi, *The Study of Man*.

[632] Cf. Michael Polanyi, *Knowing and Being*.

[633] Michael Polanyi, *Personal Knowledge*, 28 (emphasis added).

[634] Gottlob Frege, "The Thought: A Logical Inquiry", *Mind*, 65(259), 1956[1919], 289–311.

[635] Michael Polanyi, *Knowing and Being*, 134.

[636] Ibid., 16.

[637] Michael Polanyi and Harry Prosch, *Meaning*, 25.

[638] Michael Polanyi, *The Tacit Dimension*, 92.

[639] Michael Polanyi, *The Study of Man*, 68.

[640] Ibid.

[641] Michael Polanyi, *Society, Economics & Philosophy. Selected Papers*, New Brunswick: Transaction, 1997[1917–72], 343.

[642] Michael Polanyi, *Personal Knowledge*, 266.

[643] Michael Polanyi, *The Tacit Dimension*, 18–9.

[644] Michael Polanyi, *Knowing and Being*, 138.

[645] Giorgio Baruchello, "Classifying the Classics. *Gestalt* Psychology and the Tropes of Rhetoric", *New Ideas in Psychology*, 36, 2015 10–24.

[646] Michael Polanyi, "The Growth of Thought in Society," *Economica*, 8(32), 1941, 428–56.

[647] Michael Polanyi, *Personal Knowledge*, 46 & 151 (emphasis added).

[648] Thomas S. Kuhn, "The Function of Dogma in Scientific Research", in *Scientific Change: Historical Studies in the Intellectual, Social and Technical Conditions for Scientific Discovery and Technical Invention, from Antiquity to the Present*, edited by Alistair Crombie, New York: Basic Books, 1963, 347–69.

[649] Michael Polanyi, *Knowing and Being*, 105 & 152.

650 Michael Oakeshott, *Experience and Its Modes*, Cambridge: The University Press, 1933.

651 Michael Polanyi, *Knowing and Being*, 134 (emphasis in the original).

652 Michael Polanyi, *Knowing and Being*, 169.

653 Michael Polanyi, "The Growth of Thought in Society", 432 & 435; cf. also *Society, Economics & Philosophy*, Part II.

654 Struan Jacobs, "Michael Polanyi and Spontaneous Order, 1941–1951", *Tradition and Discovery*, 24(2), 1997–1998, 14–28.

655 Michael Polanyi, *Society, Economics & Philosophy*, 78 & 82.

656 Ibid., 342 (emphasis added).

657 Michael Polanyi and Harry Prosch, *Meaning*, 156 (emphasis added).

658 Michael Polanyi, *Personal Knowledge*, 281.

659 Ibid.

660 Cf. Gilbert K. Chesterton, *What I Saw in America*, London: Hodder & Stoughton, 1922; and Arthur F. Utz, *Wirtschaftsethik*, Bonn: Scientia Humana Institut, 1994.

661 Giambattista Vico, *The New Science of Giambattista Vico*, §1106.

662 Michael Polanyi, *The Tacit Dimension*, 4.

663 Ronald M. Hartwell, *History of the Mont Pelerin Society*, Indianapolis: Liberty Fund, 1995.

664 Thomas F. Torrance (2000–2001), "Michael Polanyi and the Christian Faith— A Personal Report", *Tradition and Discovery*, 27(2), 26–33.